PRAISE FOR *THE EXPENDABLES*

"Rubin . . . leverages his firm grasp of geopolitics and economics to offer not only a primer on macroeconomics, but also on how globalization— that is, the process of opening up international markets—has routed the middle class and propped up the elite. *Winnipeg Free Press*

"The latest from the author of *Why Your World Is About to Get a Whole Lot Smaller* continues his disruptive ways in this analysis of how the collapse of union membership and the near obsolescence of full-time employment is squeezing out the middle class. . . . [Rubin] is a fiercely independent thinker." *—NOW*

PRAISE FOR *THE CARBON BUBBLE*

"Rubin's argument is sleek and fluent. . . . [He] is an engaging writer." *—Financial Post*

"An astute critique of big oil." *—Quill & Quire*

"*The Carbon Bubble* is Jeff Rubin at his finest. Thought-provoking. Meticulously researched. Intelligent without pretension. I highly, highly recommend it!" **—Michael Hlinka, Business Commentator, CBC Radio**

"[A] feat of economics writer's jiu-jitsu." **—Shawn McCarthy, *The Globe and Mail***

A MAP OF THE NEW NORMAL

A MAP
OF THE
NEW
NORMAL

HOW INFLATION, WAR,
AND SANCTIONS WILL CHANGE
YOUR WORLD FOREVER

JEFF RUBIN

ALLEN
LANE

ALLEN LANE
an imprint of Penguin Canada, a division of Penguin
Random House Canada Limited

Canada • USA • UK • Ireland • Australia • New Zealand •
India • South Africa • China

First published 2024

www.penguinrandomhouse.ca

LIBRARY AND ARCHIVES CANADA CATALOGUING
IN PUBLICATION
Title: A map of the new normal : how inflation, war, and
sanctions will change your world forever / Jeff Rubin.
Names: Rubin, Jeff, 1954- author.
Identifiers: Canadiana (print) 20230468314 | Canadiana
(ebook) 20230468349 | ISBN 9780735246119 (hardcover) |
ISBN 9780735246126 (EPUB)
Subjects: LCSH: Economic forecasting. | LCSH: Twenty-first
century—Forecasts. | LCSH: Social prediction.
Classification: LCC HB3730 .R83 2024 | DDC 330.01/12—dc23

Typeset by Erin Cooper

Printed in Canada

10 9 8 7 6 5 4 3 2 1

To a clearer understanding of
what is really going on in the world.

"We're facing an inflection point in history—one of those moments in which the decisions we make today are going to determine the future for decades to come. That is what I've come to talk to you about tonight."

Joe Biden's Oval Office address,
October 19, 2023

Xi Jinping: "Right now there are changes the likes of which we haven't seen for 100 years and we are the ones driving those changes together."

Vladimir Putin: "I agree."

Moscow, March 22, 2023

CONTENTS

THE FOG OF WAR

On the morning of May 26, 1968, a young Icelandic boy set out on his bicycle. It was a quiet Sunday. He soon entered history as the only person injured by the arrival of *Hægri dagurinn*, the Icelandic name for the day the small country would switch from driving on the left to the right. Plans to make the switch had been underway for decades—centuries, in fact. Denmark, which had governed Iceland since the Middle Ages, made the switch from left to right in 1793, back in the days of horse-drawn carriages. But there was so little traffic on the island that Iceland never got around to following suit. As motorized cars and buses started appearing in Reykjavík in the early twentieth century, planners began to consider the question again and plans were drawn up. But they were interrupted by the outbreak of the Second World War, which Iceland spent under occupation by British troops, who drove on the left. A couple of decades after the British went home, Iceland was ready. A total of 5,727 traffic signs were moved from one side of the street to the other. Thirty-three million krónur was spent modifying the country's fleet of buses to allow passengers to embark from the right. Everything seemed to be ready.

And yet, when the big day arrived, at least one little boy didn't see it coming. Navigating with the misplaced confidence we all exhibit from time to time, he was struck by a car that must have seemed to come out of nowhere. If you're on the lookout for danger approaching from one side, and it materializes on the other, it can only seem as though the everyday world has been transformed into a maze full of unexpected threats. This is our experience of the new normal. It is probably inevitable, and we tend to get into it because it seems beneficial. But if we're not paying attention, we're going to get hurt.

Even if we plan meticulously, something is going to go wrong when the world flips from one way of doing things to an entirely different way. The trouble is, we don't always plan meticulously. We tend not to pay much attention at all. But then, we don't pay much attention to the old normal either. Why did Icelanders and Englishmen drive (or initially ride their horses) on the left in the first place? It made good sense in the days when people went about armed. If you're right-handed, and most people are, you want any potential enemy on your right. So horsemen passed each other on the left. Why then switch to the right? The answer seems to be that as European wagons got bigger, teamsters started riding on the back of one of the draft horses. A right-handed teamster would want to sit on a horse harnessed on the left, for the same reason a swordsman would want to pass another on the left—to allow him to wield a whip without reaching across his body. If you're sitting on the left, it's best to drive on the right, as we do in most cars in the world. So Iceland was moving from a world optimized for swordsmen to a world optimized for teamsters (and imported left-hand-drive cars). Not that any of them cared. The old normal just kind of happened that way, as did the new.

For all of the planning and debate, *Hægri dagurinn* wasn't under anyone's control. Iceland (like Sweden the year before) was more like a surfer on the shoulder of a wave than an engineer planning the future. The world was changing, shaped by forces that had first made themselves felt centuries before. The best that policy-making can do under those circumstances is adapt.

Today, we are all in the same situation as Icelandic motorists. The world is changing. It won't be transformed overnight, but it is changing fast. And we are definitely not in control. Decisions made decades and even centuries ago are presenting us—our governments, our corporations, our bankers—with novel risks and dangers emerging seemingly out of nowhere. Policies that seemed like a good idea not all that long ago have become traps. Investments that looked bullish have turned into bad deals. Allies have turned out to be rivals. Rivals have turned out to be enemies. And we may turn out to have been our own worst enemies. In this new world, where danger bears down on us from precisely the direction we are not in the habit of looking, we are going to be blindsided. That is why we need a map of the new normal to see where we are really heading.

This map will feature more than a few surprises. Things won't be where we expect them to be. Directions, even polarity, will have changed. Highways that once took us somewhere we wanted to go will lead us to dead ends. The new normal will be frustrating for many, maybe worse than frustrating. There will be broken limbs. It's all the more dangerous right now—as the street signs have not yet all been changed.

But some of them have been. In the past few years, the world has had clear signals of what the new normal is going to look like. Some signs remain in their old spots, some have been taken down, some are ambiguous, and some are even deliberately misleading.

There is a very good reason for that. The shift to a new normal is a shift to war. In the past few years we have seen the conflagration of old frictions escalate into open military conflict. But this has been preceded by other modes of warfare: economic, cyber, diplomatic, and most obviously, informational. The latter should come as no surprise. When war kindles, we find ourselves immersed in a descending informational fog. It's called propaganda.

Propaganda—or misinformation, as it is more frequently called today—is the systemic practice of providing misleading or heavily biased information in order to influence the public into supporting a particular cause or political interest. In times of war, propaganda serves only one purpose: to galvanize support for the ongoing war effort. Like a ray of ultraviolet light, propaganda is all but invisible to the naked eye. But that doesn't mean it is difficult to discern its effects. They are everywhere to be seen.

We see it in the glaring double standards in political and war news coverage. When the United States unleashed a devastating missile attack on Iraq, it was celebrated in the America media as "shock and awe" and a testament to the prowess of America's newest generation of precision guided missiles. But when Russia deployed a small fraction of that destructive force in Ukraine, it was denounced as barbaric and inhumane. When different standards are applied to different actors, we find ourselves in the fog of war.

In Western societies, it is commonplace to think of propaganda as the exclusive domain of the media in authoritarian countries. But is consensus shaped all that differently in the West than in, say, China or Russia? Of course, many things are done differently there. But powerful interests everywhere do their best to shape what is called the "narrative." And that has held true in Western democracies as much as it has held anywhere else. For example, without forceful misinformation campaigns, the Vietnam and Gulf Wars would never have gotten underway. Today we might look back on the Gulf of Tonkin incident and the phantom Iraqi weapons of mass destruction and shake our heads at our own credulity. It was as if the world shuffled into war under hypnosis, and it was only later that we came to our senses.

Recently, the US Army's 4th Psychological Operations Group released a recruiting video with the unsettling question "Have you ever wondered . . . who pulls the strings?" The answer is, as per the video, *we do*: "You'll find us in the shadows. We can deceive, persuade, change, influence, inspire. We are everywhere." The unit's motto is "*Verbum Vincit*"—"The word conquers." We don't have to guess that we are in the middle of an information war. At least one side is boasting of its prowess—and that we are its targets.

The "psywar" video also makes clear who America's enemies are. It warns, "A threat rises in the East," followed by footage of Chinese military parades and news coverage of the war in Ukraine. It paints a picture of imminent conflict. And make no mistake about it: if you live in a NATO nation, your country is at war. While military action is at least for the moment off the table, the conflict has encouraged Western governments to weaponize their economies in a manner seldom if ever seen before. And that is how the war front comes home to you, whether you are sitting comfortably at home in North America, in Western Europe, in Japan, or in Australia. Because, as you have probably already noticed, economic warfare is a two-way street. For the first time in many, many years, the West is tangling with opponents who have ample economic resources to fight back.

In the past, sanctions have been used as a weapon by the strong against the weak. But any undergraduate in an economics program should be able to easily understand that if David Ricardo's theory of comparative advantage explains why trade should be mutually benefi-cial, it also stands to reason that sanctions should be mutually destruc-tive. Deployed against larger, more productive economies, sanctions can be expected to harm those who deploy them as much as if not more than those who find themselves sanctioned (especially in the case of countries that fully expected to be sanctioned and have thus spent the better part of a decade making themselves sanction-proof). On many occasions in the long history of the practice, sanctions have boomer-anged against the very countries imposing them. So, instead of NATO sanctions on Russian energy bringing that resource-dependent econ-omy to its knees, the economic impacts ricochet back on energy con-sumers in the economies of the countries imposing the sanctions.

And that leaves you bearing much of the economic burden that is intended to be borne by the Russian and increasingly Chinese econo-mies. Whether you are one of the 20 million households in Germany that had to cut back on gas consumption during the winter heating season, or among the millions of British households that saw their energy bills soar, or among the American motorists who at one point had to shell out a record five dollars a gallon to fill up their vehicles at the pumps, or a farmer paying record prices for fertilizer, the war in Ukraine has come home to you on a variety of economic fronts.

No doubt there will be a multitude of books written about the geopolitical consequences of this particular conflict. What follows here is an attempt to explain how the conflict in Ukraine and on other emerging battlefronts between the old world order and the emerging new one signals profound changes in the way our economies are organized and how they will operate in the future—so much so that we're not just talking about the end of an economic cycle. What we are talking about is the end of an economic era—the end of what we've all come to think of as "normal" since the Second World War.

It's not our enemies who can take credit for that, at least not initially. It was instead the COVID-19 pandemic that first broke the links of global supply chains, the very arterial structure of globalization. As we will see in the chapters ahead, lockdowns gave us all a glimpse of a world in which the postwar certainties of comparative advantage, lower tariffs, offshore production, wage arbitrage, and just-in-time delivery could no longer be counted on to operate smoothly and seamlessly, as they had done for decades before. The world is still reeling from that shock.

But as damaging as the pandemic was to the free movement of goods, capital, and technology across borders, its impact, in the broad sweep of history, has been fleeting. Whether vaccines blunted the aggressiveness of the virus or COVID simply followed the path of most viruses toward lower and lower virulence is a question we can leave to others to debate. What we can say is that no one is worrying anymore about lockdowns or the risk of health-care systems being overwhelmed by COVID patients. The epidemiological story is all but over. But the shift in the way our economies operate has barely begun.

Resuming global trade after COVID is a little like resuming a game of Monopoly after someone has flipped the board. It can happen only after a mad and probably acrimonious scramble. The diplomatic, economic, technological, and cultural confrontation between the Atlantic and Eurasian powers had been going on for years. After COVID flipped the board, that confrontation entered a new phase—the sanctions war, the consequences of which will prove far more lasting than the impact the pandemic had.

The chasm that divides the global economy into geopolitical blocs grows wider and wider, and each new round of sanctions politicizes an ever-increasing share of global trade, leaving in tatters the once rules-based trading system championed by the World Trade Organization (WTO). In their wake, sanctions have not only Balkanized global trade and finance into competing regional blocs, but in the process they have also resurrected an economic demon that we thought was long extinct.

Inflation has risen from the grave and reached levels not seen for decades. And it has proven surprisingly resilient against efforts to stuff it back into its coffin. Like a cancer that begins as a localized tumour, it first manifested in food and energy prices, and as the soaring cost of living begets wage increases, it has since metastasized to impact the entire economy. And the very policies that governments successfully employed to fight the devastating economic impacts of the pandemic—record-low interest rates and record-high spending, and the resulting expansion of the money supply and fiscal deficits— have nourished inflation like it has seldom been nourished by policies in the past. In the context of yesterday's lockdowns, flooring the pedal on fiscal and monetary stimulus provided an economic lifeline to millions of households locked out of their jobs and unable to work. But in today's economic environment, it's akin to trying to extinguish a fire with gasoline.

Admittedly, getting the policy mix right for a rapidly and profoundly changing world is no simple task. The tectonic movement of massive geopolitical plates is driven by seismic forces of unprecedented proportions. The task requires, first and foremost, a clear understanding of the lay of the land that an emerging new global order brings. But our ability to map the contours of this "new normal" is made increasingly difficult by the fact that virtually everything we see is glimpsed through the fog of war.

Still, we are not blind. We are vulnerable to dangers surprising us from the fog, as was that young boy innocently riding his bike in Iceland back in 1968. But only if we're looking the wrong way. Only if we're not paying attention. In the weeks following *Hægri dagurinn*, when so much seemed poised to go so wrong, traffic accidents in Iceland actually declined. Drivers plied the streets and highways with new attentiveness. Because whichever side of the road we drive on, the real risk is complacency.

CHAPTER I

THE BIG EASY
(COMING OUT OF THE PANDEMIC)

In the time of our greatest calamity we never had it so good. While the COVID-19 virus in its various mutations cost millions of workers in G7 countries their jobs, it was simultaneously true that nobody seemed to have to work anymore. Everybody, it seemed, was on some kind of government-paid program.

Since the initial wave of the viral pandemic washed ashore, G7 countries have spent some $2.2 trillion on a bevy of programs, including direct income-support payments to households whose jobs have been lost to the economic shutdowns or generous wage subsidies to corporations to help foot their wage bill and keep employees working. The United States, for example, spent more than $1.5 trillion in pandemic offsets, including three rounds of direct payments to households regardless of their employment status. In Canada, the federal government claims to have spent over $300 billion sheltering Canadians from the economic lockdowns that the pandemic forced.

All that fiscal generosity left everyone flush with cash. Thanks to the generous support payments, North American households were financially better off during the pandemic-induced sharp recession than they were before. And when the economy finally reopened, all that pent-up demand, armed with months of benefit cheques, sent retail sales soaring through the roof.

We all, of course, liked getting a free lunch—whether we were a worker or a corporation. But was it *really* free?

As it turned out, the flip side of the fiscal generosity shown by governments around the world was a massive and unprecedented increase in the size of (peacetime) fiscal deficits. The US deficit tripled to a record $3 trillion, reaching 15 percent of its GDP, the highest level since the Second World War. The European Union (EU) had to suspend one of its founding principles—the Stability and Growth Pact, which had limited members from running a budget deficit in excess of 3 percent of GDP—as its deficit in 2020 rose to over twice that level. The pact's limits on deficit size and total debt size relative to GDP remains suspended, with fiscally wayward countries like Greece and Italy continuing to run budget deficits in the 7 percent of GDP range. In the United Kingdom, pandemic spending pushed deficits to 13 percent of GDP. And the deficit in Canada increased by a factor of ten—the largest increase as a percentage of GDP among all the Organisation for Economic Co-operation and Development (OECD) countries.

The scale of those increases in budgetary deficits leaves one wondering whether there is any limit to how much debt governments can rack up. Economists can debate that issue theoretically until the cows come home, but the real question is: Should taxpayers care? Most taxpayers in G7 countries didn't seem to be too fussed about their governments' fiscal situation. Few parties even addressed the issue during elections.

In the past, however, taxpayers would have cared plenty about fiscal deficits of this size. Back then, spendthrift governments that racked up massive deficits would have incurred huge financial penalties in terms of the interest rates payable to place their debt in global bond markets. And those increases in borrowing costs would have been passed on, in turn, to both the country's corporations and households, making everyone in the economy pay more to borrow money. Not surprisingly, the potential for that economic chain reaction used to get the attention of most voters when confronted with unwieldy government deficits.

So why weren't voters complaining about the explosion in fiscal deficits during the pandemic? The key reason for voter indifference was that the chain reaction between the size of government deficits and the price of financing those deficits in the bond market had suddenly been short-circuited. But why? What changed in the bond market that blunted if not totally nullified the impact that huge government deficits would normally have had on government borrowing rates and the yields paid to investors holding their debt?

In a nutshell, what changed was who was buying government debt in the bond market during the pandemic and in its immediate aftermath. In the past, it would have been financial institutions like pension plans and insurance companies or even individual retail investors who financed budgetary deficits by purchasing government debt sold in the bond market. And there was a very simple rule at play: the more bonds a government had to issue to cover its deficit, the higher the yield or interest rate the government had to pay those holding its bonds. The principle is called supply and demand, and it works for setting the price of government bonds in the same way that it works for setting the price of everything else.

But that rule didn't apply to central banks, which suddenly emerged during the pandemic as the principal buyer of government debt. While pension plans, insurance companies, and retail investors would have demanded those borrowing premiums in the face of unprecedented peacetime deficits, they weren't the ones buying the flood of government bonds issued during the pandemic. Suddenly, there was a new player in the game: central banks, whose purchases dwarfed those of other participants in the market.

Whether we were talking about the Federal Reserve Board, or the European Central Bank, or the Bank of Canada, or the Bank of England, or the Reserve Bank of Australia, central banks became the principal buyers of their government's debt. It was these banks that were suddenly financing all those generous support programs governments offered in the midst of the COVID-19 pandemic and the ensuing lockdowns of their economies. And as they continued to gorge themselves on tranche after tranche of government debt, their balance sheets ballooned, swollen with trillions of dollars of government-issued bonds.

QUANTITATIVE EASING (OR PRINTING MORE MONEY)

Admittedly, the size of their central bank's balance sheet isn't something the average voter spends a whole lot of time thinking about. Nevertheless, they might ask themselves where the central bank got the money it used to suddenly buy all these government-issued bonds. The answer was simple enough: they just printed it. They've been doing a lot of that lately.

The money-printing practice is known as quantitative easing, and it's given governments a licence to spend like never before. By all accounts they've made maximum use of it. Quantitative easing has effectively replaced the discipline that the bond market used to impose on government borrowing before the practice found its way into the central banks' tool box.

The Federal Reserve Board, the central bank of the largest economy in the world, set the standard for other central banks to follow with its massive purchases of Treasuries. Those purchases shielded the bond market from having to finance the tripling of Washington's budget deficit. Federal Reserve Board chair Jerome Powell authorized no less than $120 billion a month of central bank purchases, split evenly between US Treasuries and federally backed mortgages. As a result of all the money printed to buy these bonds the American money supply increased 38 percent over the two years during which the pandemic elicited emergency spending programs from Washington. That scale of monetary expansion was a multiple of normal monetary growth, roughly 7 percent a year.

North of the border the Bank of Canada pretty well followed suit. In 2021, Governor Tiff Macklem authorized the purchase of C$5 billion of Government of Canada bonds every *week* to finance the massive C\$327 billion deficit that finance minister Chrystia Freeland created in her budget.

While today it is used as a means of financing massive fiscal deficits, the practice of quantitative easing didn't start out that way. It had another purpose altogether. The term itself was coined by former chair of the Federal Reserve Board Ben Bernanke back in 2008. But the original inventor of the plan was actually the Bank of Japan, which had been practising some form of it since the 1990s—a time known as the lost decade in Japan after the country's real estate and stock market bubble burst.

Before the advent of quantitative easing, central banks had relied on adjusting their short-term policy rate to fine-tune monetary policy. Hence, in the United States market attention was focused on any announced changes to the benchmark federal funds rate. If the Federal Reserve Board lowered or raised the federal funds rate, commercial banks would quickly follow suit, passing on the central bank move to borrowers and lenders throughout the economy. But as the Bank of Japan had learned, there was nothing a central bank could do to stimulate its economy after its policy rate had approached zero. It was akin to pushing on a string.

So central banks began to focus on bringing down longer-term interest rates like mortgages. Since mortgage rates were based on what the government was paying to borrow money, the way to bring them down was for central banks to start buying government bonds and, in the process, bring down government borrowing costs. In some cases (for example, the Federal Reserve Board), the central bank bought federally approved residential mortgages as well.

That meant that central banks could not only bring down short-term interest rates through adjusting their policy rate (like the federal funds rate in the United States), but they could also bring down long-term interest rates by buying their government's bonds or mortgage bonds. It was an extraordinary change in how central banks could influence borrowing costs throughout the economy—one that allowed the monetary authorities to influence the entire yield curve and not just short-term money market rates that were tied to its target rate. As such, quantitative easing simultaneously provided an enormous boost to the stock markets that competed with government bonds for investors' capital. The housing market also got a boost, with the demand for homes turbocharged by record-low mortgage rates. And as stock and real estate prices went up, so too did the borrowing power of anyone holding those assets.

Very few of us are eager to criticize wealth that seems to fall out of the sky. So there weren't a lot of complaints when the pandemic presented governments with a new problem for quantitative easing to solve. Suddenly, stimulating the economy through cuts to the short-term interest rate target was no longer the name of the game. Now it was all about bringing down long-term interest rates otherwise determined in the bond market. And if an extraordinary amount of fiscal stimulus came as part of the deal, so much the better.

Before quantitative easing became commonplace in monetary policy, the amount of fiscal stimulus a government could provide to the economy was always circumscribed by the impact that huge fiscal deficits would have on the government's, and everyone else's, borrowing costs. That was because when governments racked up huge deficits in the past, their cost of borrowing (government bond yields) would become punitive compared to what was incurred when they exercised a greater degree of fiscal probity in their borrowing appetites.

The more bonds that the market had to absorb from an issuing government, the higher the yield that government would have to pay to place all its debt in the bond market. As a result, higher deficits quickly led to higher interest rates, and, of course, higher interest rates would in turn be an impediment to economic growth, offsetting much of the fiscal stimulus that deficit spending itself was supposed to impart. That very impact on debt-servicing costs brought a strong measure of self-restraint and market discipline to government borrowing and spending.

Soaring debt-servicing costs also had a nasty feedback impact on government deficits themselves and, therefore, fiscal policy. The higher the interest rate that the government had to pay on its bonds, the greater the percentage of its tax revenue that would have to be devoted to paying debt-servicing costs instead of paying for vote-getting program spending. Over time, program spending would be "crowded out" by rising debt-serving payments.

However, the adverse consequences of massive government spending and deficits were suddenly suspended during the pandemic, thanks to massive central bank purchases of government bonds. So, despite the mammoth size of the fiscal deficits racked up during these years, a funny thing happened. Not only did debt-servicing costs as a percentage of total government spending or government revenue not rise as would normally have been the case, but they remained near historic lows during most of the pandemic and the associated economic lockdowns. In fact, after tabling a record C\$327 billion deficit, ten times larger than originally expected, Canadian finance minister Chrystia Freeland even bragged about how low the federal government's debt servicing costs were.

Massive purchases of government bonds by central banks simply overwhelmed the natural laws of supply and demand that would otherwise have been in force in the bond market to determine the interest rate that a government would have to pay on its debt issuance. By dominating government bond purchases, quantitative easing allowed central banks to finance massive deficits at trivial interest rates and, in turn, trivial debt-servicing costs.

It would seem, then, that quantitative easing gave us the best of both worlds: cheap money provided by central banks for governments to spend freely on us. But what was lost in this novel way of funding government deficits was the market discipline that the bond market normally would have exercised on governments' spending intentions. And without that discipline, panic-stricken governments were able to amass unheard-of-sized deficits without incurring any financial penalties.

History, though, warns that a marriage of record-high deficits and record-low interest rates cannot last. But the longer it prevails, the costlier the divorce—and hence, the more unlikely it is that one will ever occur. All the more so if it's not just the government's financing costs that are being massively subsidized by runaway central bank bond purchases. During the pandemic, yours were too. Which is why no one was complaining. We were all benefiting from the "big easy."

Whether you are a corporation or a household, your borrowing rate is based on your government's borrowing rate. You, of course, pay a credit premium on top of the government rate, but nevertheless, the interest rate you are charged to borrow is based on how much your government is charged to do the same. So the lower the yield on your government's bond, the lower the financing rate on your car lease and, most importantly, the lower the mortgage rate for your home—which is far and away the biggest source of your debt. That is why you didn't hear too many homeowners or corporations complain about lax monetary policy.

In fact, not only did they not complain, but they did what record-low borrowing costs incented them to do. Corporations and homeowners gorged themselves with ever more debt. As a result, both public and private debt were being financed at artificially low interest rates—and those very same artificially low interest rates, brought about by super-accommodative monetary policy, in turn encouraged the explosive growth of more debt. It was a virtuous circle as long as central banks kept on doing what their governments instructed them to do—which was simply to print more money and use it to buy more government bonds at ludicrously low yields.

And that is why you were probably not concerned about the size of your government's budget deficit. When your government pays record-low interest rates to borrow, you also pay record-low interest rates to borrow. And if sky-high deficits don't increase your cost of borrowing, why should you care—particularly when you are receiving a generous stream of COVID-19 subsidies in one form or another?

But were such generous polices sustainable? Well, that depended on how much longer central banks around the world could keep buying their government's bonds that paid record-low interest rates.

And that, in turn, depended on one thing only: inflation.

CHAPTER 2

INFLATION

Incremental change can be hard to recognize. Things such as bio-diversity loss or rising levels of atmospheric carbon dioxide are famously impossible to spot. We generalize about decades and generations, but the eighties didn't really start on January 1, 1980, any more than someone born five minutes after the last millennial will be all that different from those who came before. This is a truth overlooked by many boiling frogs. It is hard to identify the moment we pass a threshold.

Hard, but not impossible. In the summer of 2023, economists started to notice a convergence of troubling trends in Europe. In France, red wine and foie gras consumption were markedly down. Across the border, Germans were stinting on pricy organic food. Spaniards were learning to do without their usual quotient of olive oil. The Finnish government took to asking citizens to enjoy their saunas only on windy days, when renewable energy was more plentiful. The Italian cabinet called a crisis meeting to figure out what to do about the spiking cost of pasta. It seemed as though old stereotypes had something to say about the new normal: Europeans were getting poorer.

The numbers are clear. Fifteen years ago, Europeans accounted for about a quarter of global spending on consumption. They now spend about 18 percent. Part of that is that Europeans just have less to spend. Real wages are down about 3 percent in Germany, 6 percent in Greece. But sinking incomes are only half of the story. The other is rising prices.

In the United Kingdom, inflation was running at about 10 percent through 2023, and energy costs were growing much faster than that. Some householders were forced to go without heat earlier in the year, while others—like their peers across Europe—turned to burning wood to stay warm. In late 2023, Bristol City Council brought in new bylaws to regulate the smoke from woodstoves, which the national government has called a health hazard. Said one councillor: "As we see the cost of living crisis hit more, we know people are using inappropriate means to heat and power their homes because they can't afford any alternative."[1] Those who can't afford gas will face fines of £300 for burning wood instead. But they need not worry about enforcement, as the government is broke too. "How are we supposed to [enforce the new laws] with the incredible cuts that we've had to local government?" the same councillor asked. Huw Pill, the Bank of England's chief economist, told British citizens that inflation and the decline in living standards is the new normal: "Yes, we're all worse off."[2]

Not that inflation is normally measured in foie gras or cordwood. Energy and food prices may not be considered "core" in a central bank assessment of underlying inflation, but they are pretty "core" when it comes to the budget of most households. In fact, most households consider their grocery bills to be as good a measure of inflation as there is. Yet their omission from central bank measurements of core inflation is based on the presumption that movements in food and energy prices reflect "transitory" forces that can easily distort an accurate assessment of underlying or systemic inflation.

Even so, in the initial stages of an inflationary outbreak it's usually the food and energy components of the consumer price index (CPI)—precisely the prices that central banks typically ignore—that fuel the rapid rise in headline (or all-items) inflation. As a result, the headline rate of inflation usually runs well ahead of the core measurement of inflation, at least initially. But at some point in an inflationary cycle, often after food and energy prices have peaked, core inflation starts to advance at a faster rate than headline inflation. That critical inflection point occurs when everyone from airline pilots to auto workers starts chasing those big headline inflation numbers that soaring food and energy prices have brought with demands for compensating wage increases. And wages have much to be compensated for. In 2022, grocery bills for the average American household rose more than 11 percent, over five times the twenty-year average increase of 2 percent.

While central banks are powerless to prevent food or energy price shocks, they can govern their inflationary fallout. An oil price shock, for example, doesn't have to be inflationary unless central banks choose to soften the impact by printing more money. If they refuse to monetize the shock and the money supply remains the same, soaring oil prices will force households to spend more of their money on energy and less on everything else—which means, in turn, that the prices of everything else should fall with the drop-off in demand. So while the relative price of oil will have risen dramatically relative to the price of everything else, the overall price level need not rise at all.

If, on the other hand, central banks do monetize the price shock, the positive impact of their actions on household spending could cushion the blow of higher energy prices and allow consumers to maintain their spending on everything else. In that case there would be no offsetting decline in the prices of everything else to cancel or at least partially offset the increase in energy prices, and the general price level and inflation would rise. And the higher and longer inflation rises, the more likely that it will induce workers to chase those soaring prices in their wage demands, setting off a self-perpetuating wage-price spiral long after the initial catalysts for inflation, like food prices or energy prices, began to rise.

So, while inflation typically starts with a price shock—for oil, more often than not—it quickly spreads from energy prices to all prices through wages.

ENERGY SHOCKS HAVE BEEN COMMON TO
ALL PAST INFLATIONARY EPISODES

It's certainly no coincidence that virtually all of the major inflationary outbreaks in the postwar era have had soaring fuel prices at their onset. And of all the fuel prices that have mattered in our economy, the price of oil has always mattered the most.

When the price of oil has gone up, the price of almost everything else has followed.

That was certainly the case back in the inflation-prone 1970s, when Saudi Arabia and its Arab partners proclaimed an oil embargo on countries that were deemed to be supporting Israel in the Yom Kippur War, which began in October 1973. That group included Canada, Japan, the Netherlands, the United Kingdom, and the United States, and subsequently included other countries as well. By the time the embargo was finally lifted in March 1974, the price of oil had quadrupled from $3 a barrel to nearly $12 dollars a barrel.

North American motorists lined up for hours at filling stations as fuel supplies became scarce. President Richard Nixon even lowered the speed limit on American highways in an effort to promote fuel conservation. It didn't take long for soaring oil prices to filter through to the price of just about everything. CPI inflation climbed into double-digit territory before an oil-based North American economy crashed into a deep recession.

A scant five years later the world economy was subjected to another major oil shock, with devastating consequences for both inflation and, ultimately, growth. The overthrow of the shah might have been an uplifting event for most Iranians, but the oil shock that followed in the wake of the Iranian Revolution threw into doubt the functioning of one of the world's largest oil industries. The following year, those doubts came to fruition when oil production in Iran fell markedly during the ensuing war with Iraq. Oil prices more than doubled, to almost $40 a barrel. In the space of a decade and over the course of two separate Organization of Petroleum

Exporting Countries (OPEC) supply shocks, the price of oil had increased tenfold.

Just as they had back in 1974, soaring oil prices pushed inflation into double-digit territory. This time around, however, it evoked a far more drastic response from the monetary authorities. Instead of trying to monetize the price shock, the Federal Reserve Board, under Paul Volcker's leadership, pushed its trendsetting federal funds rate up to 20 percent, triggering not one but two recessions over the 1980–81 period—the so-called double-dip recessions.

A third, albeit much lesser, oil shock occurred in 1990, when Saddam Hussein ordered an Iraqi invasion of neighbouring Kuwait, leaving many of that country's oil wells on fire. Monthly oil prices soared from $17 a barrel in July 1990 to as high as $46 a barrel. Not only were the two warring countries significant producers in their own right, but there was also concern at the time that the war might spread to the world's largest oil producer—Saudi Arabia. Those concerns quickly dissipated when a US-led coalition repelled the Iraqi invasion and oil production was quickly restored in the region. Nevertheless, annual CPI inflation, driven by surging oil prices, averaged 5.4 percent in the United States in 1990.

And last but certainly by no means least was the run-up in oil prices to an all-time record high of $147 a barrel in 2008, forcing interest rate hikes that ultimately burst the financial bubble that had grown around the fraudulent securitization of subprime mortgages into toxic collateralized debt obligations—or CDOs, as they were known on Wall Street. The ensuing recession, now known as the Great Recession, was the deepest the world economy had seen since the Second World War. And it was accompanied by a world financial crisis that bankrupted a number of major financial institutions, most notably Lehman Brothers, and forced massive government-sponsored bailouts of other crippled investment banks and insurance companies.

Given those historical precedents, it was hard to ignore what was happening in global oil markets by the end of 2021. Oil prices, having crashed during the pandemic to lows not seen in decades, had risen to over $80 a barrel, conjuring up memories of past oil shocks.

Following the economic lockdowns from the pandemic, the World Bank estimated that energy prices had seen the greatest two-year increase since the first OPEC oil shock, in 1973. While in percentage terms the price of oil may not have risen as much as it did during past OPEC oil shocks, this latest round involved much more than just the price of oil. Natural gas prices in Europe and coal prices globally had risen even more. In the case of thermal coal—the fuel that the world economy was supposedly weaning itself off—the price reached an all-time high. Ditto for European natural gas prices after supply from Russia was disrupted.

All of that left the world pondering one very troubling question: Since every energy shock over the last five decades had led to a global recession, why wouldn't current runaway energy costs lead to the same result?

The answer depended on what central banks were prepared to do about the inflation that their easy money policies during the pandemic had unleashed.

TALKING THE TALK OR WALKING THE WALK?

When you get right down to it, central banking is really a confidence game. The primary task of a central bank is to control inflation. If corporations and individuals believe that their central bank will be successful in that task, they will behave accordingly. Workers won't be worried about inflation eating up the purchasing power of their wages, so they won't have to ask for compensating increases in their remuneration. And if corporations believe that their workers' wage demands will remain modest, they won't have to hike up their prices to protect their profit margins. So confidence in your central bank's ability to manage inflation affects actual economic behaviour. And, likewise, a lack of confidence in the central bank affects the behaviour of economic actors.

In recent years, public confidence in monetary policy has been anchored by an inflation rate target that each central bank sets. The most common target is 2 percent, which is the official inflation target rate of the Federal Reserve Board, the European Central Bank, the Bank of Canada, the Bank of England, and the Reserve Bank of Australia, among many others.

The target rate is supposed to work in the same way a traffic signal does. An inflation rate below the central bank's target rate is a green light for growth-promoting policies like easy credit conditions and lower interest rates. It signals that there is slack in the economy and points to the presence of what economists call an output gap (the difference between actual GDP and potential GDP if the economy were operating at full employment). Conversely, an inflation rate above the central bank's target rate signals a red light for growth and cause for monetary tightening and rising interest rates. It indicates that the economy is overheating and needs to be cooled off through a slowing of economic growth.

In recent decades, inflation has been more or less comatose, often running below the 2 percent target rate mandated by North American and European central banks. In fact, some central banks, like the European Central Bank, have at least publicly deemed deflation to be a greater risk than inflation in recent years. In a benign inflationary environment, central banks were able to set their trendsetting policy rates at levels that by any historic benchmark were absurdly low—by some accounts, the lowest in five thousand years of recorded history.

The Federal Reserve Board set the federal funds rate in the United States at effectively zero; the Bank of Canada's policy rate was set at a quarter point; and in some instances the European Central Bank's rates were even negative, in which case depositors actually paid their banks to hold their money for them. To many investors and borrowers alike, those rates seemed like the new normal. And as long as there was no credible inflation threat, they were. But suddenly, the inflationary genie was out of the bottle, and central banks were very reluctant to force it back in.

As a general rule in monetary policy, the longer it takes a central bank to react to an inflationary outburst, the higher interest rates will ultimately have to climb to eventually collar price pressures, and the greater the toll those same interest rate hikes will ultimately have on the economy. That principle doesn't bode well for how the central banks' current bout with inflation will turn out, given how late they were to respond to it.

By mid-2021, central banks were witnessing something that hadn't been seen in decades. Out of nowhere, inflation was suddenly heating up all around the world. At first, the central bankers tried to slough off the embarrassingly high inflation numbers. Federal Reserve Board chair Jerome Powell and the Bank of Canada's Tiff Macklem both stated that the rise in inflation was "transient," citing so-called base-year effects on the year-over-year measurement of prices from artificially low levels induced by the pandemic. But as the months wore on, with each one bringing an even higher inflation rate than the one before it, that excuse sounded less and less convincing.

Having misdiagnosed the initial outbreak, central banks were slow to treat the patient. The initial Federal Reserve Board rate hike did not occur until US CPI inflation was already running at an annual rate of more than 5 percent, over twice the central bank's target rate. And even then the Fed's initial move was a paltry twenty-five-basis-point hike from a record-low near-zero setting for its key federal funds target rate. Ditto for the Bank of Canada, which has more or less taken its cue on both the timing and size of rate hikes from the Federal Reserve Board.

Having been widely criticized for not responding to inflation running at multiples of official target rates, both central banks and even the European Central Bank have switched gears in a hurry, in a desperate attempt to regain lost credibility. The subsequent run-up in interest rates, marked by a succession of jumbo-size seventy-five-basis-point hikes by the Federal Reserve Board, was the largest and quickest run-up in interest rates in four decades. But even so, central bank interest rates were certainly not high compared to any historic benchmark and were still running well behind the rate of inflation.

How long central banks will continue on a tightening course is far from assured, even though they steadfastly claim that they will raise interest rates until inflation is wrestled back down to target rates. But that task may soon become a lot more difficult. It's one thing to tighten monetary policy while the economy is still growing and creating jobs, which pretty well describes the lay of the land during most if not all of the tightening to date. It is another policy challenge altogether for central banks to continue to tighten when the economy is shrinking and voters are losing their jobs—all the more so when those same voters will soon be heading to the polls.

"CLASS WAR"

What central banks fear the most in their battle against inflation is the dreaded wage-price spiral that catapulted inflation into double-digit territory during the 1970s. And yet, by responding so belatedly and allowing inflation to take root in the economy, they have created exactly the conditions where a wage-price spiral is now very likely to take place.

Those concerns were expressed in the summer of 2022, when Bank of Canada governor Tiff Macklem urged businesses not to give in to exorbitant wage demands and promised that careful monetary management at the central bank would soon bring inflation down. Not surprisingly, his call received an immediate rebuke from organized labour, which reminded him that the inflationary threat faced by workers had been created precisely by monetary mismanagement at the central bank. As monetary policy inches ever closer to a policy-mandated recession to bring inflation down, the battle between unions and their central bank is likely to heat up.

Already some union movements—like Canada's Unifor, for example, the largest private-sector union in the country—are accusing their central bank of engaging in class warfare. That's because the Bank of

Canada, along with the Federal Reserve Board and many other central banks, is deliberately trying to *raise* unemployment in an effort to thwart a wage-price spiral that would keep inflation running along a self-sustaining course. So while politicians are always promising their constituents that they are working to create more jobs, their central banks are busily trying to destroy jobs by tightening the monetary screws on the economy in an effort to wrestle wages down. You can rest assured that even in the darkest moments of the new normal, politicians will not be campaigning on a platform of destroying millions of jobs.

In the meantime, for North American workers—if not for workers throughout most OECD economies—the good news since the pandemic is that wages are growing at their fastest pace in over a decade as workers rediscover a bargaining power that they'd thought was lost forever. At the same time, however, those same wage increases have been trailing soaring inflation, leaving workers with less and less purchasing power. Real, or inflation-adjusted, wages are falling at one of the fastest paces seen in years.

Back in the 1970s, when workers faced a similar dilemma from the inflationary fallout of the OPEC oil shocks, strikes became the norm as organized labour attempted to negotiate wage increases that would give them protection from ever-rising inflation. It's no coincidence that the inflationary 1970s (US CPI inflation averaged almost 7 percent) saw, according to the US Bureau of Labor Statistics, almost six thousand strikes—the highest of any postwar decade.

But most industrial workers at the time were unionized, and thus in a position to take strike action. Back then, one in every three private-sector workers in America belonged to a union. In some industries like trucking, unions like the Teamsters had signed up 90 percent of industry employees. And even those workers who didn't belong to a union often benefited from their presence, as their employers often felt compelled to offer near-comparable wage rates to union settlements in order to discourage their own workforces from organizing.

Today, only one in ten workers belongs to a union in the United States, one in twenty among private-sector workers. The very industries that housed much of union membership have themselves virtually disappeared. Decades of trade liberalization stripped away the last vestiges of tariff protection, leaving factory jobs vulnerable to offshoring, which, in the process, gutted union membership. In fact, unionized plants were the first to be closed, on account of the typically higher wages they paid. The word policy-makers use for this is *globalization*.

Goods-sector employment, where the bulk of private-sector union membership came from, peaked more than two decades ago in North America. Up until Donald Trump's presidency and the introduction of huge tariffs against Chinese imports, the goods sector had shed almost 5 million jobs since 2000. The story wasn't much different north of the border, or, for that matter, in any other OECD economy. The Canadian economy hadn't seen any net job creation in the goods sector of the economy for more than two decades, during which time it shed some 600,000 manufacturing jobs.

But if globalization sounded the death knell for unionization, would the collapse of global supply chains devastated by the pandemic provide opportunities for its rebirth?

So it would appear.

The outlook for union membership growth has improved markedly. During the first half of 2022, unions won 641 representation elections in the United States (a more than 75 percent victory rate), which according to the National Labor Relations Board is the most in almost two decades.

Whether this signals a decisive turning point after decades of steeply declining union membership remains to be seen. But there are at least two factors that favour a revival in union membership.

The first is the rapidly vanishing threat of the offshoring that decimated much of North American manufacturing, where the bulk of union membership had been based. Most of that offshoring went to China, which is increasingly the subject of American economic sanctions.

The second factor is the increasing ability of unions to organize in the service sector, into which, until now, they had made very limited inroads. At the same time, the new-found service industries where unions are having success are bringing a different type of worker into the ranks of union membership.

When people think of unions, they think of predominately white, middle-aged men with beer bellies driving to their union halls in beat-up pickup trucks. That was certainly the stereotype when union membership was at its strongest in the 1950s and 1960s. But today the demographics of union membership have changed markedly. More and more new union members today are drawn from the ranks of younger workers. More than anything else, this reflects which sectors of the economy new union membership is coming from.

In the past, millennials and younger generations generally had a negative perception of unions. They considered factory jobs, which accounted for the bulk of private-sector union membership, as dead-end endeavours, even though in most cases they paid a higher wage than many service-sector industries where such workers were employed. Most millennials and Generation X and Z cohorts work in the services side of the economy, or in the so-called gig economy, centred around the ever-pervasive application of digital technology.

Before the pandemic forced millions out of the labour force, most people thought it unthinkable that workers for Starbucks, Amazon, Apple, or Google could ever be organized. But now they are.

Beginning with a lone store in Buffalo, New York, three hundred Starbucks locations have now unionized. In another landmark development, the Amazon Labor Union was founded in 2021; a year later it successfully organized an Amazon warehouse in Staten Island that employed 8,300 workers. Similarly, workers at tech giant Google have formed the Alphabet Workers Union. And 90 percent of those who work in Google's sprawling cafeterias (around 4,000 workers) have organized themselves into a union and went on strike for the first time in 2023. Meanwhile, the Communications Workers of America Union has successfully organized employees in Apple stores in Towson, Maryland, and subsequently in Oklahoma.

Not only are new workers considering union membership, but those that do belong are also flexing their muscles. The historic relationship between inflation and industrial strikes that was so prevalent back in the inflation-prone 1970s seems to be reasserting itself in the post-pandemic labour market. As US inflation rates have more than tripled since coming out of the pandemic, there has been a noticeable increase in strike activity throughout the American economy.

These new union members are increasingly choosing to exercise their option to strike. The number of workers who went on strike in the United States in 2021 tripled over the year before. The surge in both union membership and strike activity continued into 2022 as US CPI inflation rates relentlessly ate away at the purchasing power of wages. During the first half of 2022, there were 180 strikes in the United States, up 76 percent from the previous year and including three times as many workers. And an act of Congress was required to prevent a national railway strike that would have paralyzed large swaths of the American economy.

As in the past, high inflation rates have been a trigger for growing labour militancy and industrial job actions. And despite the noticeable pickup in strike activity, public approval of unions is now at its highest level since 1965 (more than 70 percent compared to less than 50 percent only a decade ago).

In Britain, a million teachers, civil servants, and train drivers walked off their jobs in a coordinated strike in January 2023, adding to the worst labour unrest since the Margaret Thatcher era in the 1980s. Across the English Channel in France, unions CGT and Sud Rail called out their workforce to go on rotating strikes that temporarily closed down much of the country's rail sytem, reminiscent of the populist Yellow Vest mass protests back in 2018.

What is becoming increasingly clear on both sides of the Atlantic is that workers aren't just going to passively sit on the sidelines and watch soaring inflation eat up their paycheques. They are organizing in a manner seldom seen in recent decades and doing what they used to do during tight labour markets—striking for higher pay. And in the post-pandemic labour market, strikes aren't the only ways in which hugely dissatisfied workers are forcing up wage rates.

THE BIG QUIT

Something very curious happened in the labour market during the pandemic, defying all previous cyclical norms. Droves of workers suddenly got up and quit their jobs. In fact, they quit in such great and unprecedented numbers that the phenomenon has been dubbed "the Big Quit."

Normally, quit rates are inversely related to unemployment rates. When unemployment is rising, workers are less inclined to quit their jobs because finding a replacement will be difficult. Conversely, when unemployment is low, workers are more prone to quit and head off in search of better-paying jobs.

When the pandemic first hit and firms were closing down their plants and shedding their workforce, quit rates fell—as would be expected under those circumstances. But around the middle of the pandemic the reverse started to occur, even though unemployment rates had yet to return to pre-pandemic levels. In 2021, more than 47 million American workers quit their jobs. At the beginning of 2022, monthly quits as a percentage of US employment soared to an all-time high.

Certainly, the generous subsidies paid to households during the pandemic gave many of those workers a nest egg that they could rely on when they quit, particularly when the coincident shutdown of many retail stores during that time limited their opportunities to spend those benefit cheques. But the benefit cheques have long run out, and the high quit rates have persisted.

The post-pandemic exodus from the labour force was for the most part led by millennials and Generation Z workers. Many of those workers toiled away at low-paying jobs in restaurants and hotels. Quit rates were also uncommonly high in the retail and health-service sectors. It was at one point reported that more than half of Gen Z workers were looking for a new job.

And at the other end of the demographic spectrum, there were record numbers of workers suddenly retiring. In the United States, the share of retired people in the population rose 15 percentage points above the pre-COVID level.

Insofar as wage pressures are concerned, droves of workers suddenly quitting their jobs (or retiring) has the same impact on wage rates as if they had gone on strike. By creating so many job vacancies, quitters are forcing up wage rates in the industries that they have abandoned. And while they themselves may not have benefited from the wage increases that their record-high quit rates induced, those replacing them did.

The flip side of record quit rates is record job vacancies as firms scramble to replace exiting workers in an extremely tight post-pandemic labour market. In the US economy, job vacancies peaked at a record 11.9 million jobs in March 2022. In Canada, job vacancies rose to an all-time high of 5.6 percent in the fall of 2022, with employers unable to fill nearly a million jobs. In some sectors, like accommodation and food—sectors of the economy that have seen the greatest number of workers quit their jobs—the vacancy rate rose to almost 12 percent. Like quit rates themselves, record numbers of vacant jobs can only bid up the price of labour.

Between record quit rates and record job vacancies, the post-pandemic labour market has become fertile ground for wage growth. Both are telltale signs that labour markets are changing. Indeed, today's worker has major grievances. Not only is there decades-long resentment about wage stagnation, but now there is increasing anxiety about soaring inflation as well.

Just as profound changes in the global economy are putting much greater emphasis on using the domestic labour force, structural changes in that very labour force during the pandemic make it less likely that workers will answer the bell.

Many of them have not been seen in their workplace at work in a long time. Initially, the exodus from workplace to home had the blessing of businesses and public health officials, who viewed the practice as a helpful move to arrest the spread of the contagion. But long after the pandemic subsided, the practice of working from home has continued. A billion square feet of empty office space in the United States is testament to how pervasive and enduring it has become. Working from home may become a sustainable practice for millions of workers in the service sector, but it is easy to see that it won't work in the many manufacturing industries that are now coming back. You can't build semiconductors or vehicles from the friendly confines of your home office while keeping a watchful eye on the kids.

It certainly doesn't seem like today's labour force is going to roll over passively and become cannon fodder for the central banks' war on inflation. Yet that is precisely what central banks are asking them to do.

HOW MANY JOBS MUST BE LOST TO SECURE PRICE STABILITY?

Interest rate hikes don't just magically collar inflation. They do so by discouraging borrowing and spending in the economy, which in turn creates recessions and unemployment. It is the rise in unemployment that serves as the critical link between interest rate hikes and inflation, since it is precisely the growing number of jobless workers that prevents wages from chasing inflation and ultimately breaks any wage-price spiral that may have taken root.

But it's that very carnage in the labour market and the blowback from its political fallout that often inhibits central banks from honouring their commitment to bring inflation back under control.

If you look at the forecasts of most central banks for 2023 and beyond, they share two common expectations. The first is that inflation will remain high in the short run but gradually taper over time and return to or close to the central bank's target rates within the next two years. And the second is that this will be achieved at the cost of only a modest (normally a percentage point or so) rise in the national unemployment rate.

Most economists would consider that outcome for the economy to be fortuitous at this point. But is it credible? A Deutsche Bank study of major OECD economies over the last six decades found that every one-percentage-point decline in trend inflation required at least a one-percentage-point rise in the unemployment rate.

Measured from its peak, what is required on the inflation front is somewhere around a three-percentage-point reduction in trend or core inflation rates. A corresponding three-percentage-point reduction in employment, which stood at 158 million in the United States in 2022, would mean 4.7 million Americans would have to lose their job.

Some central banks, like the Bank of Canada, argue that record-high numbers of job vacancies in the post-pandemic labour market will cushion the ultimate rise in the unemployment rate needed to bring inflation down, since firms are likely to cancel unfilled job vacancies before they actually start firing workers. That is undoubtedly true. But at the same time, vanishing job vacancies won't moderate workers' wage demands in the same way that actual layoffs would.

Instead of requiring fewer workers to lose their jobs to bring inflation down, the record-high number of job vacancies in the North American economy may simply mean that it will take longer than would otherwise be the case for monetary tightening to temper wage demands. In other words, the high number of job vacancies won't substitute for job losses—it will merely postpone them. It won't be until those vacancies are eliminated that the real labour shedding will begin, and thus the real pressure on wage demands. But even when that process begins, it will be starting at what by historical standards is akin to full employment in North American economies. Hence, building up sufficient slack in labour markets will take considerable time and pressure on the workforce before tightening the monetary policy screws on the economy has its intended effect of moderating workers' wage demands.

Whether the Federal Reserve Board and the Bank of Canada have the stomach for such a protracted labour market response remains to be seen, particularly since both countries will soon face federal elections where the economy will undoubtedly be the major campaign issue.

STAGFLATION: THE WORST OF BOTH WORLDS

Fighting inflation is a little like a game of chicken: both doing something and doing nothing cause pain. And since policy-makers will face complaints either way—who can say whether the suffering is cause or effect?—they are torn in both directions. Stay the course, or declare victory and go home even in the face of defeat? To navigate these conflicting pressures, central banks are guided by what they call their "terminal rate"; that is, the peak interest rate before they stop tightening. The trouble with deciding ahead of time what one's terminal rate might be is that if it falls short of what is required (or is held for less time than required), monetary policy may fall well short of its task of bringing inflation back within its targeted range. Instead of higher unemployment wrestling inflation back to the central banks' target zones, we may end up with both high unemployment and high inflation—the worst of both worlds.

The name for this is *stagflation*, and we have seen it before. The coincidence of high inflation and little or no economic growth was a condition that defined normal in the economy of the 1970s. Current economic conditions are the closest to mimicking those conditions that we have seen in almost a half a century.

Back when stagflation ruled, it inspired American economist Arthur Okun to develop a measure to gauge our economic well-being. He called it the misery index, and it was simply the sum of the annual inflation rate and the unemployment rate. Stagflation brought two sources of misery—rising inflation, which denuded the purchasing power of your paycheque, and rising unemployment, which for many took away their paycheque altogether.

Full employment in the US economy is considered by the current consensus of economists to approximate a 3 percent unemployment rate. And the Federal Reserve Board's inflation target is a 2 percent rate. So the ideal value for Okun's misery index for a full employment economy operating within the central bank's inflation target is 5 percent, which is where it stood prior to the COVID pandemic shutting the economy down. Today's misery index reading in the US economy is almost double that setting. And the Canadian experience isn't far off. The misery index reading isn't quite as bad as it was back in the 1970s, but it's nevertheless the worst reading since the 1990s.

Since rising unemployment is seen as the most reliable route to lowering inflation, don't expect to see that reading improve much any time soon. Any progress on the inflation front will come at the expense of the unemployment rate. That is why Federal Reserve Board chair Jerome Powell has warned American households that they need to get used to the prospect of more misery coming their way.

But what worries Powell and the rest of the board of governors of the Federal Reserve Board is that miserable voters seldom choose to vote for more pain.

CHAPTER 3

BROKEN LINKS

In November 2022, the Los Angeles Police Department (LAPD) made local and national news when it announced the end of a successful yearlong investigation into a string of train burglaries that had targeted the Union Pacific Railroad Company—to the tune of a 160 percent increase in rail theft across the country, with ninety-plus containers being broken into every day. After countless hours of surveillance and forty-nine search warrants, twenty-two people were arrested on charges of burglary, cargo theft, and receiving stolen property. In addition, $18 million worth of stolen merchandise was recovered. Prior to the bust, that merchandise had been stored in homes, cars, and other warehouse facilities, awaiting resale in LA County and as far away as Arizona.

For Robert Vega, owner of A&A Auto Wrecking in Los Angeles, the train burglaries were more than just a news item. The railway passes right in front of his business in Lincoln Heights, and he often saw debris from merchandise that was meant to arrive at warehouse facilities around the United States. He'd even seen the thieves breaking into containers and hundreds of packages.

"It was a joke because these guys are hanging on to the trains while they are running or when they stopped," he told a local reporter. "They had tools, they're opening up all the containers, throwing everything out. It was like a free for all."[1]

Train burglary rings like the one Vega witnessed and the LAPD busted up would seem to be an unintended consequence of globalization. The previously steady stream of containers full of high-value goods in the port of Los Angeles created both an economic ecosystem rich in targets for thieves and an underclass of expendables perfectly positioned to exploit it. The system came into sharp focus during the early days of the COVID-19 pandemic, when consumers all over the world realized just how dependent they had become on far-flung supply chains.

But the good times are coming to an end for Angeleno thieves as American ports that were bustling only months ago are suddenly silent. Even in the lead-up to Christmas 2022, normally the busiest time of year, things were quiet. Orders from Chinese factories were down 40 percent. The global shipping industry was forecasting an 80 percent decline in profits for the coming year as containers stacked up on distant shores lay empty. By early 2023, the cost of shipping a forty-foot container from a Chinese port to Los Angeles had fallen to a little over $1,500—just a tenth of what it cost back in September 2021. When you have ten times more container capacity than you do cargo to ship in them, you know that global supply chains are in deep trouble.

It wasn't so long ago that globalization was touted as both inevitable and inevitably prosperous. The more markets were globalized, the richer and happier we would all be. All we had to do was get out of the way. Today that seems like a quaint idea from some golden age in the past.

Whether globalization's demise is a positive or negative development depends largely on where you stand. If you are a corporation outsourcing your production to make use of cheap overseas labour, it is nothing short of a calamity that threatens your bottom line. But if you are one of the few remaining workers in an OECD economy still making things instead of delivering food for Uber Eats and earning below the minimum wage, the breakdown of overseas supply chains gives you a new and totally unexpected lease on life.

When you get right down to it, globalization is just a fancy term to describe wage arbitrage leveraged by low transport costs. When China was admitted to the World Trade Organization back in 2001, the world's most populous country added half a billion low-paid workers to a world economy that was searching for cheap labour. It quickly became the choice destination for corporations all around the world in the race to the bottom—a place to build the world's factories and take advantage of the lowest possible wage rates. Those same corporations then used low-cost oil to ship the goods made by cheap labour in those far-flung factories to supply your market at the lowest possible cost.

OFFSHORING

While central bankers typically take the credit, the real heroes behind vanishing inflation over the latter decades of the postwar era turned out to be the trade negotiators. It was their unrelenting drive to dismantle trade barriers—first under the General Agreement on Tariffs and Trade (GATT), and subsequently under its successor, the World Trade Organization—that made it possible to move high-paying jobs in developed economies like the United States, Canada, the United Kingdom, Australia, and the European Union to low-paying jobs in developing countries like China and India.

When nearly everything you buy is suddenly made by workers earning a tenth of the wage of those who used to make those products, you don't need a graduate degree in monetary theory to figure out which direction inflation will be heading. Outsourcing, as it came to be known, didn't just mean that at any moment in time inflation would be lower; it basically immunized the economy from catching inflation by eviscerating the once powerful Phillips curve.

The Phillips curve, first espoused by an Australian economist in the 1950s, posited that there was a direct trade-off between inflation and unemployment that policy-makers could actually choose between. The curve plotted wage increases against the unemployment rate and the data showed that as the economy got closer to full employment the rate of wage increases would accelerate, which in turn fed directly into a rising inflation rate as firms passed those increases in labour costs on to consumers in the form of higher prices. Conversely, as the unemployment rate rose, the rate of wage increases would slow, as would the resulting rate of inflation.

This relationship allowed governments to make policy trade-offs between inflation and unemployment by adjusting the monetary stance taken by the central bank accordingly. They could encourage lower unemployment by permitting higher inflation, or vice versa.

But the relationship between wage rate increases and unemployment that was so prevalent in the early postwar period in the industrial economies of North America and Western Europe suddenly started to fade around the 1970s and then vanished entirely in more recent decades—at least until now.

The reason the relationship between the unemployment rate and wage gains no longer held was simple enough. In the global economy that emerged under the GATT and WTO, employers weren't just hiring from their local labour market like they used to back in the 1950s or 1960s. Thanks to the dismantling of trade barriers, they could hire from a global labour market. So, if their domestic workforce all of sudden ratcheted up their wage demands in line with a tightening local labour market, there was a very simple solution to the problem: close down the factory and move production to some offshore labour market where not only were wages not rising as quickly, but—even better—those wages were a mere fraction of what they were at home. Once that offshoring option became available to employers, the once venerable Phillips curve was no longer relevant to managing either unemployment or inflation. Governments no longer had to choose between a low rate of unemployment or a low rate of inflation. They could have both.

The good news about this brave new world brought by globalization was that central banks could operate the economy at full employment or pretty well close to it without triggering what traditionally would have been an inevitable rise in wages and inflation—the old Phillips curve trade-off.

This was particularly good news for companies, because it meant that when demand for whatever it was they were selling was surging—as it would be in the case of a full-employment economy—there was no accommodating increase in wage costs that would eat away at profit margins. The profit share of national income rose to record heights at the expense of wages' share in most OECD economies.

It was also good news for central bankers, because they no longer had to slam the brakes on economic growth to defuse what otherwise would have been surging wage pressures as the economy got closer to full employment. In turn, this meant growth cycles could be extended well beyond what had previously been possible, as economies could operate with lower rates of unemployment without risking a resurgence of inflation. And it spared central banks from what they dreaded the most: having to engineer recessions to collar runaway inflation and then incur the wrath of those who lost their jobs, risking serious voter blowback against their government masters.

And it was even better news for the stock market, which no longer had to worry about central banks such as the all-powerful Federal Reserve Board tightening and inducing policy-mandated recessions that typically devastated corporate earnings. A few hiccups aside, it looked as if globalization had put bear markets into permanent hibernation.

Of course, it wasn't such great news for workers' wages, at least not when it came to those workers in the developed economies like the United States, Canada, Western Europe, and Australia. Their employers' ability to move their jobs to offshore labour markets robbed them of whatever bargaining power they might once have had, even during times when a tight domestic labour market would have otherwise favoured higher wage demands. As a result, their wages didn't grow, no matter how strong the economy was growing or how low the unemployment rate fell.

Workers whose jobs and wages had been protected for decades by once powerful unions suddenly found themselves expendable. The participation of former steel, auto, and other manufacturing workers was no longer required in the new services-based economy that outsourced most of the jobs in the sectors that had once produced goods to cheap offshore labour markets.

In America, those expendables found an unlikely champion in real estate billionaire Donald Trump, who campaigned for the Republican nomination and later the presidency in 2016 on a vow to ignore WTO rules that gave preferential tariff treatment to so-called developing countries such as China. Contrary to WTO rules, Trump sought to impose punitive tariffs to bring back long-lost manufacturing jobs that had fled there to take advantage of much lower wage rates overseas. And, true to his word, once in office he imposed the most punitive tariffs (20 percent plus) on imports from China since the Smoot-Hawley tariff of the early 1930s. At the same time, President Trump's refusal to allow the filling of vacant appellate judge seats at the WTO effectively crippled the organization's ability to adjudicate trade disputes—a critical role if the global trade body was to enforce its so-called rules-based trading system.

Trump lost the election in 2020, but his trade policies—which were so maligned and fiercely denounced by the Democrats in Congress— have been maintained in full measure by the succeeding Joe Biden administration. Not only has President Biden maintained Trump's double-digit tariffs on Chinese goods, but he has also, like his predecessor, refused to fill vacant appellate court seats at the WTO, starving the institution of legitimacy. Without judges to adjudicate trade disputes between member states, the WTO has been paralyzed. Since it was set up to oversee the "rules-based" order, the message seems to be that the old rules no longer matter very much, and the WTO is not going to play a role in coming up with new ones.

And if the largest tariffs since the 1930s and an effort to denude the enforcement capacity of the WTO wasn't enough of a monkey wrench thrown into the smooth functioning of global supply chains, the rolling economic lockdowns following the COVID-19 pandemic brought the whole system to a standstill.

The pandemic turned the functioning of a global trade system upside down. The virtues of just-in-time inventories provided by highly complex supply chains of interlinked and interdependent factories around the world suddenly became a liability. Everything from bicycle parts to washing machines to semiconductors became unavailable as the global sweep of the pandemic shut down those interconnected factories. An outbreak of COVID-19 among the workforce in a factory on one side of the world meant that a factory on the other side was idling, waiting for parts that never came. It, in turn, couldn't supply still other factories that were dependent on whatever its contribution to the production chain happened to be. What caught the attention of most people was the failure of global supply chains to deliver desperately needed medical supplies—like the respirators and vaccines needed to combat recurring waves of COVID-19 infections.

As the pandemic severed more and more global supply chain links, it at the same time provided a powerful incentive for reshoring. Another unintended consequence was the weird policy convergence between the outgoing American president and the new one, supposedly elected to steer the country on a radically new course. President Biden responded to the failure of overseas supply chains to deliver during the pandemic by calling for the American economy to become self-sufficient in a wider range of industries, ranging from semiconductors to pharmaceuticals. In other words, he sounded an awful lot like President Trump. He may have talked much less about bringing back long-lost manufacturing jobs than the outgoing president did, but he was no less protectionist. His Inflation Reduction Act, which actually had nothing to do with containing inflation, was chock full of all kinds of buy-America provisions designed to spur domestic production in a wide range of industries.

———

The pandemic and the economic lockdowns that followed in its wake exposed just how fragile global supply chains had become. Just-in-time inventory deliveries—the catchphrase of commerce in the global economy—suddenly became just-too-late deliveries or no deliveries at all.

Those broken links in global supply chains have outlasted the economic lockdowns that first ruptured them. Much to the dismay of retail chains and North American consumers, backlogged orders for everything from bicycles to smartphones quickly became the new normal.

Few industries felt the impact more acutely them the auto industry, which relies critically on semiconductors that for the most part are supplied from Taiwan and South Korea. Today's vehicle has become a computer on wheels. Even a gasoline-powered vehicle comes equipped with a thousand different semiconductors; an electric vehicle has twice as many. Not surprisingly, then, shortages of chip shipments created havoc for major automobile manufacturers, underlining their vulnerability to far-flung supply chains, no matter what cost advantages they might provide.

Many of the key chip manufacturing plants in Asia were shut down because of COVID-19 outbreaks among the workforce. To make matters worse, demand for chips from the electronics industry soared during the pandemic as cooped-up consumers turned increasingly to gaming devices to pass the time. Lastly, easing lockdown restrictions unleased a pent-up demand for vehicles, and hence a stronger than normal demand from the automotive industry for the chips that go inside those vehicles. As low man among the semiconductor industry's customer base, sitting well behind military and electronic customers, auto manufacturers were the last to have their orders filled.

Auto producers estimate that they produced 7.7 million fewer vehicles in 2021 than planned due to the chip shortage, resulting in an over $200 billion loss of revenue. The chip shortage got so bad in the auto industry in 2021 that General Motors had to idle some of its North American plants and curtail production. The resulting shortage of new vehicles for sale pushed used car prices up by an astounding 24 percent that year. The resale market got so hot that many leasing companies were giving complementary upgrades to existing leaseholders just so they could get their hands on already leased cars and sell them into the used car market.

And broken supply chains boosted the price of not only semiconductors but also a whole raft of vehicle components supplied by low-wage countries. When Ford announced in September 2022 that supply chain issues would raise production costs by $1 billion, the venerable American automaker lost more share value in one day (12 percent) than in any day over the last decade—a poignant reminder of just how vulnerable North American vehicle producers had become to offshore parts suppliers.

Central banks such as the Federal Reserve Board were quick to blame broken supply chains for reflation, noting that the phenomenon was beyond their control and the reach of monetary policy. But the Fed and other central banks insisted on referring to the rupture of global supply chains as a temporary phenomenon. What they didn't seem to realize was that the world they had known and come to rely on to dependably hold inflation down was fundamentally changing. And to make matters worse, their easy money response to the economic challenges brought about by the pandemic created a ready-made runway for inflation to take off.

The signs that the global superorganism was coughing up blood were all around us. During the pandemic, the supply backup at key American ports was so immense that President Biden ordered the ports of Long Beach on the Pacific Coast and Long Island on the Atlantic Coast to stay open twenty-four hours a day, seven days a week. Supertankers were lined up for miles awaiting entry, while the ports themselves were clogged to the brim with stacked containers that could not be moved in time because of a critical shortage of truckers to haul them to their onshore destinations. At one point, President Biden even considered deploying the National Guard to alleviate the trucker shortage, which was pegged at an astonishing sixty thousand drivers in the United States and twenty-five thousand in Canada. Overseas supply chains had become a logistical nightmare.

"FRIENDSHORING"

COVID-19 had broken supply chains all around the world. But new supply chains would not necessarily sprout in the same places where they'd broken. As global tensions mounted, once reliable offshore supply sources were suddenly seen in an entirely different light than in globalization's heyday. While offshoring's labour-cost advantages were as great as ever, the practice had nevertheless lost much of its appeal, and was shrouded in a cloud of growing geopolitical uncertainty and tension. Nowhere more so than with China, home to most of the supply chains in the world.

American officials such as Treasury secretary and former Fed chair Janet Yellen called for a new world trading order based on "friendshoring," which means trading with your allies instead of relying on your enemy (i.e., China) for supply chains vital to the functioning of your economy. Her call to minimize commercial dependence on China through economic decoupling has resonated with many of her colleagues among America's allies.

Germany's economic minister Robert Habeck said his country was considering a raft of economic measures aimed at China—its principal trading partner—to reduce dependence on Chinese raw materials, batteries, and semiconductors. He pledged that there would be "no more naivety"[2] in Germany's trade relations with China, although he never articulated what was particularly "naive" about the existing trading relations between the two countries. The reason China had become Germany's number one trading partner was that the country was the cheapest supplier of goods that the German economy needed and, at the same time, a not insignificant market for German exports.

Only months later, senior Canadian cabinet minister François-Philippe Champagne echoed similar sentiments by declaring that

Canada must decouple its trade from China on national security grounds. The statement was a far cry from the stance he'd taken in 2017, when, as minister of international trade, he was the point man for Ottawa in trying to negotiate a Canada-China free trade agreement.

Not only is any trade deal with China off the table, but Canada's trade relations with the United States now also require it to abide by restrictions that the United States has imposed on its own trade with China. These include unprecedented export controls now sanctioned by the Department of Commerce on US-made semiconductors and semiconductor technology.

That is how far the goalposts in Canada have moved on commercial relations with China. And they did likewise in the United States. The National Retail Federation, the American Apparel & Footwear Association, and the Council of Supply Chain Management Professionals have all urged their membership to reduce their reliance on Chinese suppliers in view of mounting Sino-American political tensions and the growing danger of economic warfare between the two powers.

And friendshoring, as it is now called, won't just apply to trade. It will also apply to investment, undermining yet another one of globalization's key pillars: cross-border capital flows.

In step with the Biden administration's policies, Canada has warned that any transactions involving state-owned companies (thinly veiled code for "Chinese companies") operating in Canada's critical minerals sector would be permitted only in exceptional circumstances. Moreover, the Canadian government is now forcing state-owned Chinese companies to divest from their current holdings in the sector. Sinomine Rare Metals Resources Co., Chengze Lithium International Ltd., and Zangge Mining Investment Co. have been asked to sell their shares in, respectively, Power Metals Corp., Lithium Chile Inc., and Ultra Lithium Inc. Other government-forced divestures are likely to follow.

Chinese investment, a previously important source of funding to many Western companies, will no longer be allowed, at least not in sectors that are deemed strategic, like critical minerals. As friendshoring spills over from trade practices to investment practices, heightened geopolitical tensions will not only divert trade flows but capital flows as well. And as with all things in economic warfare, the measures cut both ways.

Earlier in April 2022 China's oil giant CNNOC announced it was divesting from assets held in Western countries, including its operation in the Alberta oil sands, acquired in its $15.1 billion acquisition of Canadian oil firm Nexen in 2013, for fear that they could be expropriated at some point in the future (perhaps in retaliation over a possible Chinese invasion of Taiwan). For CNNOC and no doubt other Chinese resource conglomerates, reducing economic liabilities to potential enemy countries becomes the only effective means of immunizing yourself from those types of expropriation risks. But it makes for a much smaller world for Chinese energy giants—as does the decision by Exxon, BP, and Shell, on the other side of the geopolitical divide, to abandon their Russian assets and withdraw from the Russian energy market, in the process denying themselves access to one of the world's largest oil and gas reserves.

But the biggest problem with friendshoring is that while it may make sense in a time of conflict, it doesn't make any economic sense otherwise. Virtually all of America's allies—the European Union, Canada, Australia, Japan—are high-wage countries, precisely the places from which American companies like Apple don't want to source their products or components. If they did, they might as well just bring production home and pay American wage rates. In 2023, California, Apple's home state, had a minimum wage of $15.50. Its largest supplier in China, Foxconn, paid a little over a $1 an hour. If you were an Apple customer, where would you want your iPhone made?

Friendshoring may make supply chains a lot more secure in a world where economic warfare has suddenly become the norm. But at the same time, the realignment of supply chains along geopolitical contours as opposed to cost considerations is going to make the world a whole lot more expensive for generations of Western consumers who have grown accustomed to reaping the benefits of cheap overseas labour.

No longer will trade be driven by market imperatives. Instead, international trade will be driven by geopolitical considerations. Suddenly, the foreign policies of a country's government, and not the cost competitiveness of its industries, will determine the flow of trade. At least from an economist's perspective, the emerging new world order will be a lot less efficient than the old world order it is rapidly replacing.

CHAPTER 4

LOOKING FOR OIL IN
ALL THE WRONG PLACES

The essential prerequisite for globalization was the dismantling of postwar tariff walls. But the system also needed something else to run smoothly. In order to access cheap labour from far-flung countries, you need cheap transport costs to ship those goods to wherever they are going to be sold. And no matter how you move the goods—either by ship, truck, rail, or air—you need to burn one fuel and only one fuel: oil. While billions are currently being invested to replace it, oil remains the world's primary transit fuel. So the price of oil matters. If transport costs are high, suddenly relative wage costs aren't the only consideration governing where production should be located; distance ends up costing money.

Since the collapse of triple-digit oil prices in the world financial crisis and ensuing global 2008/2009 recession, cheap oil has kept transoceanic transport costs in check. You can largely thank the shale revolution in America for that; within a few years, the US more than doubled its oil production, catapulting itself to the front ranks of global production. And then the pandemic hit, and the impact on travel sent oil prices plunging to lows not seen for decades.

The dramatic fall and equally dramatic subsequent rise in oil prices (as well as coal and natural gas prices) between 2020 and 2022 had been conditioned by the stranglehold that the pandemic lockdowns had on much of the world economy. World oil demand collapsed during the lockdowns, falling by almost 10 million barrels a day, or almost 10 percent, from pre-pandemic levels. To put that decline in historical perspective, global oil demand declined by only 1.4 percent during the 1974 recession, by 4 percent in the 1980 recession, by 3 percent in the 1981 recession, by 2.7 percent in 1982, and by little more than half a percent in the 2008 global recession and world financial crisis. So the magnitude of the decline in global oil demand brought about by the COVID-19 pandemic was literally off the charts, dwarfing any previous demand adjustment in history.

The reason for the severity of the decline was plain enough. No recession had grounded the world's airline industries as the travel restrictions around COVID-19 did. Nor had any recession emptied the streets, highways, and public transit systems as the pandemic did, when all of a sudden nearly everyone worked from home or didn't work at all, and in many cities around the world people were not even allowed to leave home for fear of spreading the contagion.

Faced with that unprecedented scale of decline in world oil demand, oil prices plummeted. At one point, contract prices for West Texas Intermediate (the US benchmark price) briefly became negative as capacity at the critical storage hub in Cushing, Oklahoma, was almost full; that is, oil companies would pay you to take oil off their hands. While that anomaly proved to be a one-day wonder, the price of West Texas Intermediate nevertheless languished around $20 per barrel for several months during the depths of the COVID-19 lockdowns. At that price, most of North American oil production becomes unprofitable.

But the decline in world oil demand, as dramatic as it was, proved to be just as short-lived. And the subsequent recovery was just as dramatic as the prior decline.

The V-shaped recovery that most economies experienced in the aftermath of the pandemic-induced global recession burned a lot of oil. Two years after COVID-19 had shut down large swaths of the world economy, global oil demand had just about recovered all the ground it had lost. The global economy was once again burning around 100 million barrels per day of the fuel. But while demand had recovered, supply growth had fallen way behind.

It is often said that high oil prices kill oil demand, but it is just as true that low oil prices kill oil supply. While low prices encourage households and businesses to consume more oil, they simultaneously encourage oil producers to produce less.

Low oil prices not only lower current production by rendering much of what is being produced unprofitable, but they also impact future production by discouraging new investment in the industry; in turn, this reduces growth in future supply. And that is precisely what happened to the global petroleum industry as it weathered the collapse in demand during the COVID-19 economic shock.

As world demand crumbled, refineries were shut down and production cutbacks became commonplace across oil fields all around the world—the result of an industry scrambling to refit itself to the contours of an unprecedented contraction in the world oil market. But as OPEC and other oil producers would soon discover, once you turn off the tap, it's not always so easy to turn it back on—particularly when industry investment collapses.

Globally, capital investment in the oil industry fell by 30 percent during the pandemic. In the United States, it fell by more than 60 percent and registered the lowest levels in a decade. And if low oil prices during the pandemic weren't a big enough impediment to investment, and hence future production growth, the industry suddenly faced an even more daunting challenge on this front.

STRANDED ASSETS OR TOMORROW'S FUEL?

An essential feature of past oil cycles was that soaring prices could reliably be counted on to trigger aggressive industry capital expenditure (CapEx) spending that would inevitably usher in new supply. Today, that traditional industry response has been severely muted—and not just in North America. It's played out in oil industries around the world with few exceptions (Saudi Arabia and Russia being two notable ones).

Instead of allowing for the diversion of a healthy proportion of soaring earnings to develop reserves and bring on new production, the stock market has instead encouraged oil companies to turn themselves into veritable instant teller machines for the benefit of their shareholders. For the most part, the revenue bonanza from soaring oil prices has been paid back to shareholders in the form of either generous dividend hikes or large-scale share buybacks, or a combination of both. As it turns out, that marked change in industry behaviour is motivated by an equally marked change in the share ownership of oil companies themselves.

Despite soaring energy prices, and thus soaring earnings, the current investment climate for fossil fuel firms has soured measurably in recent years as more and more institutional investors started looking at the oil industry through an environmental, social, and governance (ESG) lens. And what they saw from that perspective was not exciting investment prospects to develop badly needed reserves but a grim future where they will spend billions of dollars developing what will ultimately prove to be stranded and therefore worthless assets.

A central tenant of the fossil fuel divestment movement is that a capital expenditure on developing new hydrocarbon reserves—be they coal, oil, or natural gas—is an investment in stranded assets. The reserves that new investment seeks to exploit will be stranded because the emissions created from their combustion is incompatible with achieving the global emission reductions mandated by the Paris Agreement on climate signed in December 2015 by 191 countries, as well as subsequent international agreements. (Of course, they will be stranded only to the extent that those ambitious but far-off emission reduction targets are reached.) Even the International Energy Agency has come around to this viewpoint, cautioning that no new carbon fuel infrastructure should be built going forward if countries are to adhere to their emission-reduction pledges.

As a result of the growing influence of the ESG movement in the wealth management business, many institutional investors who had routinely owned oil, gas, and coal stocks no longer do. They are part of the fastest-growing divestment movement in history, which as of July 2023 had already seen more than 1,593 financial institutions around the world, managing over $42.5 trillion worth of assets, divest or start the process of divesting from fossil fuel stocks. And banks are coming under increasing pressure to stop financing exploration and new production in their lending practices.

What started out as a fringe movement with a handful of university endowment funds has become mainstream. The ESG movement today includes some of the largest fund managers in the world. For example, Larry Fink, founder and chief executive officer of BlackRock—the world's largest asset manager, with holdings of some $10 trillion worth of assets—warns CEOs whose companies BlackRock holds in its many funds that climate risk is investment risk. Companies held in BlackRock portfolios must now disclose how they will be able to operate in a world of net-zero carbon emissions and, if unable to do so, face potential divestment from BlackRock funds. BlackRock has projected that by 2030 the percentage of companies it invests in with a clear plan to cut emissions to zero by mid-century will rise from 25 percent to 75 percent.

Whether BlackRock hits that target or not, one thing is clear: as atmospheric carbon levels continue to rise, and with them increasingly graphic evidence of global climate change, the ESG movement is unlikely to dissipate.

However, in financial markets as in nature, vacuums are quickly filled. As increasingly ESG-conscious institutional investors have bailed out of fossil fuel stocks, legions of retail investors have just as quickly jumped in and filled the gap. But retail investors have very different investment preferences than institutional investors. Those differences have already had and will continue to have a huge impact on future CapEx spending in the industry and, in turn, on investment in future supply growth.

Retail investors gobbling up oil, gas, and even coal stocks are far more concerned with short-term financial returns than with ESG considerations. At the same time, and unlike institutional investors—who typically look at a longer-term time horizon for their investments, which readily accommodates investment in business growth—retail investors just want to be paid now. They aren't concerned about investing in future supply growth. From their perspective, the less supply growth the better, because that implies even higher oil prices and thus even bigger dividends and share buybacks in the future.

But if oil firms have to continually cater to the wishes of an anti-CapEx retail investor base, where will industry spending come from to secure new supply growth? Without supply growth, prices would seem to have only one direction in which to move.

While global recessions will still be able to rein in prices by temporarily clobbering demand, as they always have, without robust investment in supply growth, prices will quickly rebound, just as they did in the post-pandemic oil market. Without ample reinvestment in supply growth, high oil prices will become a permanent feature of the economic landscape.

Unfortunately for Western oil consumers, the two places where neither ESG concerns nor the dictates of retail investors will constrain supply growth are Russia and Saudi Arabia. Although the two are the largest oil-exporting countries in the world, neither will be supplying much oil to Western markets—in Russia's case because its oil is sanctioned in Western markets, and in Saudi Arabia's case because it has long since pivoted toward supplying China and other Asian markets.

Sanctions have banned as much as 800,000 barrels per day of Russian oil from the American market and about 2 million barrels per day of oil and refined petroleum products from EU markets. With no end to the hostilities in Ukraine in sight, those sanctions are not likely to be dropped any time soon. Even if they were, Russia has already found new markets in China and India to replace the demand for the oil it once sold to American and European markets.

Moreover, the sanctions have abruptly ended the long-time involvement of Western companies in Russia's massive oil and gas sector. BP, Shell, and Exxon have all abandoned their very substantial operations in Russia. In early 2022, BP, which has operated in Russia for over three decades, unloaded its 20 percent ownership share in Russian oil giant Rosneft, and in the process had to swallow a $25 billion write-down on its Russian assets. Similarly, Shell's exit from the Russian natural gas and oil sectors—including the company's 27.5 percent share in the massive Sakhalin-2 liquified natural gas (LNG) facility and its 50 percent share in Salym Petroleum Development—resulted in a $5 billion write-down. And Exxon announced that it would be exiting the $4 billion Sakhalin-1 offshore oil and gas project that it operated on behalf of a consortium of Japanese, Indian, and Russian companies. In addition, all three Western oil giants announced that they would no longer be investing in Russia.

Whether the loss of foreign capital and technology will impede future production growth in Russia's oil industry remains to be seen. But as the country has already learned from its natural gas experience, revenues can grow even if production doesn't—as long as prices rise enough. Given Russia's weight in world oil exports, an inability to grow production could limit world production growth. If this happens, Russia may well get the same revenue growth from the resulting increase in world oil prices.

Neither Saudi Arabia nor, for that matter, any other OPEC producer is likely to make up the shortfall from banned Russian fuel. After repeatedly turning down President Biden's many pleas for the cartel to boost production, Saudi Arabia actually led a 2-million-barrel-per-day cut in cartel production beginning in November 2022. The move was both an open defiance of Washington and a brazen attempt to raise world oil prices, which had fallen from triple-digit levels to around the $80-a-barrel mark as a result of massive releases of oil inventories from American and other OECD fuel stockpiles. It subsequently led to another 1-million-barrel-per-day OPEC cut in production in June 2023.

All told OPEC and its allies (OPEC+) have cut production by about 5 million bpd. While it's not an outright export embargo as was the first OPEC oil shock back in the early 1970s, it's nevertheless the closest the cartel has come to that in squeezing global supply.

Moreover, as Saudi energy minister Abdulaziz bin Salman Al-Saud has repeatedly warned, the OPEC supply picture will for the foreseeable future remain constrained by a lack of investment in new capacity. Aside from Saudi Arabia, which plans to ramp up CapEx to $50 billion, few other members are following suit. And even Saudi Aramco's announced investment in new capacity will result in only a modest increase in production (up to 13 million barrels per day from 12.1 in 2021), and that isn't expected to be achieved until 2027.

BIDEN'S DESPERATE SEARCH FOR MORE FOREIGN SUPPLY

Having been spurned by Saudi Arabia, President Biden went looking to replace the banned Russian oil whose loss had at one point pushed American pump prices up to a record $5 a gallon. But he went looking in all the wrong places. He even turned to Iran (itself a long-time subject of American sanctions that had crippled production in what used to be one of the world's primary oil producers) and offered to drop the sanctions imposed against its nuclear arms program in exchange for more oil. To no one's surprise, the two long-standing adversaries failed to reach a deal.

Biden then turned to President Nicolás Maduro of Venezuela, whom only a few years ago Washington was encouraging Venezuelans to overthrow. But even if the Maduro administration was so inclined, and it certainly wasn't, Venezuela is producing less than a third of what it once did and is in no position to replace the lost 800,000 barrels of imported Russian oil.

But where the Biden administration *didn't* turn for more oil was as notable as where it did. America's friendly and oil-rich neighbour to the north was largely ignored in the president's around-the-world quest for more fuel.

After all, in one of his first acts after taking office, Biden cancelled Washington's earlier approval of the transborder Keystone XL pipeline that would have brought some 900,000 barrels per day of crude from Alberta's oil sands to Gulf Coast refineries. And it wouldn't have done so for only a couple of months or quarters, as was requested from OPEC, but reliably for the next three to four decades. Which is precisely why the president was so keen to make sure it never got built. Building new energy infrastructure like pipelines will only perpetuate the use of fossil fuels in the American economy—a prospect that the Biden administration is dead set against.

Instead, he chose to tap his own country's Strategic Petroleum Reserve (SPR) at a record rate, releasing 1 million barrels per day of oil for 180 days, coincidentally leading right up to the mid-term congressional elections in November 2022. The move marked Biden's third withdrawal from the SPR since assuming office. A fourth was announced shortly after another OPEC production cut. The Biden administration then authorized another 1-million-barrel-per-day release in 2023, in an effort to moderate pump-price increases as the peak spring/summer driving season approached.

Established by Congress in 1975 following the first OPEC oil shock, the SPR was designed to insure against future oil shocks like the supply disruption back in 1973. But in this case the supply disruption was self-inflicted by the Biden administration's ban on the importation of Russian oil.

While it can certainly be argued that the SPR need not be as large as it was back in the 1970s, given how much domestic oil production has increased thanks to the shale revolution, the reserve nevertheless remains a finite resource and is nearly half depleted. Since coming to office and immediately cancelling the Keystone XL pipeline, the Biden administration has reduced the SPR by almost 45 percent—from 638 million barrels to 400 million barrels by December 2023. As a result, the reserves have been whittled down to just over half of the original endowment. A 400-million-barrel inventory would feed the American economy's 20-million-barrels-a-day fuel habit for 20 days. Moreover, the Biden administration intended to release an additional 140 million barrels from the SPR as a revenue-raising measure between 2024 and 2027, until Congress nixed the plan.

Of course, in President Biden's vision, the US economy won't be using oil within a decade, and hence there will be no need for storing millions of barrels of oil in the Strategic Petroleum Reserve. Instead, the United States will need strategic reserves of lithium and rare earth elements (REE) to foster the transition to a green economy.

If he is right, Washington can continue to run down the SPR over the next decade with relative impunity. It can be used as a bridge while millions of American drivers ditch their gas-guzzling SUVs and switch to zero-emission vehicles like plug-in electric cars, plunging oil use in the American economy to all-time lows.

But if President Biden's utopian vision takes decades longer to unfold than planned, exhausting the Strategic Petroleum Reserve may ultimately leave the American economy in the same position it was in back in 1973, when Saudi Arabia and OPEC turned off the tap.

CHAPTER 5

DELEVERAGING

While Toria Neal slept on the night of November 21, 2022, she received a text message she didn't read until she woke up next morning. What she learned would soon make headlines. She, along with everyone else at United Furniture Industries of Tupelo, Mississippi, had been laid off. All twenty-seven hundred employees had received the same text message: Don't come to work. If you are on the road in a delivery truck, turn around and bring it back. No notice, no severance, no company-paid health care. It was only three days before Thanksgiving.

Of course, what happened to United Furniture was part of an economic chain reaction. Within hours, Seagrove Lumber—which built the frames for United Furniture—was laying off its entire workforce. Those workers, like the ones at United had been, were dominoes, and more would continue to fall. North of the border, major Canadian lumber producers such as Canfor and West Fraser Timber, which provided much of the lumber framing for newly built American homes, closed mills, laying off more than four hundred workers.

All of these events had a single origin: a real estate crash. In the United States, new real estate listings in November 2022 had fallen over 25 percent from the year before. Some once red-hot Canadian markets were hit even harder. Sales in Toronto were down 49 percent, while Canadian housing prices nationally dropped by almost 20 percent that year.

With fewer houses sold on the market, it was no surprise that construction companies were buying less timber framing and households were buying less furniture. They were all just dominoes.

But the question on everyone's mind—from lumber companies to furniture manufacturers—was why a once booming housing market in North America was suddenly collapsing. And the answer had very little to do with what was happening in North America but everything to do with what was happening in far-off Ukraine. As we will see, the North American housing market had become collateral damage in the ever-escalating economic war between Russia and NATO.

Not that good times can go on forever. It shouldn't come as any surprise that the lowest interest rates in recorded history (going back five thousand years) would spawn a housing-market boom and the longest-running bull market in history. What is surprising is that both homeowners and shareholders had come to regard those conditions as the new normal. They were anything but. And more important, they weren't sustainable.

Easy money policies have always nurtured speculative bubbles: the Roaring Twenties (1924–28); Japan's real estate and stock market bubble of the 1980s; the dot-com bubble in 2000; and, most recently, the subprime mortgage bubble back in 2007/2008—to name a few of the major ones in recent history. When you can borrow for free, a lot of otherwise questionable investments suddenly become alluring. The massive monetary easing that took place around the pandemic was no exception in this regard.

In the United States, the money supply grew by almost 40 percent over the course of the pandemic, compared to a long-term average of just 7 percent a year. In Canada, the money supply (as measured by the monetary aggregate M1) grew by 35 percent after the pandemic compelled quantitative easing by the Bank of Canada.

The fact that inflation has soared during a period of rapid monetary expansion will come as no surprise to followers of the late American economist Milton Friedman, the father of the monetarist school, whose famous dictum "inflation is always and everywhere a monetary phenomenon" has never rung more true. The massive increase in money supply created through quantitative easing and the attendant rise in financial market liquidity quickly spawned asset inflation. Whether it was tech stocks, Bitcoin, or collector baseball cards, asset bubbles were sprouting up all over the place, nourished by virtually free borrowing rates. And central banks, whose policies spawned these bubbles, seemed indifferent.

Central banks ignored such bubbles at their own peril. Asset inflation doesn't just affect the price of stocks, crypto currencies, or collectables. Like a virus that can jump species, asset inflation can jump into the real world of prices for goods and services.

Double-digit money supply growth—which is how central banks paid for their massive purchases of government bonds—was a powder keg just waiting to be lit. And sweeping economic sanctions about to be imposed against the world's largest resource producer would provide all the sparking power to blow that powder keg sky high.

A SHRINKING HOUSING MARKET

Before the dominoes started falling, the North American housing market had been one of the biggest beneficiaries of the easy money policies that the Federal Reserve Board and the Bank of Canada had pursued for their economies through quantitative easing. The more mortgage rates fell, the higher housing prices rose. There was a simple but nevertheless very powerful direct drive relationship between the cost of borrowing and the cost of what you were borrowing to buy.

The housing market created by record-low mortgage rates was a great deal for homeowners, except perhaps first-time buyers, whose savings for a down payment often couldn't keep up with soaring housing prices. Even if you didn't have a mortgage, you as a homeowner benefited from falling mortgage rates because the more those rates fell the more your house was worth. But those halcyon days were predicated on record-low mortgage rates, which in turn were grounded by low inflation rates—rarely above the central banks' 2 percent target and often below that threshold.

As homeowners were soon to discover, that direct drive relationship between mortgage rates and housing prices works just as powerfully in the opposite direction. Which is why a sharp upturn in interest rates was felt more painfully in the housing market than anywhere else in the economy.

The economic impact of falling housing prices can be felt far beyond the real estate market. Since your house is typically your most valuable asset, a housing market correction doesn't just make your house worth less—it makes you worth less too, which affects what you spend on everything else. And, at the same time, rising mortgage rates make the cost of borrowing (for the thing that is making you poorer in the first place) a lot more expensive and therefore burdensome to carry.

Think of mortgage rates as a gateway to the housing market. When interest rates fall, more households are able to qualify for mortgage financing and can therefore bid on a house. The more buyers that bid on a property, the higher the price that property will ultimately sell for. Conversely, rising mortgage rates disqualify more potential buyers from obtaining or affording financing, and as marginal buyers drop out of the market and fewer bidders bid on a property, the price that property will sell at drops too.

For those homebuyers who do qualify for a mortgage, changes in interest rates also have an impact. Not only do they determine how big your monthly mortgage payment will be, but they also affect how much of that payment goes to paying off what you borrowed (the principal) and how much is simply spent paying interest to carry the loan. The higher mortgage rates go, the more of your monthly payment is spent on the interest, which can make owning a home look and feel more and more like renting.

As inflation has soared, so too have mortgage rates. For prospective American homebuyers, the cost of a 30-year fixed-rate mortgage skyrocketed from a record low of 2.65 percent in July 2020 to 7.3 percent by November 2022. According to Black Knight, a mortgage data company, the monthly mortgage payment on a median-priced home in the United States has increased by $930 over that period, an increase of more than 70 percent.

As interest rates continue to rise, more and more homeowners who financed their homes through popular variable-rate mortgages hit the dreaded trigger rate, a threshold at which the actual size of your monthly payment has to increase. By the fall of 2022, half of the variable-rate mortgage holders in Canada had already reached that threshold. Trigger rates hit the housing market at both ends. As soaring mortgage rates disqualify more and more prospective buyers, trigger rates may force some mortgage holders to sell their homes because they can no longer afford the increase in monthly payments.

Some lending institutions allowed homeowners to capitalize soaring interest costs by increasing the size of their mortgages and extending the length of the loan. In effect, they are increasing the amount that the homeowner owes on their mortgage by adding unpaid interest to the principal. So, instead of gradually paying off your mortgage, the amount you owe actually grows over time as more and more of your interest costs are capitalized in a bigger mortgage. Instead of getting richer every year by paying off a little bit more of your mortgage, you're actually getting poorer.

By September 2023 three of the largest banks in Canada (Bank of Montreal, Toronto-Dominion Bank, and Canadian Imperial Bank of Commerce) disclosed that 20 percent of their residential mortgage borrowers, representing nearly $130 billion in loans, were seeing the size of their mortgage increase as their monthly payments could no longer even cover the interest cost of carrying the mortgage. Negative amortization, as it is commonly called, is a growing phenomenon in the mortgage market, putting more and more homeowners in financial peril and duress. And it's also putting the country's top lending institutions at risk. Their regulator, the Superintendent of Financial Institutions, has instructed them to put more reserves aside to ensure against the increasing likelihood of rising mortgage defaults.

Shocked homeowners who find themselves a lot poorer today as a result are no doubt wondering what happened to the housing market in the years since they bought their home. What changed was the cost of borrowing.

It may seem like a long way from the battle lines in Ukraine to your neighbourhood bank, but the mortgage rate you pay and the war in Ukraine are more closely linked than you might think. At the end of the day, your mortgage rate depends on inflation, which central banks are ultimately forced to respond to with multiple rate hikes. So when the price of everything from oil and natural gas to grain and fertilizer suddenly rises because of the pervasive impact of economic sanctions, those impacts are in turn woven into your mortgage rate and the cost of home ownership.

STOCKS ARE NO LONGER A ONE-WAY BET

Quantitative easing created many winners: record-low government-debt servicing costs; record-low mortgage rates for homeowners; near-zero financing rates on car loans and leases for consumers. But the biggest winner hands down was the stock market. And that made the wealthiest households in our society a lot wealthier.

Make no mistake about it: ever since the global financial crisis of 2007/2008, monetary policy has been very friendly toward the stock market. It's no coincidence that after the Federal Reserve Board adopted quantitative easing, Wall Street enjoyed its longest-running rally in history—right up until the pandemic. And while the economic shock and panic selling that the pandemic triggered quickly felled the stock market, it took no time at all for stocks to rebound and go on to new record highs as the Fed shifted its quantitative easing program into overdrive.

In this respect not a lot has changed since the Federal Reserve

Board bailed out Wall Street by scooping up $700 billion worth of toxic securities backed by delinquent subprime mortgages under its Troubled Asset Relief Program (TARP) and depositing $125 billion onto the balance sheets of nine American banks deemed too big to fail. (Instead of being lent out to households and businesses, that money ended up being paid out in record bonuses.) Back then, the rationale for such lavish central bank support for Wall Street was to avoid an outright collapse of the financial system as some of America's largest financial institutions teetered on the brink of bankruptcy. The support was also intended to spur an economic recovery from the recession that had engulfed not only the US economy but most of the world economy as well. But even when the crisis was well over, the Federal Reserve Board kept buying government bonds for the next five years, effectively underwriting massive asset inflation in both the housing market and the stock market. And when the central bank resuscitated quantitative easing in response to the pandemic, it engaged in it on a scale never seen before, compelling other central banks around the world to follow suit.

It seems that the one constant in an ever-changing world of monetary conditions—whether intended or not—is that the stock market has been the prime beneficiary of Federal Reserve Board policy.

The main reason stocks benefit so much from quantitative easing is that they are the primary investment alternative to bonds in the composition of any investor's portfolio. When bond yields fall to record lows because of massive central bank bond purchases, private money flows from the bond market to the stock market. That flow of funds, measured in the trillions of dollars, can only move stock values in one direction—up!

Over the last forty years, that flow has pretty well been one way. At first this was due to globalization's success, mainly through offshoring, in wrestling down inflation and hence interest rates. Since 2008, it has also been driven by the massive outright purchasing of bonds by central banks under the cover of their quantitative easing programs.

As interest rates fell continuously over decades, the value of stocks soared. Consider, for example, the opposing trajectories of the yield on 10-year Treasury bonds, a common benchmark for the US government fixed-income market, and the S&P 500, historically the benchmark for US stocks. Bond yields peaked in the early 1980s when Paul Volcker, renowned chairman of the Federal Reserve Board at the time, launched an all-out attack on raging inflation following the second OPEC oil shock. Volcker hiked the federal funds rate up to as much as 20 percent. During that time, the yield on 10-year Treasuries peaked at around 16 percent.

Now turn the clock forward some four decades. By 2021, thanks to massive quantitative easing, the yield on the 10-year Treasury bond had nosedived to a scant 0.5 percent. Meanwhile, over the same period the S&P 500 index had increased by more than thirtyfold. The lower the yields paid by bonds, the higher the price investors will pay for competing stocks.

The steady, almost unrelenting decline in government bond yields and the attendant rise in stock market returns had a profound impact on investor behaviour. Traditionally, the rule of thumb in the invest-ment industry was that a portfolio should hold 60 percent of its assets in stocks and 40 percent in bonds. The thinking behind this ratio was that since bonds and stocks usually move in opposite directions, and stocks have generated historically higher returns, this split would ensure an adequate return over time.

But as bond yields continued to plummet to new record lows, that traditional rule of thumb failed to hold true for more and more inves-tors. The interest rate on bonds had fallen so low that the coupons (interest payments) they paid individual retail investors yielded too meagre a return to justify holding them. And for institutional inves-tors such as pension plans, bond market yields no longer provided returns adequate to cover their future actuarial liabilities, forcing them to find more attractive alternatives elsewhere—like investments in infrastructure, real estate, private equity, and, most of all, stocks.

As bond yields continued to fall, the 60/40 rule gave way to much higher proportions weighted to stocks. In other words, the more bonds

the central bank bought at hugely discounted interest rates (and exces-
sively high prices) through quantitative easing, the less private investors wanted to buy them.

Central banks had a seemingly insatiable appetite for their own
government's bonds. Coming out of the pandemic, central banks collectively held a staggering $36 trillion worth of bonds on their balance
sheets, almost 30 percent of the total value of all outstanding bonds.
When questioned about that practice, the central banks defended their
massive purchases by claiming that they were not deliberately manip-
ulating bond yields, given that they'd bought the bonds on the open
market, just like everyone else.

That was true, in so far as it went. But what they neglected to mention was that they'd outbid all other participants, driving bond yields
(which are inversely related to bond prices) to record lows so that their
governments would pay only trivial financing costs on the massive
deficits they had racked up during the pandemic.

So while it was true that central banks had bought their bonds in
the market, it was equally true that they were playing by different rules
than the other participants. Unlike private investors or fund managers, who have to worry about their portfolio's performance, central
banks didn't have to worry about the performance of the huge fixed-
income portfolio they held on their suddenly bloated balance sheets.
At least, they didn't think they ever would.

In other words, while the central banks did indeed buy the bonds
at market prices, they also massively distorted that market. What's
wrong with that? After all, if warping the bond market makes homeowners richer, drives record stock market gains, and allows governments to finance record deficits at trivial interest rates, why don't
central banks just keep doing it?

The answer, of course, is that rigging the markets is a game as old
as markets themselves. The problem is that they can't stay rigged
forever. Financial assets such as stocks and bonds eventually find their
true level. At times of low inflation, central banks can distort the bond

market and get away with financing huge government deficits by providing huge bond-buying subsidies, but they can't do the same when inflation is soaring to highs not seen in four decades. When that happens, the emperor is suddenly seen to be wearing no clothes!

Inflation is the bondholder's enemy, given that it devours the real value of the coupon payments over time. A bond pays its owners a series of set payments over a fixed time period—hence the name "fixed income." Those payments are worth less and less as inflation erodes their real value—and the higher the inflation rate, the more value is eroded. So, in order for anyone to buy a bond whose coupon payments don't even cover inflation, the price of the bond itself must fall. Say a bond that was to mature at $100 previously sold at $95 but suddenly inflation rose. That bond would now have to sell at a lower price, say at $90, to compensate for the fact that its coupon payments had been eroded by inflation. In other words, the buyer would get it at a discounted price, and the more that inflation robbed the real value of the coupon payment, the bigger the price discount that would have to be offered to the investor. And the longer those coupon payments stretched out into the future, the greater the impact inflation would have on the underlying value of the bond, and thus the greater the decline in the price of the bond. Which is why the price of longer-term bonds (20-years-plus) are more vulnerable to inflation than the price of short-term bonds (1 to 5 years).

So, if your bonds are losing money because they no longer protect your investment against inflation, why not just sell them? Private investors can do just that, and they did. But the option wasn't as simple for central banks.

If central banks stopped buying their governments' bonds at artificially low prices, the market would find its true value; that is, other participants in the market would force up bond yields in response to soaring inflation rates, leaving central banks facing even bigger losses on the bonds they were already holding. And if those same banks stopped subsidizing their governments by buying their bonds at artificially low yields, the cost of servicing the government's debt—which had ballooned with record fiscal deficits during the pandemic—would suddenly soar, ultimately leaving taxpayers on the hook. But if central banks didn't sell the bonds they had bought during the pandemic, their losses would grow as bond yields continued to rise with inflation.

If holding the bond is going to hurt you, and not holding the bond is going to hurt you, you are going to be in a very uncomfortable position. And it'll be that much worse knowing how much is at stake.

But what was vexing for central banks was euphoric for shareholders. While all stocks benefited from the record-low bond yields that quantitative easing engineered, the stocks that benefited the most were the so-called growth stocks—mainly technology stocks listed in the NASDAQ, which investors were betting would post exponential growth in a market that had lost all fear of central banks ever applying the monetary brakes. Many of those stocks also benefited from the retail lockdowns that followed in the wake of the pandemic, when all of a sudden e-commerce got a quantum but temporary boost. Between record-low bond yields thanks to quantitative easing and the sudden lift to e-commerce thanks to the pandemic, the NASDAQ posted spectacular gains (43.6 percent in 2020, and 21.39 percent in 2021).

Those stellar gains were in turn largely driven by five surging mega stocks, the so-called FAANG stocks—Facebook (now Meta), Amazon, Apple, Netflix, and Google—whose capitalization became GDP-like in magnitude. Apple's market capitalization was over $3 trillion, while back in 2021 Amazon posted a peak valuation of $1.7 trillion. To put those valuations in perspective, only nineteen countries in the world have a GDP greater than a trillion dollars.

In theory, a rising tide should lift all boats—which means a soaring stock market should make everyone richer. But unlike soaring housing prices, which benefit roughly two-thirds of North American households, soaring stocks mostly benefit only the top 10 percent of households. This is because that 10 percent owns more than 80 percent of all publicly listed shares. So, as the value of shares soared, the distribution of wealth became ever more concentrated in the hands of the wealthiest. The two trends, of course, were integrally related, since the above-average returns from the stock market during the longest-running bull market in history accrued disproportionately to the wealthiest households in society. Their wealth grew relative to the majority of households, which owned little to no stocks.

Whether this was intended or simply a consequence of monetary policy, it cannot be denied that the top 10 percent of households were clearly the prime beneficiaries of quantitative easing. Perhaps not surprisingly, this has spurred criticism that from a distributional standpoint the stock-market-friendly posture of the Federal Reserve Board has been highly regressive; that is, it favours the wealthiest segment of society.

That may well have been true in the past, but multi-billionaires such as Amazon's Jeff Bezos or Tesla's/X's Elon Musk have quickly discovered the same lesson that homeowners did: leverage is a two-way street. What free money inflates, soaring interest rates deflate—and that includes once high-flying tech stocks that seemed headed for the moon.

It's not hard to see why this is the case. All of a sudden, the American economy went from one in which anyone could effectively borrow for free to one in which even the best credit, the US Treasury, was paying 5 percent for short-term credit, and homeowners were paying more than 7 percent for long-term mortgages. Rapid-fire Federal Reserve Board rate hikes and net selling in the bond market (quantitative tightening) had led to the sharpest rise in interest rates since Paul Volcker was at the helm of the Fed four decades ago.

And just as record-low interest rates had a huge impact on valuations, so too did one of the most rapid increases in borrowing costs in history. Whether it was the nearly 80 percent decline in the value of Bitcoin, the 33.4 percent decline in the NASDAQ in 2022, or the double-digit decline in North American housing prices, the air was rapidly escaping from the asset bubbles that easy money had created.

At their worst, the meltdown in the value of tech stocks and the mounting layoffs in the tech sector were reminiscent of the implosion of the dot-com bubble over two decades ago. The decline in the share values of the FAANG stocks at one point resembled the share losses of Pets.com or Global Crossing in the pre-dot-com era. As of early January 2023, Facebook had lost two-thirds of its market capitalization, while Amazon and Netflix were down more than half, and Google was down more than 40 percent. Apple had fared the best among the FAANG stocks, but it was still down more than 40 percent and had lost almost a trillion dollars from its market value. Other NASDAQ darlings had taken a hit as well. Canadian e-commerce platform provider Shopify (briefly the largest market cap listing on the Toronto Stock Exchange, where it was cross-listed along with the NASDAQ), lost more than 70 percent of its former market cap, as did Tesla—once the stock market darling of the electric vehicle industry.

While these extreme losses were subsequently pared back in the much-hyped artificial intelligence rally during 2023, it has taken the stock market two years to climb back to its pre-COVID highs. And now the stock market has reluctantly come to accept that it will face higher interest rates for much longer than it had earlier hoped.

For years, stock markets had been swimming downstream, riding a strong current of ever-falling bond yields. Now, however, they would be forced to swim upstream, fighting against a current of rising bond yields as inflation rooted itself ever deeper into the economy. As with real estate, stocks looked a lot less alluring when borrowing money was no longer free.

QUANTITATIVE TIGHTENING: CAN GOVERNMENTS AND THEIR CENTRAL BANKS AFFORD TO DELEVERAGE?

A central bank's raising or lowering of short-term target interest rates used to pretty well define the totality of monetary policy shifts. But that was before quantitative easing came to play such a prominent role in central bank policy. The principal difference between the two policy levers is that while adjustments to short-term interest rates go up and down over the course of a business cycle, quantitative easing has typically been a one-way street.

But not anymore. A number of central banks, including the all-important Federal Reserve Board, are now traveling in the opposite direction, having embarked on a quantitative tightening program where they are now net sellers instead of massive buyers of government bonds. This course could provide a powerful new source of braking power on the economy and inflation, and on the prices of assets such as stocks and real estate.

As its name implies, quantitative tightening is the polar opposite of quantitative easing. Instead of buying bonds, the central bank sells the bonds it once gobbled up and stuck on its balance sheet, spitting them back out for the bond market to digest. Just as central bank purchases of government bonds lowered both bond yields and connected long-term interest rates (such as mortgage rates), central bank sales of government bonds would raise yields and rates. And they would do so quite apart from whatever action the central bank was taking in terms of adjusting its short-term target at the time.

In theory, of course, quantitative easing could be reversed through quantitative tightening, just as cuts in central bank short-term interest rate targets could be reversed through rate hikes as changing economic conditions warranted. In practice, however, quantitative tightening has never been tried before, save for an attempt by the Fed back in 2018, when it briefly sold bonds it had amassed during its initial qualitative easing program between 2008 and 2013 back into the marketplace. That exercise didn't last very long.

The Federal Reserve Board abruptly terminated its one and only attempt at quantitative tightening when it sensed a sudden loss of liquidity in the bond market, a sign that the market was having trouble digesting what the Fed was feeding it. Except for that very brief and unsuccessful monetary experiment, quantitative tightening has not been tried on a sustained basis. At least, not until now.

The Fed certainly has a lot more motivation to stick with the policy today than it did back in 2018, when US CPI inflation was running at only 2.3 percent, barely above the central bank's target rate. But with inflation, particularly the all-important core inflation, still running at almost twice the Federal Reserve Board's target rate, and with the Fed's balance sheet more than twice the size it was back in 2018, the central bank now believes it has no choice but to begin to reverse the massive bond purchases it made during the pandemic

After announcing in March 2022 that it would be ending its quantitative easing program, the Fed commenced in June the long and uncertain process of shrinking its bloated $9 trillion balance sheet by no longer rolling over up to $30 billion worth of maturing Treasuries bonds and up to $17.5 billion worth of federally backed mortgage securities each month. In September 2022, the central bank upped the ante by ratcheting up its monthly sales of Treasuries to $60 billion and mortgage-backed securities to $35 billion.

The Federal Reserve Board—or, for that matter, any central bank—could in principle sell any part of its bond portfolio back into the market at any time. But in order for its actions to cause the least possible disruption to bond markets, it has chosen to simply not roll over bonds as they mature. In this way, all of the other participants in the bond market don't have to guess which bonds the Fed will be dumping. And while the Fed hasn't sold bonds directly, it has nevertheless shed maturing bonds from its portfolio, and in doing so has forced the bond market to absorb the replacement issues.

The Fed has yet to indicate to what degree it wishes to shrink its $9 trillion balance sheet. By March 2023, it had shed roughly $700 million worth of bonds. If the central bank wanted to pare back to pre-pandemic levels, the task would take years of quantitative tightening at the current pace of $1.1 trillion a year. The sustained pressure on bond yields, and hence on housing prices and the stock market, is one reason it may choose not to go that course.

Another reason is that the Federal Reserve Board and other central banks who would follow this path could very well go broke in the process.

MARKING TO MARKET

"Marking to market" is how portfolio managers keep score on their investments. It is a way of comparing the value of the securities at the time they were bought with their current value in the marketplace. The results are usually reported to clients monthly or, at a minimum, on a quarterly basis.

Central banks also have to report their holdings quarterly, and what they have recently reported has never been reported before. For the first time in their history, they are hemorrhaging red ink as they try to finance the massive bond portfolios they acquired during their quantitative easing programs. And the losses will continue to pile up for years to come.

Under normal conditions, central banks actually make money for their governments through the bonds they hold on their balance sheet. They typically remit those earnings every year to their country's finance department. Not anymore. Now they are incurring mounting losses and many need to be bailed out.

Consider, for example, the position in which the Bank of Canada finds itself. In 2022, for the first time in its nearly nine-decade history, the central bank was forced to declare a loss in its third-quarter statement, to the tune of C$522 million. That loss was the direct result of the carrying cost of the massive C$3 billion worth of Government of Canada bonds that the bank had bought at egregiously high prices (and thus low yields) during the quantitative easing program enacted during the pandemic. The bank bought the bonds to finance the massive and record-high C$327 billion budget deficit that the Canadian federal government racked up during that time. Over the course of 2020 and 2021, the central bank purchased C$350 billion worth of Government of Canada bonds; in the process, it assumed ownership of almost half (45 percent) of the government's bond debt.

For the most part, the Bank of Canada bought the bonds from the country's large commercial banks and paid for them through so-called settlement balances, where the banks would be paid interest at the prevailing overnight target interest rate that the central bank itself sets. The settlement balances were, in effect, money supply creation by another name. When the Bank of Canada started this process, it enjoyed the benefit of "positive carry" on its huge bond position. In other words, the bonds that the Bank of Canada held paid a coupon rate (around 1 percent) that was higher than the 0.25 percent overnight rate the bank was paying the commercial banks on their settlement balances. But as inflation soared, forcing the Bank of Canada to continually hike rates, so too did the rate it was paying the country's largest banks on their settlement balances. As of July 7, 2023, that rate had risen to 5 percent.

Even when the overnight target rate was only 3.5 percent, the Bank of Canada managed to rack up that C$522 million loss mentioned above. The bank has warned that further losses will be pending over the next three years, depending, of course, on the interest rate trajectory. A study by C.D. Howe Institute, a major Canadian think tank, estimates that the losses will cumulate somewhere between C$3.6 and C$8.8 billion over that time period, depending on the Bank's overnight target rate. With that rate already sitting at 5 percent by the fall of 2023, the losses are likely to be at or near the upper limit of that range.

Every major Western central bank is encountering the same problem the Bank of Canada faces. During the pandemic, they all bought massive amounts of their government's bonds at ridiculously high prices (and thus low yields) in an effort to ease the financing burden on the huge fiscal deficits governments were racking up during the pandemic. Had they not done so, the cost of financing those record-sized budgetary deficits in the bond market would have skyrocketed—so much so that the financing might not have been affordable, in which case, governments couldn't have been so generous dispensing benefit cheques during the pandemic.

But now it's the central banks' carrying costs that are skyrocketing. The Federal Reserve Board, which remitted $100 billion to the US Treasury back in 2021, incurred an operating loss of a roughly comparable amount.

The story is no different in Switzerland, where the Swiss National Bank reported a loss of 132 billion Swiss francs in 2022, the largest loss since the central bank was founded in 1907. And the Bank of England, which has paid the British government more than £120 billion in net revenue since 2009, will require an £11 billion bailout from the government to cover carrying losses. Morgan Stanley estimates that the central bank will require cash infusions of £30 billion in both 2023 and 2024 to make up for the shortfall between the interest income it normally receives from government bonds and the interest it pays to the financial institution it bought the bonds from. And the more the Bank of England hikes rates to fight inflation, the more it will have to pay those commercial banks, and the bigger those losses will be on carrying its huge bond portfolio. Morgan Stanley estimates that every percentage point hike in interest rates by the Bank of England lowers the central bank's remittances to the treasury by a whopping £10 billion per year.

Eurozone central banks are in no better shape. Morgan Stanley estimates that central banks in the eurozone collectively incurred around €40 billion in losses from carrying the bond positions that they held on their balance sheets in 2022.

But as it turns out, the carrying losses being incurred by central banks are just the tip of the iceberg. They are simply the cost of financing the banks' current bond portfolios. While these losses are unprecedented in their own right, they are paltry compared to the horrific investment losses that have been incurred due to the change in the value of the bonds themselves.

It turns out that those massive central bank purchases of government bonds at record-high prices took place on the eve of one of the biggest corrections the bond market has ever seen. As bond yields soared, the prices of the bonds that the central banks had bought plunged.

By the fall of 2023 the price of the benchmark 10-year Treasuries had fallen around 25 percent since the summer of 2020, when its yield fell to as low as 0.5 percent. The value of longer-term Treasuries (20-plus years) fell by over 40 percent. While declines of this magnitude have often been seen in stock prices during bear markets, they are unheard of in the supposedly much safer government bond market. According to the Bank of America, the current sell-off in the Treasuries market is the greatest of all time, surpassing even the 19 percent decline in the 10-year Treasuries in 1860, before the American Civil War.

As bond yields have soared, triggering one of the worst bond market sell-offs in history, the price of the bonds that central banks so generously bought at record-high prices has plummeted. By September 2023, if marked to market, the bonds bought by the Bank of Canada during its quantitative easing program would have dropped by more than C$31 billion. And Government of Canada bond prices have continued to fall since then, pointing to an even greater loss.

The Reserve Bank of Australia (RBA) finds itself in a similar predicament. In 2022, if marked to market, its bond portfolio would have incurred an AU$36.7 billion loss, leaving the central bank with a AU$12.4 billion negative equity position.

If the RBA or the Bank of Canada were a private bank saddled with their current negative equity positions, they would be heading for the same ending that befell Silicon Valley Bank in early 2023—the third-largest bank failure in American history and the largest bank failure since the 2007/2008 financial crisis. It too bought massive quantities of long-term Treasuries in the mistaken belief that record-low bond yields were sustainable. When they weren't, massive losses starting to accrue on the bank's balance sheet.

When depositors catch wind of problems on a bank's balance sheet, they head for the exit. This sets off a run on the bank as depositors try to withdraw their money, which then forces the bank to liquidate its Treasuries holdings and, in the process, realize the huge losses that have accrued. If the bank's bond redemptions can't cover the deposit withdrawals, the bank will either need to be bailed out or will have to declare bankruptcy, as was the case with Silicon Valley and would have been the case with PacWest Bancorp, if it hadn't been bailed out by the much larger J.P. Morgan.

Yet, as dramatically as government bond yields have risen since the end of quantitative easing, they, much like the central banks' short-term interest rate targets themselves, are by no means high compared to historical norms. The severity of the sell-off in the bond market is a testament to how low yields had fallen in the face of massive central bank buying, not how high yields are today now that quantitative easing has stopped.

The problem for investors is that no one really knows what normal will look like in tomorrow's bond market. Without all those central bank purchases, bond yields would have been hundreds of basis points higher all around the world, and in particular in the Treasuries market, where the Federal Reserve Board led all central banks in bond buying. With quantitative easing no longer on the table, the days of 0.5 percent 10-year Treasury yields are all in the rear-view mirror. With the bell-wether 10-year Treasury yield touching as high as 5 percent in the fall of 2023, even current bond yields may still be unsustainably low.

While yields have already climbed back up to their highest levels since the last recession, inflation back then was running at little more than half of what it's at today. And that bond market didn't have to worry about the prospect of the Federal Reserve Board and other central banks potentially unloading trillions of dollars of bonds from their bloated balance sheets. Instead, that was when the Bernanke-led Fed started its bond buying program in the first place.

The fact of the matter is that any time you get a massive swing in interest rates like the current one, things tend to get broken in financial markets. In 2008, it was Wall Street investment banks that held toxic securities (collateralized debt obligations), which were chock full of delinquent mortgages. Today, it's regional banks, at least so far. But this time around, the toxic securities aren't defaulted subprime mortgages but US Treasuries, supposedly the safest investment in the world but whose value nevertheless plunged in one of the worst bond market sell-offs in history.

American banks typically hold vast quantitates of US Treasuries that they fund with their depositors' money. While Treasuries have always been considered the safest investment instrument in the world from a default standpoint, this doesn't mean that they can't blow up on a bank's balance sheet if their price suddenly plummets. When the yield on a 10-year US Treasury bond soars from 0.5 percent to 5 percent, a lot of balance sheets get blown up.

Fortunately, this is not a problem that the Reserve Bank of Australia, the Bank of Canada, or, for that matter, the Federal Reserve Board has to face. Unlike Silicon Valley Bank, central banks don't have to worry about a run on their bank caused by fleeing depositors. And they hold a unique option to cover losses—one that no private bank has access to. In the candid and telling words of the RBA's then deputy governor and now governor Michele Bullock, the central bank can simply "create money. That's what we did when we bought the bonds."[1]

It's admittedly the most obvious solution to the central banks' new-found dilemma of insolvency. And it's certainly a much more politically palatable option than making taxpayers pick up the tab for billions of dollars of bond losses. And so the solution to the problem turns out to be the very same practice that created the problem in the first place: just print more money.

But if the printing presses go back to working overtime, what does that mean for inflation?

Free money not only encourages households and corporations to borrow, it also encourages governments to do the same. When tax cuts or spending hikes can be financed over a ten-year period by a bond that pays only a 0.5 percent annual interest, as was the case during the pandemic, why not? But when inflation suddenly makes it more and more expensive to borrow, governments have to think twice about racking up huge deficits. At least, this is true for governments that don't have to massively subsidize their country's skyrocketing energy bill.

For energy-exporting countries like Canada, the termination of pandemic support programs will allow record deficits to shrink rapidly. However, this isn't the case for Western European countries like

Germany or Great Britain that are paying huge energy-use subsidies to households and corporations—payments that rival what was doled out during the pandemic. High prices will push deficits in the opposite direction. The United Kingdom has earmarked about £60 billion to deal with the country's energy crisis. Its budget deficit is expected to be close to 7 percent of GDP in 2023. Such large budgetary deficits will persist and will have to be financed at steadily rising borrowing rates.

What that means is that while COVID-era spending is going to leave us all generally poorer, some of us are also going to be a lot colder.

CHAPTER 6

WINTER IS COMING

The image Germany projects to the rest of the world is that its renowned status as a manufacturing powerhouse and the third-largest-exporting country in the world is due to the prowess of its engineers, the inventiveness of its scientists, and the discipline and dedication of its skilled workers. What isn't usually mentioned is that Germany's economic success—so envied around the world—has been in large measure predicated on cheap imported labour and, most of all, cheap imported energy.

The postwar German economic miracle—Wirtschaftswunder, as it was called—saw the meteoric rise of a German economy resurrected from the ashes of Second World War devastation. But by the early 1960s, the miracle was running out of labour. The construction of the Berlin Wall in 1961 cut off an important source of economic migrants from East Germany, leaving the booming West German economy seriously undermanned.

The solution to German labour force shortages turned out to be an agreement with Turkey in 1961 that allowed for hundreds of thousands of Turkish citizens to come to Germany for up to two years as guest workers.

There was no shortage of applicants. Even though German guest workers did not qualify for minimum-wage protection—and thus provided a plentiful source of cheap labour to German industry—the wages they earned in Germany were still a multiple of what they could earn back home. From Turkey's perspective, the wholesale export of surplus labour took pressure off the country's unemployment rate, while the steady stream of income that guest workers sent back to their families was a welcome source of remittances into the Turkish economy.

German industry, which quickly became enamoured with their guest worker labour force, lobbied hard for the repeal of the two-year limit, and it was lifted, allowing guest workers to become permanent residents. Many of them subsequently brought their wives from Turkey and started raising families in Germany.

The reunification of the two Germanys in October 1990 suddenly gave West German factories a huge labour force to draw from, and imported Turkish workers were no longer needed. Nevertheless, those who had arrived were given either permanent residency status or citizenship, along with the families they'd brought with them. Not all Germans, however, welcomed them. The Turkish population remains a target of right-wing parties like the Alternative for Germany, which decries the new multicultural look of the country. Nevertheless, Germany quickly became the largest region for the Turkish diaspora, and Turks became the most populous ethnic minority in Germany, numbering by most recent estimates around 7 million.

A steady stream of Turkish migrant workers may have filled the labour market void facing the postwar German economy, but there was an even bigger void to fill—an energy void. And when it came to filling this void, Germany didn't look to the Middle East but instead to its Second World War adversary, the Soviet Union.

Back in the 1970s, the newly elected chancellor, Willy Brandt, advocated a new concept in German politics—"Ostpolitik." It was an attempt to thaw the Cold War relations between West Germany and the Soviet Union, in the hope that a better relationship would open a pathway to reunification. And energy trade lay at the heart of the initiative.

Huge reserves of natural gas had been found in western Siberia, putting the Soviet Union in the position of becoming a major exporter of the fuel. However, there were no pipelines to export the fuel to gas-hungry Western European markets. So Brandt proposed the construction of a massive pipeline network—using, of course, German steel—that would connect Siberian gas with German markers. It was a win-win. On the one hand, Russia got an important new market for its natural resource and a source of hard currency earnings. On the other, Germany was able to secure a cheap supply of vitally needed energy, while Russian pipelines became an important new customer for German steel.

But with the collapse of the Soviet Union in 1991, those Russian pipelines connecting to Germany were suddenly running through an independent and increasingly hostile country—Ukraine. Disputes over the transit fees Russia would pay Ukraine for the right to pump its gas through what had become Ukrainian pipelines reached a climax in 2008, when Russia suspended gas shipments for twenty days during the winter.

That was a huge problem for Europe's industrial powerhouse. By the mid-1990s, Germany had come to rely on Russia for 40 percent of its natural gas supply. It needed an assured pipeline network where gas could not be blocked by transit-fee disputes with a third country. So it was in both Russia's and Germany's interests to circumvent Ukraine and avoid any further conflicts that could interrupt the flow of Russian natural gas to German markets.

To that end, the two countries agreed to build a series of pipelines under the Baltic Sea that were designed to deliver Russian natural gas to a terminus in Lubmin, in northeastern Germany. Running for 1,222 kilometres (759 miles), Nord Stream 1 was the longest sub-sea pipeline in the world, carrying a total annual capacity of 55 billion cubic metres (1.9 trillion cubic feet) of natural gas. It was by far the single most important pipeline that connected Russian gas fields to millions of European households and businesses.

The pipelines were as much the brainchild of former German chancellor Angela Merkel and her predecessor Gerhard Schröder as they were of Russian presidents Dmitry Medvedev and Vladimir Putin. Today, both former chancellors are under attack in their country for rendering Germany so dependent on Russian gas exports, and hence vulnerable to Moscow's political dictates. But at the time, successive German governments (both Social Democrat and Christian Democrat) quite rightly recognized that the country could not maintain its status as a global manufacturing powerhouse without cheap and abundant energy to power its industrial base.

Germany didn't build pipelines from Russia because its government liked Russia's leadership, any more than the United States imported oil from Saudi Arabia because it favoured a repressive autocratic monarchy that still staged public beheadings at the time. Germany imported Russian natural gas for the same reason it had earlier imported Turkish labour: because the lower your costs of production, the more competitive your export industries. Since the German economy lives or dies according to its exports—particularly energy-intensive ones like cars, appliances, and chemicals—Nord Stream 1 was a no-brainer, no matter which party was in power.

Schröder and Merkel championed Nord Stream 1 because they wanted to supply German companies and German households with the cheapest gas possible. And the cheapest gas possible for the German market was Russian gas. It still is today.

Not every country, however, was a fan of the Nord Stream project. The United States aggressively lobbied against it, fearing it would give Russia undue political leverage over NATO's largest and most important European power. And while Germany is a NATO ally of the United States, it is also an industrial rival. Certainly American industry wouldn't lose sleep if German exports were to suddenly become less competitive.

Washington actually tried to halt Nord Stream by first prohibiting any American companies from being involved in laying cable under the Baltic Sea, and then later threatening German firms involved in

its construction with sanctions. In the end, though, German push-
back got its way and the United States had to walk back the threat of
sanctions.

Of course, the country that objected the most but was powerless
to stop the pipeline's construction was Ukraine. After all, Nord Stream
was designed to sidestep Ukrainian pipelines, which generated billions
of dollars in transit fees for Kiev. With the opening of Nord Stream 1,
the percentage of Russian gas exports passing through Ukraine fell
from around 60 percent to around 25 percent.

Both Russia and Germany would have been happy to see that
number fall even farther. So why not build another pipeline, paralleling
the original, that would double gas throughput to Germany? To no
one's surprise, both Ukraine and the United States bitterly opposed
Nord Stream 2. Its construction occurred against the backdrop of the
Russian occupation of Crimea and the revolt of Russian-speaking
regions in the wake of the American-led overthrow of the Moscow-
friendly government in Kiev. The Americans renewed their threats to
sanction any company doing work on the project and pressured
European allies to buy American gas instead.[1] In fact, the Americans
went so far as to say that they would never let it come online. "If Russia
invades Ukraine, one way or another," said US State Department under-
secretary Victoria Nuland, "Nord Stream 2 will not move forward."[2]

Sure enough, it didn't. German diplomats proved unable to repeat
their earlier accomplishments in placating American pressure. When
construction was complete in early 2022, the German government
refused to certify Nord Stream 2, despite what at the time were already
rapidly rising European natural gas prices, and the $11 billion invest-
ment in the pipeline, much of it made by German utility companies.

The Russians didn't seem to mind. They were in no hurry to resume
gas exports to a country that had aligned itself against them. If Berlin
could weaponize the opening of Nord Stream 2 to deny Russia export
earnings to finance its war effort in Ukraine, Russia could play that
game too. In a series of staged reductions, gas flows to Nord Stream 1

had been entirely shut off by the end of the summer, reducing Russian gas supplies to Germany by 90 percent.

The looming gas shortage threatened Germany with its greatest energy crisis since the Second World War. In Germany, political pressure to open up the new pipelines was mounting. Nothing the United States or its other NATO allies could do would change the underlying economics: Germany needed Russian gas. As important as Russia was to world oil supply, it was even more important to natural gas supply, particularly for Europe. Russia is the world's largest gas exporter, and Europe has been its primary export market, relying on Russia for more than 40 percent of its gas supply. Germany was even more heavily reliant, depending on Moscow for over half its gas.

That economic lifeline snapped on September 26, 2022. Denmark and Sweden reported leaks in both the Nord Stream 1 and Nord Stream 2 pipelines following explosions on the floor of the Baltic Sea. The leaks temporarily created a bubbling cauldron of leaking gas that at one point measured a kilometre (just over half a mile) in width.

The explosions rendered both pipelines inoperable, ripping gaps of more than forty-five metres (148 feet) in each one. The damage removed any remaining hope that a negotiated settlement between Russia and Ukraine or its NATO allies could lead to the restoration of Russian natural gas supplies to Western Europe. Both NATO and Russia have accused each other of sabotaging the pipelines.

The West was quick to point the finger at Russia, claiming that Putin was crazy enough to destroy his own multi-billion-dollar investment and simultaneously throw away one of his best bargaining chips. More objective analysts pointed out that if Putin had really wanted to cut off Europe's gas supply, all he had to do was shut off the tap, like he'd already done with Nord Stream 1.

Meanwhile, American secretary of state Antony Blinken was gloating that the Nord Stream sabotage presented the United States with a "tremendous strategic opportunity."[3] At a January 2023 Senate hearing, Nuland was just as pleased: "I think the administration is very gratified to know that Nord Stream 2 is now . . . a hunk of metal at the bottom of the sea."[4] The United States did not seem heartbroken by the disaster that had befallen its ally.

While Nord Stream methane was still gushing from the sabotaged pipeline, Norwegian and Polish officials cut the ribbon on a new pipeline connecting their two countries. It seems unlikely these NATO allies would have been disappointed by the disaster that had befallen their much bigger competitor (and historical rival). Neither would American LNG exporters. After all, there was plenty of American gas available. And if it happened to cost much, much more than what Russia could provide, that was Germany's problem, not theirs.

A few weeks later, Pulitzer Prize–winning American journalist Seymour Hersh—who broke stories like the My Lai massacre in Vietnam and the Abu Ghraib torture in Iraq—published a story called "How America Took Out the Nord Stream Pipeline." According to his sources, US Navy divers used the cover of joint exercises to lay mines on the sea floor, which could be remotely detonated. Hersh claimed the secret operation reported directly to Joe Biden. Later reports suggested that Ukrainian divers were to blame.

But in the end, the question of responsibility misses the much larger point. No one should be surprised by cynical ruthlessness in war. What marks the Nord Stream attack as a signpost on the landscape of the new normal is who the ultimate victim of the attack was. Because it wasn't really who it appeared at first glance to be: Russia.

To be sure, the destruction of the pipelines meant that Russia couldn't sell its gas to Germany anymore (which it already wasn't at the time anyway). But the loss of the German market certainly didn't mean that Russia couldn't sell its gas elsewhere. The real victim of the sabotaged pipelines turned out to be Germany and the rest of the EU economy.

Whether the divers who planted the charges were American or Ukrainian is no more than a footnote to the much bigger story. All that really matters is that from the moment those explosions detonated, the European economy, and in particular the German economy, was cut off from its energy lifeblood. It had been sucked into the war. And suddenly, there was no turning back.

LOCKING IN THE FUTURE

Economic shocks are by their very nature ephemeral. Some might argue that the war in Ukraine is a shock. Chances are that at some point in the future there will be a treaty between Russia and Ukraine and its NATO allies, and that sanctions against Russia could even be scaled back or lifted. Governments change, alliances shift. New issues arise. Nothing lasts forever. But that doesn't mean that energy flows will go back to the way they were before the sanctions were imposed on Russia.

The energy infrastructure landscape has changed markedly since sanctions were first imposed. Germany, which had no LNG terminals before the invasion, has hastily leased three floating LNG terminals at an estimated cost of nearly €10 billion and has several more planned that will be land-based. They are part of the no less than nineteen new LNG terminals that are being hastily constructed in Europe to replace the lost natural gas supply from Russia.

And just as Germany has pivoted toward LNG, Russia has pivoted toward the huge Chinese market to sell its gas. The pivot began over a decade ago with the construction of the Power of Siberia natural gas pipeline (originally called the Yakutia-Khabarovsk-Vladivostok pipeline) that connects Siberian gas with Chinese markets. The project was financed by a thirty-year, $400 billion contract. The pipeline first became operational at the end of 2019. Annual supply has grown from 113 million cubic metres (4 billion cubic feet) of gas in 2019 to 436 million cubic metres (15.4 billion cubic feet) in 2022. By 2025, the volume through the pipeline is expected to rise to a peak level of 1 billion cubic metres (38 billion cubic feet)—roughly what Russia supplied Italy, its largest European customer after Germany.

Just prior to the Beijing Olympics, Russian energy corporation Gazprom announced a thirty-year deal to supply Chinese state energy firm CNPC with natural gas exports via a new planned pipeline, connecting Russia's vast Yamal natural gas deposits in Siberia with northwest China. Construction of the 2,700-kilometre (1,677-mile) Power of Siberia 2 pipeline, which will run through Mongolia, is expected to commence in 2024, and the pipeline should be operational by 2030. Power of Siberia 2 is expected to more than double the amount of Russian gas piped to Chinese markets through the first pipeline delivering 50 billion cubic metres (1.7 trillion cubic feet) annually. Russia, which supplied only about 10 percent of Chinese gas imports before the conflict in Ukraine began, will become by far China's largest supplier when the next pipeline is built, supplying almost half of its natural gas imports by the end of the decade. If we keep in mind that the German economic "miracle" was fuelled by cheap labour and Russian gas, it is not hard to see what the world's biggest exporter has in mind.

Neither Germany nor Russia undertook these investments as a short-term fix to the problems that sanctions brought. You don't spend €10 billion on building LNG terminals for just a year's supply of gas. For example, German utility company SEFE, a former unit of Gazprom that was seized by the German government, signed a deal to import 2.25 million tonnes of LNG a year for the next two decades from a export terminal in Louisiana. Nor do you spend billions of dollars on building pipelines to China as a temporary alternative to piping gas to Western European markets. The German turn to the East for an energy partner was called "Ostpolitik." Now Russia has an Ostpolitik of its own.

In addition to the construction of new pipelines, Russia intends to reconfigure its existing pipeline network so it can redirect oil and gas flows from traditional European markets to newly opening Asian markets.

Over time, as Russia commits an ever-increasing share of its gas exports to supplying the Chinese market, there will be less and less surplus gas to export to Europe, even if at some point in the future European sanctions against Russian energy are dropped and relations between Germany and Russia improve. Similarly, the construction of

LNG receiving terminals commits Germany to a new-found dependency on LNG imports.

Both Germany and Russia have committed billions of dollars to building new energy infrastructure—the usage of which will be required for decades in order to justify the expenditures involved. As such, LNG terminals in Germany and China-bound pipelines in Russia lock in a tectonic long-term shift in European energy supply and an equally tectonic long-term shift in the direction of Russian oil and gas exports. The economic impact of those shifts will be felt for decades.

EUROPE'S ENERGY LOSS IS AMERICA'S ENERGY GAIN
American opposition to the Nord Stream pipelines, which dates back to the Obama administration, wasn't only geopolitical. It was very much in the United States' economic self-interest to oppose pipelines from Russia in an effort to create demand for what has become the most dynamic part of America's energy industry: the large-scale export of shale gas in the form of LNG. New liquefaction trains at Calcasieu Pass and Sabine Pass suddenly gave the United States the largest LNG export capacity in the world.

Whether it was simply fortuitous or part of a carefully schemed master plan, the United States bulked up its LNG export capacity just as the Ukrainian conflict and the sabotage of the Nord Stream pipelines cut off European markets from Russian gas supply. Literally overnight, turbocharged European demand for American LNG catapulted the United States to the front ranks of global LNG exporters, alongside traditional heavyweights Qatar and Australia.

Europe's LNG imports soared in 2022, up an astounding 65 percent from the previous year, as EU countries scrambled to make up for the loss of the Russian gas on which they had been so heavily dependent. And the US natural gas industry was one of the prime beneficiaries of soaring European LNG demand, with about two-thirds of record-high American LNG exports going to European markets.

The LNG export boom was certainly the long-sought-after game changer for the US gas industry. Whereas US natural gas exports were almost entirely via pipeline to continental neighbours Mexico and Canada, LNG exports are now greater than pipeline exports. And it's been a very profitable transition. Since the loss of Russian gas flows, European LNG prices have soared, surpassing Asian prices to become the most attractive market in the world. Thanks to LNG shipments American gas producers were getting four times more from selling their product in post-Nord Stream Europe than they were getting paid in the North American market.

Europe's replacement of Russian natural gas with LNG has been nothing short of a bonanza for America's natural gas industry. From virtually zero a decade ago, by 2022 LNG exports claimed 15 percent of American natural gas production, and that percentage could easily more than double over the next decade with the addition of as many as ten new LNG export terminals proposed along the Gulf of Mexico coastline.

But for Europe's energy consumers, it's anything but a bonanza.

DE-INDUSTRIALIZATION

There was never any question that spiking energy costs would fuel inflation in Germany, or that recession loomed. No economy can absorb a shock like 11 percent inflation without it affecting growth. But recessions, as traumatic as they may be to workers who lose their jobs, usually last only a couple of quarters. What Germany's highly vaunted manufacturing industry faces is a lot more challenging than a brief cyclical downturn. It instead faces the prospect of secular decline.

German manufacturing accounts for an oversized 20 percent of the country's GDP, but until recently, its factories ran on power derived for the most part from burning cheap Russian natural gas. That reality wasn't lost on either Germany's business community or its labour unions. In April 2022, a joint statement by the employers' group BDA and the country's trade union confederation DGB argued that the loss of Russian natural gas supply posed a mortal risk to the industrial core of the German economy. According to the Federal Statistical Office of Germany, power prices charged to industrial users were already the highest by far on record, as the largest economy in the European Union and one of the world's biggest manufacturing hubs suddenly found itself saddled with some of the most expensive power rates in the world and certainly the most expensive in Europe.

The most vulnerable victims in the German economy, and indeed the EU economies in general, are very energy-intensive industries like glass and steel. These industries, once the mainstay of the German economy, are no longer economically viable in much of Europe at today's power prices. You don't locate energy-sucking industries like steel and glass in a country when power costs have surged to as high as €500 per megawatt (the Btu equivalent of $600 per barrel of oil!). Soaring gas prices in Italy, which uses about half of the natural gas it imports to generate electricity, have already caused widespread production cutbacks in a growing list of energy-intensive industries, including steel, pulp and paper, and glass.

Since 2019, German glass producers have faced a tenfold increase in energy costs. Similar increases have forced ArcelorMittal SA, the world's second-largest steelmaker, to announce that it would have to shut two blast furnaces at its giant facilities in Bremen.

Steel and glass are both important industries in Germany, but what German manufacturing is most known for around the world is producing high-end motor vehicles. How much longer will Audi, BMW, Porsche, and Mercedes be able to afford to pay soaring German power prices and continue to produce cars in their native country? At stake are some 800,000 jobs in Germany that depend directly on auto manufacturing, and hundreds of thousands of others indirectly.

And if soaring power costs aren't enough of a death knell for the industry, consider Brussels's edict that by 2035 only electric-powered vehicles can be sold in the European Union. If the EU adheres to that mandate, it will mean surrendering the vast majority of the European market to Chinese auto producers, who, given their chokehold over car battery production and the material to produce them, are expected to dominate electric vehicle production by then. And keep in mind that batteries are not a source of energy. They *store* energy. Most of the electricity that car batteries store is generated by burning natural gas. If the price of natural gas goes up, so does the price of driving electric vehicles.

The German vehicle industry may be pivoting toward producing electric cars in order to comply with EU policy, but there is nothing green about the way Germany produces vehicles. It takes fifty-five thousand megajoules of energy to produce a single vehicle. Volkswagen, the country's largest car producer, derives 80 percent of that required energy from burning natural gas. BMW relies on the fuel for 60 percent of the energy used in its factories. By contrast, on-site renewable power sources account for just 1 percent of the energy used in German vehicle manufacturing.

Will soaring power costs force a migration of vehicle production to jurisdictions that can provide cheaper and more reliable power, just as high wages forced a migration of American and Canadian vehicle production to low-wage Mexico? Germany is already starting to look like a very unlikely location to locate a new energy-sucking auto plant. Not to mention an unlikely location to build a mega plant to produce batteries for electric vehicles. Maybe that's why—Canadian government subsidies aside—Volkswagen decided to locate its new multi-billion-dollar mega battery factory in Ontario, where power costs are a fraction of those in Germany.

There was never any question that spiking energy costs would fuel inflation, and that the economy would ultimately roll over into recession. It wasn't long after inflation hit 11 percent—the highest clocking in seven decades in Europe's supposedly inflation-proof economy—that Germany fell into recession, over the last quarter of 2022 and the first quarter of 2023. The rest of the eurozone economy followed suit.

Germany's economic minister Robert Habeck blamed the inflationary impact of soaring energy prices, which, in his words, brought the

German consumer to their knees. Recession aside, the head of the German Institute for Economic Research, Marcel Fratzcher, estimated that the impact of the war in Ukraine on German energy prices had already cost the German economy some €100 billion, or about 2.5 percent of GDP. Peter Adrian, president of the German Chamber of Commerce and Industry, pegged the loss at €160 billion. Both warned that higher energy prices would remain a major competitive disadvantage for Germany for decades to come.

And if seven-decade-high inflation and the first recession since the 2008 global financial crisis isn't bad enough, there is the fiscal cost to consider. All of a sudden, the eurozone's inflation and fiscal hawk has become of one the community's outliers. The German word of the year in 2022 was *Zeitenwende*. It means "the end of an era" or "epochal change." When Chancellor Olaf Scholz used it, he was referring to Germany's supposedly new and clear-eyed foreign policy, which now sees China and Russia as bona fide threats. But he could just as easily have been talking about the epochal shift in the German economy from manufacturing powerhouse to one shackled with some of the highest energy costs in the world. Suddenly, the meaning of *normal* has changed dramatically in Europe's largest economy. And most Germans aren't going to like how the new normal feels.

CHAPTER 7

GLOBAL CLIMATE CHANGE ACTION
WILL JUST HAVE TO WAIT

When the sabotaged Nord Stream pipelines started belching hundreds of thousands of tonnes of methane into the atmosphere, activists were quick to note that the consequences were not merely geopolitical. The victims couldn't be identified by their passports. The whole planet would pay the price. Methane is eighty times more potent than carbon dioxide when it comes to changing the climate, and Nord Stream was pumping out 220,000 tonnes of the stuff, which would have made it the biggest industrial methane leak in American history. Whether you "stand with Ukraine" or are cheering for Russia, massive discharges of powerful climate-forcing agents are a loss for everyone. But as it turns out those emissions were dwarfed by what was to follow. Scientists estimate that the first year of the war in Ukraine was responsible for a net increase of between 120 million and 150 million tonnes of greenhouse gas emissions, roughly equal to the annual emissions of a country the size of Belgium or the Netherlands. But that measures only the impact in Ukraine itself. Those estimates don't capture the impact that the war or associated sanctions have had on the emissions triggered by the energy choices of Ukraine's allies due to the loss of Russian fuel supply. As we have seen in the case of Germany and most of its EU and NATO partners, those energy choices have been very significant and will be continue to have an impact on emissions for decades to come—unfortunately, all in the wrong way.

That's not good news for hopes of mitigating the growing impact of global climate change. The brief reprieve from ever-rising emissions during the pandemic (global emissions dropped 4 percent as huge swaths of the global economy were suddenly locked down) proved as fleeting as the lockdowns from the pandemic themselves. No sooner had economies reopened than emissions started to rebound. And the sanctions war against Russia, with its many unintended consequences, gave emissions an additional boost.

By 2022 atmospheric carbon had reached a 4-million-year-high of 424 parts per million. And the following summer, global temperatures rose to the highest ever recorded in 125,000 years. At the current pace of emission growth, global temperatures will have risen over two degrees by the end of the century. In the world we are heading toward, the need for adaptation to global climate change would quickly eclipse today's focus on mitigation.

Notwithstanding the urgency for action, the conflict in Ukraine and its rapidly growing international ramifications have thrown new road blocks in the way of halting the relentless rise in global emissions.

ENERGY SECURITY VERSUS SUSTAINABILITY GOALS

When sanctions were first imposed on Russia's fossil fuel exports, it was widely argued in the European media and among EU governments that such measures would help wean EU member economies off their dependence on fossil fuels, since Russia was their main supplier. As a result, sanctions against Russian fossil fuels were initially packaged with a thick coat of greenwash.

But as we quickly learned, climate change policies take a back seat to concerns over energy security whenever people start to worry about whether they'll be able to heat their homes in the winter or if the lights will turn on when they flick the light switch. For all intents and purposes, energy security equated to governments trying to secure alternative fossil fuel sources for their suddenly energy-starved economies, to make up for the loss of now sanctioned Russian supply.

The choice between energy security and the need to mitigate emission-driven climate change has never been starker than during the conflict between Russia and Ukraine. The war and its attendant sanctions changed priorities all across Europe. Instead of the implementation of the next scheduled round of aggressive emission-reduction measures, the new top item on every country's policy agenda was suddenly energy security.

The energy choices made from Berlin to London to Brussels were unambiguously clear. Aside from European energy consumers themselves—who were suddenly forced to pay huge, record-setting prices—the biggest casualty of the sanctions war between Russia and NATO is the European Union's world-leading emission-reduction targets, which the community so proudly champions as a standard for the rest of the world to adopt. And as we have seen, those choices, once made, are not subject to sober second thoughts by future administrations; they are locked in for decades to come by massive sanctions-induced induced spending on new energy infrastructure.

Today's overriding imperative for energy security has sent EU economies heading in precisely the opposite direction from what their very ambitious emission-reduction targets (a 55 percent reduction in emissions below 1990 levels by the end of this decade, and net-zero emissions by the middle of the century) would require them to take. While European governments solemnly proclaim that despite the current U-turns in energy policy, they are still deeply committed to those very ambitious emission-reduction targets, their recent energy choices are sending their economies off on a very different trajectory.

The German Environment Agency has already acknowledged that the country's much-publicized 2030 emission target is not likely to be met, putting in doubt Germany's longer-term goal of achieving net-zero emissions by 2045. The admission stems from recent energy choices made in response to the war in Ukraine. What holds for missed German targets holds for most EU government emission targets.

For example, and as we saw in an earlier chapter, billions of dollars are being spent in Germany and throughout the European Union on constructing LNG terminals—and this during a decade in which the EU was intending to shift infrastructure spending to renewables and retire many of its existing oil-, gas-, and coal-burning facilities. Instead, a big chunk of new energy spending won't be on renewable energy at all, but on replacing infrastructure that used to service Russian natural gas, oil, and coal with new infrastructure to handle alternative sources of supply of those very same emission-spewing hydrocarbon fuels.

As LNG becomes the de facto alternative to Russian pipeline gas, the required investment in new receiving terminals signals a renewed investment in future fossil fuel consumption. It was precisely that tie between new energy infrastructure and continued fossil fuel usage that led President Biden to reject the construction of the Keystone XL pipeline from Canada. In his view, building the pipeline would only perpetuate the use of fossil fuels in the American economy—a prospect his administration is adamantly against.

But when it comes to using American fuel (like LNG, for example), as opposed to Canadian bitumen, it's another matter altogether—at least from Washington's perspective. The same Biden administration that nixed the Keystone XL construction expresses no similar concerns about the new LNG infrastructure being built in Germany and elsewhere in Europe, as long as the fuel is supplied by America. The projected economic lifetimes that justify the massive investment in these types of energy infrastructure require their continued operation over decades, committing Germany and its EU neighbours to long-term fossil fuel use—precisely the energy future that their emission targets are intended to prevent.

At the same time not only is the consumption of LNG boosting the EU's greenhouse gas emissions but its production has had a significant impact on emissions where the fuel is produced. CO_2 emissions from American LNG facilities have jumped 18 million tonnes per year, up 81 percent from 2019. That is equivalent to the emissions from several large-scale coal-fired power plants. And while LNG is touted by advocates as a bridge to a carbon-free future, it can be a pretty long bridge, depending on where the power comes from to turn gas into a liquid form. LNG may take up to six hundred times less volume than the fuel in its gaseous state, but it requires a lot of energy to cool gas to –160 degrees Celsius (–256 degrees Fahrenheit) to make the conversion, not to mention the fuel required to power the ships that carry it over the high seas. If the power needed to convert gas to a liquid state is produced by combusting coal, LNG can be ten times more carbon-intensive than natural gas delivered through a pipeline.

And while the construction of as many as nineteen new LNG terminals throughout the European Union guarantees the fuel a long-term presence in Europe's energy plans, an even greater carbon polluter has suddenly gotten a new lease on life in the continent's power grid.

RETURN OF THE COAL AGE

If you listen to the environmental, social, and governance movement, coal is a dead man walking. If true, that would be very welcome news for the atmosphere, since no energy source creates more carbon pollution than coal. Per unit of energy, coal emits 50 percent more carbon than natural gas (in its gaseous state). As the dirtiest of the fossil fuels, coal single-handedly accounts for over a quarter of the carbon that the global economy emits into the atmosphere every year.

For that very reason, coal is usually pointed to as the single most important immediate target for replacement in the transition to renewable energy alternatives and the ultimate achievement of a net-zero-emission economy. To that end, seventy-five countries, who between them account for 95 percent of global coal consumption, have pledged to phase out all coal-fired power by either 2050 or 2060.

But if you look at world coal prices and global coal consumption today, it hardly seems like a dying industry. In fact, times have seldom, if ever, been better. Since the economic lockdowns from the pandemic have passed, global usage of the fuel is on a record-setting run. Already at all-time highs, coal prices at one point were quadruple their pre-pandemic levels.

Like the demand for oil, global demand for coal fell during the pandemic. The price of Australian Newcastle—widely seen as the benchmark for supplying the huge Asian coal market—crashed to as low as $50 a tonne. But since then, global coal prices have soared to record highs. At a recent peak, coal was trading at over $400 a tonne, compared to a previous all-time high of just over $100 a tonne.

By 2022 global coal demand set a new all-time high, erasing a decade's worth of steady progress in reducing global consumption of the world's dirtiest fuel. While the post-pandemic rebound in Asian demand is the main driver of the turnaround, there has also been a renaissance in coal consumption in the most unlikely of places—Europe. And that renaissance turns out to be all about the war in Ukraine and the energy choices in Europe that the loss of Russian fossil fuel have compelled.

The loss of Russian natural gas supply has induced a wholesale shift among Germany and other EU countries back to, of all things, greater use of coal-fired power. Coal consumption in Europe is up over 20 percent since the conflict in Ukraine broke out (the flip side of a nearly 20 percent decline in natural gas consumption from the loss of Russian supply)—and this during a time in which many of the continent's coal-fired power stations were scheduled to have been permanently shuttered. Suddenly, the goalposts for emission policy have shifted dramatically for the world's most polluting fuel.

Energy shocks, if dramatic enough, can induce profound changes in energy usage. In turn, these changes can have a significant impact on future emissions, even long after the initial shock has passed. For example, oil supply shortages during the OPEC shocks of the 1970s induced North American households to switch to burning a cleaner fuel by replacing their oil-burning furnaces with natural gas–burning models. But today, the loss of Russian natural gas supply is forcing many

EU countries to switch back to burning far more emission-intensive coal, turning the clock back on decades of world-leading environmental policy and practice.

The return to greater reliance on coal-fired power has meant that instead of entirely phasing out coal plants from their grids, as mandated by their aggressive emission-reduction targets, most EU countries are cancelling scheduled closures of currently operating coal fired power plants. Some are also considering reopening long-closed coal-fired generating plants in a desperate attempt to prevent widespread power outages.

Nowhere is this more true than in Germany, the European Union's largest economy and biggest coal burner. Coal, which generates about 30 percent of all power in the country, was slated to disappear entirely from Germany's energy mix by 2030—a key condition in meeting the objective of reducing emissions that year to 55 percent below 1990 levels. Chancellor Olaf Scholz's government has stoically said it will stick to the 2030 coal-exit timetable. But in the meantime, at least twenty coal-fired power plants nationwide are being resurrected or extended past their closing dates in order to ensure Germany has enough energy to replace what was previously provided by imported Russian natural gas. Far from being expunged from the country's energy mix, then, coal-fired power is about to post an impressive comeback as it fuels the supposedly green German economy. Coal-fired power's share of electricity production in Germany has grown each year of the conflict in Ukraine, reaching over 33 percent by 2023. And when it comes to Germany's energy sector emissions, the impact of the switch back is already apparent, having increased by 4.5 percent in 2022 as a result of the war-induced switch from natural gas to coal.

FUKUSHIMA'S LONG SHADOW

In addition to the loss of Russian natural gas, coal combustion has received another powerful boost via Germany's closure of the last of its operating nuclear power plants. Back in 2011, following the

Fukushima disaster, Chancellor Merkel decided that the country would close its huge fleet of seventeen nuclear power plants by 2022, even though they had operated safely for decades. At the time, the decision enjoyed popular support and today is one of the bedrock conditions that cements the current coalition government between the ruling Social Democratic Party and the Green Party. With no Russian gas flowing through the sabotaged Nord Stream pipelines, the only alternative for Germany as it closes its last three nuclear power plants—which supply about 13 percent of the nation's power—is to reopen mothballed coal-powered plants.

Germany is by no means the only EU country returning to the coal age. The United Kingdom, also facing natural gas shortages and soaring natural gas and power prices, has decided to do the same. Power utility Uniper pushed back the planned closure of its Ratcliffe-on-Soar coal-fired power plant until the end of 2024. The move follows similar decisions made by EDF (Électricité de France SA) to keep open its Burton power plants, originally scheduled to close in September 2022, and Drax Group PIC's decision to keep its last two coal-fired power plants operating as well. And in December 2022, Britain's Conservative government approved the first new coal mine in the country in three decades, anticipating growing demand for thermal coal from the nation's power sector. Austria, the Czech Republic, the Netherlands, Greece, and Poland have also extended the operating life of coal-fired power plants.

Not only have sanctions and commercial sabotage of Russian natural gas supply boosted demand for coal, but the economic war between NATO and Russia has simultaneously made the supply of coal that much harder to secure. In August 2022, the European Union imposed its earlier announced sanctions on its roughly €4 billion-a-year trade in Russian coal, its largest source of supply.

The only problem with the Russian coal ban was that the European Union was as dependent on Russia for its coal supply as it was for its natural gas. And the timing of the decisions couldn't have been worse from a price standpoint. When Germany and other EU countries looked to far-away producers like Australia to replace now-sanctioned Russian supply, they faced price increases that were just as challenging as replacing Russian gas after it stopped flowing through Nord Stream.

In 2022, Australian Newcastle was trading at an all-time high of $457 a ton, over three times the price from only a year earlier. And European coal prices weren't far behind, trading at the Rotterdam coal hub at around $400 a tonne. For German power utility generators, who were paying around $60 per tonne for coal at the beginning of 2021, that amounted to an almost sevenfold increase in fuel costs. Like soaring natural gas prices, soaring coal prices quickly translated into soaring power prices for German businesses and households alike, in addition to radically higher costs for the roughly 20 million German households that relied on natural gas to heat their homes in the winter.

Meanwhile, on the other side of the sanctions wall, Russia was easily able to sell the coal it would normally have sold to Europe to China and India (the two largest coal-burning countries in the world). Both markets have doubled their import of Russian coal since the European sanctions went into effect. When you have virtually unlimited access to the world's two largest coal markets—which, combined, account for 70 percent of global consumption of the fuel, more than twice as much as the rest of the world combined—EU markets become expendable.

And as Western countries turn their back on nuclear energy in the post-Fukushima era, Russia has very quickly filled that gap. Its nuclear conglomerate, Rosatom State Nuclear Energy Corporation, has become the world's largest contractor to build nuclear power plants and provides a cradle-to-grave service that includes designing, building, operating, and even decommissioning nuclear power plants. Additionally, Rosatom is the world's largest exporter of the enriched uranium that nuclear power plants operate on. (It also manufactures Russia's nuclear weapons, but fortunately those are not for export!)

Given that nuclear power remains the most viable option available for the wholesale decarbonization of the world's electricity system—an essential prerequisite for meeting future global emission reduction targets—Rosatom has positioned Russia to play a leading role in the coming global energy transition. And whereas in the past nuclear power plants were largely built in the developed world, in the future they will be needed most in the developing world, where most of the world's coal is now being burned to generate power.

SOARING POWER COSTS DARKEN THE OUTLOOK FOR ELECTRIC VEHICLES

The loss of cheap Russian natural gas and the attendant rise in coal combustion not only compromises Europe's near-term emission targets, but also puts in doubt the even more ambitious longer-term goals. The latter are predicated in large measure on the assumption that gasoline and diesel will be eliminated from the fuel mix of vehicles by the mid-2030s. So confident was the European Union in meeting the objective of having its roads carry electric vehicles alone that they, like the state of California, planned to ban the sale of gasoline- or diesel-powered vehicles by 2035.

Given how high electric power prices in Europe have ranged since the war began in Ukraine, that ban would leave a lot of European highways pretty empty. The highly anticipated wholesale replacement of gasoline- and diesel-powered vehicles with electric ones was largely based on the expectation that it would be much cheaper for motorists to charge an electric vehicle than to fill a gasoline-powered one at the pumps. Prior to Russia's invasion of Ukraine, that seemed like a reasonable expectation. (Don't forget that, owing to much higher carbon taxes, pump prices in Europe can be as much as double what North American motorists are accustomed to paying.) It is certainly no longer the case, even with the big run-up in pump prices.

Britain's Royal Automobile Club noted in late 2022 that after a greater than 40 percent rise in public charging fees in the United Kingdom, the fuel cost of driving an electric car had risen to parity with the fuel cost of driving a gasoline-powered vehicle. Even in

Norway, a country where abundant hydroelectric power provides one of the lowest power prices in Europe, the price of electricity has soared. The cost of charging the nation's huge fleet of electric cars (almost 80 percent of all vehicle sales are electric) had increased by 50 percent, while home-based electricity bills have soared even higher, in some cases tripling.

At the end of 2022, only about 12 percent of the passenger vehicles on the road in the European Union were solely battery-powered. What will happen to those charging-price increases if the entire vehicle fleet becomes plug-in electric, as is ultimately mandated by policy? Given that most electricity grids in Europe are already running close to capacity, the notion that tens if not hundreds of millions more European drivers will switch to electric cars over the next decade doesn't seem possible without triggering massive and sustained blackouts across the continent. Right now, the only way those blackouts could be averted is by bringing back online enough mothballed coal-fired generating plants to provide the necessary charging power. But in that case, what would be saved in tailpipe emissions would be more than offset by the stuff coming out of smokestacks.

And given what has happened to coal prices since the pandemic, Europe's coal-fired power plants can't provide power at prices anywhere close to what they have in the past. Burning coal used to be a cheap but environmentally dirty alternative to generating electric power by using much-cleaner-burning natural gas. While coal is still as dirty as it ever was, it's no longer cheap.

As with global oil demand—which was expected to rise to an all-time high of 102.1 million barrels a day in 2023—soaring Asian demand together with Europe's new-found appetite for the world's dirtiest carbon fuel should drive global coal combustion to a new record high as well. And with coal combustion poised to reach a new record, so too will global carbon emissions. That is bad news for the atmosphere. But with coal now costing a multiple of what it did before the sanctions war began, it's bad news for power prices as well.

It was typically normal for governments to face a trade-off between short-term economic growth and longer-term environmental sustainability. But thanks to today's sweeping sanctions against the world's largest energy exporter, that trade-off is no longer available. Today's EU governments are now compelled to follow policies that simultaneously sacrifice both economic *and* environmental objectives. That is what happens when energy becomes a battleground in economic warfare. And there are even more casualties when the battleground shifts to food.

CHAPTER 8

THE HUNGER GAMES

Since antiquity, food has been a part of warfare. The Romans salted the earth and destroyed the irrigation systems of their enemies' land, as they did against Carthage during the Punic Wars. Centuries later, Parisians were reduced to living off rats during the siege that ended the Franco-Prussian War.

Russians and Ukrainians know hunger at least as well as anyone in the world. During Stalin's program of "forced collectivization," as many as 10 million Soviet citizens died of hunger. Between 30 and 45 percent of those victims were Ukrainian, leading some to believe famine was a deliberate genocide (others contend the cause was mismanagement, or a cynical effort to accumulate foreign currency through grain exports, in order to keep the regime afloat). Either way, the Holodomor, as it was called, is remembered as a national crime and a searing horror.

Things in the USSR just got bleaker from there. More than a million Russians starved to death during the five-hundred-day German siege of Leningrad (St. Petersburg) during the Second World War, more than the number of people killed as a result of the Allied fire-bombing of Hamburg and Dresden and the American atomic bombs dropped on Hiroshima and Nagasaki combined. During the siege, the city's inhabitants were forced to live off a daily ration of 125 grams of bread, which many supplemented with boiled carpenter's glue.

It would be reassuring to think that history has moved on from the industrial-scale inhumanity that marked the twentieth century. Certainly, the two countries locked in the lethal struggle in Ukraine remember hunger as a curse that can blight entire generations. And yet, hunger looms not far down the path the world is currently travelling.

THE RUSSIAN-UKRAINIAN BREADBASKETS

Given that both combatants in the war between Russia and Ukraine house major breadbaskets, it is perhaps no surprise that food supply is poised to be a major casualty. Russia is almost as important a food and fertilizer exporter as it is an energy exporter. Its 85.9 million tonnes of wheat production in 2020 ranked it as the third-highest in the world, behind only China and India, both of whom have massive populations to feed. With a relatively small population of 144 million—less than a tenth of China's or India's—Russia is far and away the world's largest exporter of the crop, followed by Canada and the United States.

Ukraine is a breadbasket in its own right, with its fertile soils around the Black Sea serving as home to another 24.9 million tonnes of wheat, ranking it eighth in the world in production and fifth in export. Together, the two countries account for almost a third of total global wheat exports and about 20 percent of total corn exports. In addition to grains, Russia and Ukraine are major exporters of edible oils used widely in cooking. Ukraine alone accounts for about half of global sunflower oil export, and with Russia about two-thirds of world supply. For billions of people in the developing world, the loss of that food supply would have a much greater impact than the loss of 8 million barrels a day of Russian oil exports, or the loss of Russian natural gas supplies. Only 2.5 million people in Cairo drive a car. But all 22 million of its inhabitants eat.

Like oil prices, the price of food was soaring even before the Russian invasion began. The widely followed United Nations Food and Agriculture Organization (FAO) Food Price Index, which tracks the international prices of items such as vegetable oils, dairy products, and grain, was already running at ten-year highs due to global harvest issues, including a disastrous drought on the Canadian prairies. But one month into the invasion those prices skyrocketed. World food prices jumped nearly 13 percent in March 2022 to a new record high as the war in Ukraine caused widespread global shortages of staple grains and edible oils.

Harvesting wheat and corn while missiles are exploding all around your tractor is a distraction most farmers don't have to contend with. Yet Ukraine's principal wheat-growing region, the area that lies south of Kiev to Kherson and east of the Dnieper River, found itself in the midst of a raging war zone. At best, the country was expected to be able to harvest only about two-thirds of the 6.4 million acres it sowed. Moreover, most of what was harvested had no way of getting to world markets. During the first four months of the war, some 22 million tonnes of Ukrainian grain sat trapped in storage bins. Unlike oil, grain doesn't keep when stored indefinitely.

With Ukrainian-controlled ports closed, Kiev had no way of getting its grain to world markets, even if it had been able to harvest all of its crops. During the initial months of the war, grain and oil-seed shipments from Ukraine fell by about 80 percent compared to what they'd been the previous year.

That wasn't just a problem for Ukrainian farmers and grain merchants. It soon became a problem for households around the world, especially those in the developing world.

Through interlinked grain markets, crop shortages in one part of the world quickly get translated into higher prices for that grain all over the world. In Western Europe and North America, the impact of the conflict on world grain markets was etched into soaring rates of food inflation, which along with soaring oil prices would soon be fuelling consumer price increases the likes of which hadn't been seen for decades.

In Canada, food prices climbed by 10.3 percent between November 2021 and September 2022. In the United States, food prices had risen by 11 percent year-over-year in October 2022, while in Britain they had risen by 16 percent over the same period.

But as challenging as the price increases were to Western shoppers, they weren't the ones facing the greatest threat. Those most affected were those least able to afford the price increases—almost all of whom live in developing countries. In North America, households typically spend around 10 percent of their income on food. In the developing world, in countries such as Egypt and Lebanon, that figure can be as high as 80 percent. Without massive government-paid subsidies, that doesn't leave a lot of wiggle room to feed yourself and your family when food prices soar.

Approximately fifty countries in the Middle East and Africa rely on Ukraine and Russia for most of their grain. Egypt, for example, relies on them for about two-thirds of its wheat imports. Lebanon depends on Ukraine for 80 percent of its grain, while war-torn Yemen relies on both Ukraine and Russia for 97 percent of its grain imports. In April 2022, the United Nation's World Food Programme warned that the world was facing the worst food insecurity since the Second World War. It predicted that the increase in world hunger would be felt the most in Africa, where 40 million people were expected to join the millions who were already living with acute hunger.

As wheat prices soared, food subsidies, typical in many developing countries, became fiscally untenable. When it comes to basic staples like baladi bread in Egypt, subsidies reduce the price to the poor by as much as 95 percent. Without them, hunger becomes a pandemic. And authorities in those countries haven't forgotten that food riots were the catalyst for widespread social unrest during the so-called Arab Spring uprisings back in 2010, which began with bread riots in Tunisia and then swept across the Middle East. Throughout the developing world, soaring food prices mean growing food shortages, and empty stomachs often lead to hungry and angry people in the streets.

To make matters worse, the threat of global food shortages unfortunately provoked many food-exporting countries to restrict exports, fearing that there would soon not be enough produced to safeguard the food supply for their own population. Exports bans, which first arose around masks, ventilators, and vaccines during the COVID-19 pandemic, began sprouting up around agricultural produce in a growing list of countries including Indonesia, Serbia, Moldova, Hungary, Argentina, and Turkey—yet another sign of the breakdown in the global trading system.

In July 2022, in response to a looming world food crisis, Turkey and the United Nations brokered a deal between Russia and Ukraine that would allow Ukraine to ship grain through mutually agreed-upon corridors in the Black Sea and on through the Bosporus Strait. The increased access to Ukrainian grain would allow prices to retreat from record highs. The Black Sea Grain Initiative was intended to allow some 20 million tonnes of Ukrainian wheat and corn to avoid spoilage and instead avert starvation in developing countries like Yemen, which is almost entirely dependent on the Black Sea region for grain. However, as Ukrainian officials were quick to point out once the grain started moving, most of it was already covered by commercial contracts and could not simply be doled out to hungry people around the world. "The destination for the cargo has been negotiated between the supplier and the buyers, and they are totally commercial activities," an official said. "We don't decide where it goes. It is a free market."[1] Most of it was contracted to go to Turkey and Europe.

In fact, as little as 15 to 30 percent of Ukrainian grain exports found their way to the developing countries where they were most needed. Hunger-stricken Sudan received only 65,000 tonnes, while Spain received 2.9 million—much of which was reported to have been fed to Spanish pigs to produce its world-famous jamón.[2]

Most of the rest flooded the local markets of Ukraine's neighbours. The European Union had dropped its tariffs on Ukrainian grain in an effort to allow it to be exported through member countries to the Middle East and North Africa, where it was desperately needed. But instead, the grain was sold in local EU markets, saturating them with product and driving down crop prices, to the dismay and anger of local farmers. Poland, Hungary, and Slovakia halted all grain and food imports from Ukraine in response to pressure from local farmers. Kiev in return has filed lawsuits against Poland, Slovakia, and Hungary with the WTO in protest over their bans on Ukrainian grain.

NOT JUST FOOD PRICES BUT FERTILIZER PRICES AS WELL

The disruption of Russian and Ukrainian grain supply was a bad enough threat to global food prices. But a potentially even worse threat is the inability of the rest of the world to grow more of its own food to make up the difference.

Ever since the Green Revolution began in the 1960s, seeds have been engineered to offer much higher yields. This technology has been widely credited with saving hundreds of millions of people, if not billions, from starvation in the developing world. Global grain production has tripled since, but in order for the genetically modified seeds to produce those coveted higher crop yields, fertilizer is needed—and in much greater quantities than their natural predecessors required. And Russia just happened to be the world's largest exporter of fertilizer.

This should come as no surprise, considering that natural gas is the major feedstock used in the production of fertilizer; both ammonia and nitrogen fertilizers are derived from it using the Haber-Bosch process. Russia's vast natural gas supplies put it in a position to be the world's largest exporter of fertilizer, accounting for 23 percent of world ammonia exports, 14 percent of world urea exports, and 21 percent of world potash exports. Together, exports of urea, potash, and nitrogen-based fertilizer garner Russia over $9 billion a year.

While Russia may have lots of natural gas to produce fertilizer, other countries in Europe don't these days. Gas shortages have had a domino effect on the continent's ammonia production, which has fallen by half, while its nitrogen production has fallen by a third. As a result, fertilizer prices have soared even more than food prices. Nitrogen-based fertilizer prices more than doubled after the outbreak of the war in Ukraine, rising from $1,200 a tonne in the fall of 2021 to $2,600 a tonne in the spring of 2022.

A global shortage of fertilizer had by April 2022 sent world fertilizer prices soaring by 66 percent to an all-time high. As of fall 2023, they remain over double the levels seen prior to the war. And to make matters worse, as with food itself, some major fertilizer producers, like China (among the top five global producers), have shut down exports of key fertilizer components such as phosphate, keeping supplies for use in their own domestic markets.

Although Russian fertilizer has escaped American and EU sanctions (except for potash), most international shipping companies have suspended their service to Russian ports, reducing exports. Moreover, Russia itself has taken actions to limit export sales through a variety of measures including export taxes, restrictive licensing practices, and outright bans.

Whether Russia's or China's curtailment of fertilizer exports is a retaliation for Western sanctions or the result of a genuine need to preserve key agricultural inputs to meet the food requirements of its own population is a debatable point. Either way, the restrictions only exacerbate the pressures on food prices that the war has unleashed.

Those price impacts have reverberated around the world. For North American farmers, soaring fertilizer and energy costs meant that the 2022 crop was the most expensive ever planted. Typical planting costs of $200 soared to as much as $700 an acre in Canada's wheat breadbasket on the western prairies.

Eastern Canadian farmers fared even worse. Just weeks before the planting season in March 2022, finance minister Chrystia Freeland and international trade minister Mary Ng announced that Canada was imposing a crippling 35 percent tariff on the nitrogen fertilizer from Russia and Belarus (among other products) that growers rely on to boost crop yields. Up until the imposition of the tariff, Russia had been a reliable source of fertilizer for eastern Canadian farmers, who imported

660,000 tonnes a year—roughly 90 percent of all the fertilizer imported into the region.

In a market already squeezed by soaring energy costs, this 35 percent hike in fertilizer prices could only drive Canadian food prices—which were already increasing at the fastest rate since 1981—even higher. Few Canadian consumers connected the dots between the war in Ukraine, the resulting Western sanctions, and the price of growing the food they were eating, but the soaring cost of food in NATO-allied countries certainly won't have escaped the Kremlin's attention.

LEVERAGING ITS AGRICULTURAL POWER

Between soaring energy input prices and soaring fertilizer prices—both resulting from the economic war between Russia and the West—the FAO Food Price Index jumped 14 percent in 2022, posting record highs since record-keeping began in 1991. Four of the main five subindexes—cereals, meats, dairy, and vegetable oils—all recorded historic highs.

And food prices were once again on the rise in 2023, after Russia cancelled its participation in the Black Sea Grain Initiative in retaliation for an attack on the Togliatti-Odessa ammonia pipeline and what it says were Western failures to abide by the original deal. Grain was once again prevented from leaving Ukrainian ports. Just as is the case with energy, there is no way the rest of the world can suddenly make up for the loss of supply from the Black Sea region. Grain prices, which had retreated to close to pre-war levels as the Black Sea Grain Initiative opened up shipping, suddenly shot up almost 15 percent.

That scale of global food leverage puts Russia in a position where agricultural exports could potentially yield even more of a geopolitical advantage than its energy exports furnish. As former US secretary of state Henry Kissinger is purported to have once quipped: "Control oil and you control nations; control food and you control people."

Russia and Ukraine are already vital breadbaskets for the world's population, and they are likely to become even more so as ongoing climate change relocates areas of crop cultivation around the world. Mid- to high-latitude countries (such as Russia, Ukraine, and Canada) are expected to be able to extend cultivation to new areas blessed with suddenly longer growing seasons, and to shift cultivation to more value-added crops, like corn, that previously could not have been grown on a commercially viable basis. At the same time, agriculture in lower-latitude countries (including the United States, which is the world's top food exporter) is expected to be adversely affected by climate change, as a result of both the increasing frequency of drought in its primary grain-growing areas and temperature increases beyond thresholds that become harmful to crop yields, particularly corn.

The impact of the conflict in Ukraine on world grain supply and prices provides only a glimpse into the new world order. It's only natural that in an increasingly hungry world, countries will want to be on friendly terms with the world's largest grain and fertilizer exporter. This dependency already explains why 70 percent of the world refuses to condemn the Russian invasion of Ukraine. And if most of the world has already come to view the Russian food supply as vital to feeding its population, even more countries can be expected to do so as climate change rearranges the contours of world food production.

It's already apparent who the winners in this geographic lottery will be: Canada, Scandinavia, and, above all, Russia. Rich countries such as Great Britain, France, Germany, Korea, and Japan are expected to at least be able to feed themselves—and while Ukraine is not exactly "rich," it will too, given its ample agricultural endowments. But Pakistan and India, Mexico, the Caribbean, and Central America, and large swaths of Africa and the Middle East will find it increasingly difficult to do so.

Food supply is already becoming a major political issue in many of those countries, just as soaring grocery prices have in Western countries. That is why India, the world's largest rice exporter, announced in August 2023, shortly after Russia's cancellation of the Black Sea Grain Initiative, that it had ordered a halt to its largest export category of non-basmati rice, which accounted for almost half of the country's

22 million tonnes of rice exports in 2022. A month later the FAO All Rice Price Index soared to a fifteen-year high. The impact was felt the most in Asian countries, which consume 90 percent of global rice supply. Some governments, like the one headed by President Ferdinand Marcos Jr. of the Philippines, have imposed a ceiling on rice prices. But the ceiling is a double-edged sword. While it limits price increases, it discourages desperately needed domestic rice production.

India's export ban underscores the extreme sensitivity of Narendra Modi's government to food inflation ahead of a general election in 2024. In addition to the restrictions placed on rice, the Modi government extended a ban on wheat exports and put a cap on sugar exports. Modi is betting that fed voters will be happy voters.

Two of the world's superpowers, China and the United States, may soon follow suit, in their own ways. The North China Plain—the agricultural heartland of what will soon be the world's largest economy—is drying up. Rainfall is dwindling, and its aquifer has been all but pumped dry. Meanwhile, the Huang He (Yellow River) is carrying less and less volume, and the meltwaters that feed the Yangtze will diminish to a trickle as the glaciers and snowpack that feed it melt away as a consequence of global warming. China is already buying up farmland around the world, particularly in Africa. They see hunger coming, and are spending their reserves of US dollars to avoid it.

It could be even worse for China's neighbours, whose food production is located downstream of the melting glaciers on the country's Tibetan plateau that feed rivers like the Mekong, Salween, Irrawaddy, and Brahmaputra. When China builds dams upstream, like the twenty-two it has built on the Upper Mekong, there is less flow downstream. These and other rivers originating in China flow into eighteen nations that together house a quarter of the world's population. Hydropolitics is bound to become an increasingly important diplomatic tool for China to apply to relations with its downstream neighbours.

China won't be the only superpower concerned with water and resulting food supply. The United States is in a similar boat. Rainfall is diminishing across the High Plains, and the famous Ogallala Aquifer is just about dry. The glacial runoff that feeds California's farms, which produce about a quarter of the food grown in the United States, is tapering off. In a warmer world, the mountains get rain rather than snow, which means that precipitation rushes downhill to the sea rather than being stored as snow that will run off when warmer weather arrives. Experts predict that the United States will be out of the food-exporting business once global warming reaches 2 degrees Celsius. American billionaires, like the Chinese government, are buying up all the farmland they can.

It is not hard to see that these conditions could potentially lead to massive instability, both within countries and between them. Hungry citizens will demand that their governments do *something* to alleviate hunger, and that something could be drastic and violent. No one expects the masses to quietly starve. Looking back to Ireland's Great Famine provides a hint of what might lie ahead. Even as the poor were dropping dead of hunger, ships filled with food were sailing out of Irish ports. Like the Ukrainian wheat bound for the wealthy countries of the West, that food was already owned by a merchant in a distant city. It was not available for charity. That is how the free market works.

The famine is remembered in Ireland today as a genocide, and it fuelled generations of political upheaval that led to independence for the Republic of Ireland and left a festering wound in Northern Ireland. More than 150 years later, the political fallout is still being felt as Brexiteers attempt to square the circle of a Northern Ireland both outside of the European Union and yet integrated into the Republic of Ireland.

And in some ways, Ireland represents an optimistic scenario, even though a million people are estimated to have died from starvation and related disease. It could have been far worse. Another million Irish avoided starvation by migrating to the new frontiers opening up in North America. Between starvation and migration, the island lost about a quarter of its population between 1845 and 1851.

That gives us a glimpse of the volatility of the new world order. The hungry will demand to be fed, and their governments will have powerful motivation to placate them. That imperative will leave tomorrow's breadbaskets wielding enormous geopolitical power. If energy can be used as a weapon, so too can food. Exporting countries may choose to supply only "friendly" markets.

When Western countries denounced the suspension of the grain deal on the grounds that the world's poor would go hungry as a result of Russian intransigence, Russia promised to ship grain and fertilizer free of charge. This did little to silence its critics in Kiev and Washington, but it made Russia a lot of new friends in Africa, none of whom have denounced its invasion of Ukraine. In the new normal, major food exporting countries will have lots of hungry friends.

CHAPTER 9

SANCTIONS

The sanctions game is a little like playing hot potato with a hand grenade. You may be able to take the other guy out, but there is a chance you may both get hurt. And there is always a chance the whole thing will blow up in your face.

Just ask the executives at any number of Western airlines. When the United States and its European allies closed their airspace to Russian airlines in 2022 to punish the Kremlin for its incursion into Ukraine, Moscow shrugged and followed suit. The problem for Western carriers was that Russian flights, for the most part, don't fly over Western Europe or North America. But just about any flight to Asia must fly over Russia. Once the new sanctions kicked in, only airlines based in countries aligned with Russia could use its airspace.

Suddenly, a British Airways flight from London to Shanghai was 11,140 kilometres (6,922 miles), while a China Eastern flight was only 9,750 kilometres (6,058 miles). An Air France flight to Beijing was 9,700 kilometres (6,027 miles), while an Air China flight path over Russia was 8,300 kilometres (5,157 miles). That translates into two hours of additional flight time.[1] About 10 million Chinese tourists visit Europe each year. Do you think they will want the longer, more expensive flight, or the shorter, cheaper one? NATO-aligned airlines are no longer competitive. When travel restrictions were lifted by Beijing, the French government opened negotiations with China to increase tourism, only for Air France to realize that raising the number of flights would actually hurt the company.

Of course, Emirates and Qatar Airways continue to enjoy Russian overflight rights, as do airlines from Egypt, India, and Turkey. Turkish airlines have increased their number of flights to Asia since the sanctions regime came down. For these countries, the world got (relatively) smaller.

What about airlines based in the United States? In May 2023, the US Department of Transportation approved four new weekly flights between US and China. That brought the total number of flights to twelve. The American airlines had been lobbying the Biden administration to ban Chinese flights, which were much more competitive. US carriers were losing $2 billion a year in market share to airlines allowed in Russian airspace.[2]

But why is international air travel important? When the dust settles from this dispute, the arm-wrestling reveals what is at stake in the new world order, and who is likely to benefit.

Consider another example from the world of aviation. It's doubtful that either Boeing or Airbus, the world's two largest aircraft manufacturers, were consulted before the decision was made to sanction Russian airlines and aerospace industries. But neither could have been too pleased when they discovered the role they were to play in the economic war against Russia. Patterned after actions taken earlier against Iran, the United States and the European Union targeted Russia's avionics sector. What is bad for archenemy Russia should be good for the USA, no?

Well, not exactly. The selective no-fly zone over Russia meant that Western leasing companies were told all existing leases with Russian airlines had to be cancelled immediately. That left some 515 jets, worth $10 billion, leased by Russian airlines from the leasing arms of Boeing and Airbus, in limbo. If those planes were returned to their leasing company owner, Russian airline services like Aeroflot would have virtually no planes to fly, even domestically. In effect, the return of leased planes from Western aircraft manufacturers would turn Russia into a veritable no-fly zone.

Facing that prospect, Russia passed a new law allowing Russian airlines to nationalize their leased planes. And since Russian planes were banned from flying to Western countries, where the planes could be confiscated upon landing, leasing companies had no way of repossessing the planes they had leased to Russian airlines. That meant a $10 billion write-off for the associated leasing companies of the world's two largest aircraft manufacturers—or their insurers, like Lloyd's of London.

In retaliation, both manufacturers ceased servicing the planes and refused to sell Russian airlines replacement parts for the now confiscated leased planes, forcing Russian airlines to strip down the planes idled by the ban on foreign flights to service the planes used for domestic travel.

If sanctions were to continue indefinitely, at some point Russian airlines would run out of parts from stripped planes and put the safety of air travel in jeopardy, as happened in Iran when Boeing stopped supplying their airlines with replacement parts as part of American sanctions against that country. So Russia decided to do what so many embargoed or sanctioned countries have done in the past when the supply of essential imports was suddenly blocked: they began a program of import substitution. That is decoupling from western aircraft manufacturers.

Despite its significant aircraft manufacturing capacity, 95 percent of the commercial aircraft flying in Russia had been supplied by Airbus and Boeing before the Ukraine conflict. Not because Russia can't produce avionics, but because it is much easier to get international safety certification for airliners using systems that have already been certified. But that Western duopoly was doomed when the sanctions were imposed. Not many countries can decouple from Western technology and engineering. But it is possible in a country like Russia and in an industry like aircraft manufacturing.

Any country that can build a Su-57 (an advanced fighter jet with stealth technology) can build an airliner. In response to Western sanctions,

Russian minister of trade and industry Denis Manturov announced that Russian aerospace manufacturers would ramp up production and be ready to deliver more than 1,000 domestically made airplanes to the country's airlines by 2030. That target included all the aircrafts' parts, from engines to wings. The Russian PD-14 jet engine is reportedly between 10 and 17 percent more efficient than anything made by Pratt & Whitney.[3] The single-aisle MC-21 airliner is the first commercial aircraft in the world to use a composite wing.[4] The commitment to boosting the country's commercial aircraft production was a clear indication that Moscow did not see its relations with the West improving anytime soon. The world was changing, and Russia's Ministry of Trade and Industry wasn't expecting it to ever return to what it had been before the war in Ukraine. For Russia's avionics sector, this meant a future without Boeing or Airbus planes.

However, Russia's avionics sector wasn't exactly starting from scratch. Back in 2007, Putin, perhaps in anticipation of what was to come, ordered the creation of a state-owned Russian aerospace conglomerate called Rostec. With the withdrawal of Boeing and Airbus from the Russian market, the Russian conglomerate now has an effective monopoly on producing commercial aircraft in the country. It has been contracted by Russian airlines to produce 142 Superjets, 270 MC-21s, 70 turboprop Il-114s, 70 medium-haul Tu-214s, and 12 wide-body Il-96 jets between now and 2030. Aeroflot has already ordered 89 Russified models of the regional SSJ100 jet, and the export market for it is expected to be huge.[5]

As these newly ordered Russian-manufactured planes are delivered, Airbus and Boeing planes will drop out of Russian airline fleets. In the words of Sergey Chemezov, head of Rostec, "Boeing and Airbus planes will never be delivered to Russia again."[6]

Moscow's directive to provide more than 1,000 new commercial aircraft over less than a decade is nothing short of the largest prod to Russia's commercial aircraft manufacturing industry in history—a prod that is a direct response to Western sanctions. In the largest acquisition in its history, Russia's national carrier, Aeroflot, announced that it would be more than doubling its fleet by 2030 through ordering 339 new planes. But instead of Airbus A320 family-type planes or Boeing B777s, they would be buying a new fleet of entirely Russian-manufactured planes. Out of the airline's current fleet of 305 aircraft, aside from 76 Sukhoi, none are Russian-built.

Targeting Russia's avionics industry didn't force Russians to do without air travel. Instead, by denying Russia the ability to lease imported planes from Boeing and Airbus, sanctions have compelled Russia to develop its own civilian aerospace sector. In the short run, the sanctions will cost Boeing and Airbus (or their insurers) billions of dollars to write off the leased planes now confiscated by Russian airlines. But in the long run, the sanctions could cost them much more. They have spurred the rapid development of an unwelcome competitor that not only will shut Boeing and Airbus out of the Russian market, but in time could compete with them for sales in other markets as well.

What has happened to Boeing and Airbus in the Russian market may soon happen to them in another larger and more important market—China. China isn't passively waiting for similar sanctions to be imposed against its airlines' leases from Boeing or Airbus. Indeed, every sanction thrown at Russia can be viewed by Beijing as a dress rehearsal for what is inevitably coming China's way, and they've been preparing for it. Back in 2017 the Commercial Aircraft Corporation of China launched the Comac C919, designed to compete with the Airbus A320 and the Boeing 737 MAX. On September 30, 2022, the 169-seat passenger plane with a range of 2,200 nautical miles received official certification from the Civil Aviation Administration of China, clearing it for use by Chinese airlines. President Xi personally attended the certification ceremonies, signalling the importance that the development of a domestic aerospace industry holds with the country's leadership. It has since been introduced into service by several Chinese airlines.

American exports of aircraft and parts to the Chinese market have already plunged from $18 billion in 2018 to a little over $5 billion in 2022. And now, with the development of the Comac C919, they are expected to fall farther. Meanwhile Embraer, the largest aircraft manufacturer in BRICS, is expecting to expand sales in the Chinese market, principally at Boeing's and Airbus's expense.

With the sanctions-induced prod to Russian and Chinese civil aircraft manufacturing, the world is about to get a whole lot smaller for both Boeing and Airbus. They can thank their governments' sanctions for spurring the development of commercial competitors among their geopolitical rivals.

But unintended consequences aren't the only legacy of sanctions. Sheer brutality is another of its trademarks. Consider the sanctions imposed during the First World War when the practice reached its zenith.

WHAT SANCTIONS ACCOMPLISH

The First World War introduced the world to new horrors. But when peace finally returned, it was not the new weapons of industrial slaughter—the tanks, machine guns, heavy artillery, and barbed wire—that shook most people's sense of dignity. The new weapon that seemed most devastating wasn't even military. It was economic: the sanction.

Today, sanctions tend to be seen as a diplomatic Swiss Army knife—more of a peaceful tool than a weapon. Sanctions are announced as a means to bring wayward nations to their senses. Those who impose them can say, *At least we didn't go to war*. But history shows us that sanctions *are* war. They are every bit as lethal. And, like air raids and the manoeuvres of armies, they are meant to cripple nations, topple governments, and crush civilians.

Economic warfare was not, of course, a new concept. The first recorded use of sanctions was almost twenty-five hundred years ago, during the Peloponnesian War, in 431 BCE, when Athens imposed a commercial ban on merchants from the Greek port city of Megara.

During the American Civil War, the Union blockade of Confederate ports denied the Confederacy the ability to finance their war effort through the lucrative cotton trade with Great Britain, ultimately contributing to their defeat.

But it wasn't until the First World War that the full devastating force of sanctions—or "the starvation weapon," as it was called—was felt by the civilian populations that they targeted. US president Woodrow Wilson, an ardent fan of such measures, described them glowingly as "an absolute isolation . . . that brings a nation to its senses just as suffocation removes from the individual all inclinations to fight."[7] While the Allies could do little to dislodge the Germans from Belgium and France during the brutal trench warfare that defined the conflict, they could nevertheless bring the fight to the defenceless civilian population of their enemy. By December 1918, the National Health Office in Berlin calculated that 763,000 people in Germany had died as a result of the Allied naval blockade. Another 300,000 perished in the Ottoman Empire, whose ports were also blockaded.

When the dust cleared and the consequences of the blockade were made clear, the victors were aghast at what they had done to Germany. Even Wilson admitted that "while war is barbarous . . . the boycott is an infinitely more terrible instrument of war." One British bureaucrat involved in the administration of the blockade recoiled from the way the Allies had won: "We tried, just as the Germans tried, to make our enemies unwilling that their children should be born; we tried to bring about such a state of destitution that those children, if born at all, should be born dead."[8] The interwar years saw the acknowledgement that the effects of sanctions would be felt for generations, in poor health, stunted children, and social fragility. Just as anti-war sentiment after the Second World War crystallized around the abhorrence of nuclear weapons, the peace movement after the Great War took the position that sanctions were just too awful to actually use.

But this sheer awfulness could be strategically useful. So devastating was their impact that it was reasoned no country would be so rash as to risk having sanctions applied against them. To do so would be to bring upon oneself assured self-destruction. Hence, sanctions were seen as a deterrent to war much in the same way that nuclear weapons are today.

But pacifists weren't the only ones to parse the horrors of the Great War for lessons. Anyone could see that vulnerability to sanctions left a country at the mercy of those with the power and the willingness to use this terrible weapon. The best defence against sanctions, it followed, was self-reliance—or autarky.

In retrospect, the consequences are obvious. Any country that was not self-reliant had a strong incentive to become so. Germany had starved in the Great War because of a lack of farmland and fertilizer. Not surprisingly, it made the acquisition of land a priority. While the United States and the British Empire had plenty of oil, Germany, Italy, and Japan could not say the same. They concluded that the only way to be sovereign was to go out and aggressively acquire the resources of their neighbours. The lesson of the sanctions of the Great War was that only this approach would allow them to better withstand the otherwise suffocating grip that sanctions could hold on their populations. Economic self-sufficiency quickly became the top priority for countries ostracized by the international community and targeted for sanctions.

In other words, sanctions helped to create a new normal in the 1930s. Now, nearly a century later, fully one-third of the world economy is subject to sanctions. In the early 1960s, only 4 percent of countries were subject to economic sanctions imposed by the United States, the European Union, or the United Nations, covering less than 4 percent of global GDP. Fast-forward to today, and fifty-four different nations—a quarter of the countries in the world—are subject to some form of sanctions, affecting almost a third of global GDP.

In addition to national sanctions, there has been a marked rise in the number of individual or entity sanctions. In the United States, sanctions imposed by the Office of Foreign Asset Control soared from 540 a year under the Obama administration, to 975 a year under Trump to 1,151 a year under Biden. As these numbers indicate, sanctions have become increasingly popular over time at the White House—and it doesn't seem to matter if the administration is Republican or Democratic. Without question sanctions have become part and parcel of the new normal. We would do well to consider what the consequences might be.

LIVING WITH THE NEW NORMAL

We don't have to look to the future to consider the effects of Western sanctions on Russia. The Russians have been living with them for more than a hundred years. Following the conclusion of the First World War, Western powers, led by the United States, turned sanctions that had previously been targeted at a now defeated Germany toward the new Bolshevik government in Moscow and the newly formed Communist government in Hungary, led by Béla Kun.

At the time, the governing economic and political elites in Western Europe and America felt threatened by the Russian Revolution, fearing that worker unrest might spread to their own countries. (Indeed, at the time there was widespread labour unrest in the United States and the Winnipeg General Strike in Canada, and the newly formed Labour Party organized the largest general strikes in history in the United Kingdom). Crushing the newly formed Soviet state was a high priority for both the American and British bourgeoisie. Although Western powers were not technically at war with Soviet Russia, Britain and France sent 200,000 troops to fight against the Bolsheviks in the Russian civil war that followed the 1917 revolution.

Even back then there were many doubts about whether the crippling sanctions would actually promote the regime change that they were intended to achieve. Many opponents of sanctions in the West feared that further impoverishing the Russian people through economic warfare against their government would serve only to strengthen the Bolsheviks' hand and their fight against the czarist White Army that was still operating in many parts of the country and challenging the new Soviet government.

In addition to its trade ban with the newly formed Soviet state, Great Britain—at the time the most ardent advocate of economic warfare against the new Bolshevik government in Russia, as it is today—forbade any ships that had been supplying Bolshevik-controlled ports from being loaded with British coal. That restriction created a major disincentive for shipping countries to service any Russian ports, since British control over the production of bunker coal, which was the primary fuel used for shipping at the time, was much greater than Saudi Arabia's control of today's oil market.

Over time, however, support for continued sanctions began to wane. Scandinavian merchants were the first to lobby for a repeal of the trade blockade, but other voices were soon heard, on both humanitarian and commercial grounds. Russian resources, particularly wheat, were highly coveted by European governments cognizant that hungry stomachs among their own labour force had the potential to feed the same kind of social unrest they'd seen unfold in Russia, while both European and American industrialists were eager to sell their wares to a backward and still largely rural Russian economy desperate for foreign technology.

Eventually their voices were heard and enthusiasm for the three-year-old economic war against the Bolshevik regime waned. It had clearly not achieved its intended effect of bringing down the revolutionary Bolshevik government in Russia. By 1922, czarist forces had been annihilated, and the Bolsheviks were the undisputed rulers of Soviet Russia.

Fast-forward a hundred years, and Russia and its people find themselves in a similar position to where they were at the end of the First World War. But Russia today is not a backward, semifeudal nation. It's an industrial and military power that has been preparing for Western sanctions for years.

From a Russian perspective, Western sanctions are just a fact of life. Russia was already subject to them. And they were already at war with the West—an economic, diplomatic, and information war that had been going on for decades. While no one knows for sure how long he had been planning it, some have speculated that if not for the COVID outbreak, which hit Russia as hard as anywhere in Europe, Putin would have moved sooner. By the time the crisis in the Russian-speaking part of Ukraine reached its boiling point, Putin had clearly calculated that proceeding with the special military operation was less risky than the status quo.

NATO'S RELENTLESS EXPANSION INTO RUSSIA'S BACKYARD

In a strong sense, the conditions for the new normal were born when the USSR was dismantled. Back in 2000, only five years after taking power, Vladimir Putin had made no bones about how he felt about the breakup of the USSR orchestrated by Mikhail Gorbachev. Putin publicly declared it to be one of the greatest geopolitical catastrophes of the twentieth century. Most Russians agreed with him. Before he died, Gorbachev was regaled in the West for his liberal reforms of glasnost and perestroika and perhaps most for his decision to break up the USSR. His fellow Russians took a different view, rating him a worse leader than Joseph Stalin. And Yegor Gaidar, architect of the International Monetary Fund (IMF)–imposed "shock therapy," has gone down in Russian memory as a scoundrel and a fool. According to a 2020 poll, 75 percent of Russians believed that the Soviet Union represented the greatest time in Russian history. The 1990s, by contrast, were a time of despair, corruption, and decay.

NATO had promised Gorbachev that the alliance would not expand an inch farther east if the Soviet Union disbanded, and yet it immediately set out to do just that. Russians saw the mighty achievements of previous generations stripped by oligarchs and Western investors, neither of whom left much for anyone else. Life expectancy plummeted. Western prosperity quickly came to look like a cynical hoax. From the perspective of many Russians, perestroika and its aftermath looked like a tragic betrayal.

This was particularly true when the West clearly did not reciprocate post-Soviet Russia's attempt at integration. When a humbled Russia asked to join NATO in 1991, it was quickly rebuffed. When NATO instead expanded into Poland, Hungary, and the Czech Republic in 1999— despite explicit promises to the contrary made by US secretary of state James Baker in 1990—Russia realized Gorbachev had been duped. Russian diplomats warned that further expansion would be a provocation, but NATO expanded again in 2004, this time into Baltic countries that had been part of the USSR itself (rather than Warsaw Pact allies). Despite warnings from both Russian diplomats and American statesmen, NATO expanded again in 2007, 2009, 2017, 2020, and 2023. It would be easy for Russians to feel they were being hemmed in by enemies. And given the serial betrayals, the Russians felt they could not trust the West, and therefore could not negotiate with them. They have a word for it: недоговороспособны. It means "incapable of agreement." Having been burned badly by the West's attitude toward Russia since the 1991 dissolution of the Soviet Union, most Russians came to believe there was no point trying to deal with the United States or NATO. The West simply couldn't be trusted to keep any commitments it may have made. When former German chancellor Angela Merkel admitted in an interview that the two rounds of negotiations in Minsk had been ploys to buy time for Ukraine to further arm itself, Russia believed that it had been duped yet again into negotiating in good faith.[9]

A naive Gorbachev hadn't seemed to realize that most of the former Soviet republics he was letting become independent would soon be headed by virulently anti-Russian nationalist governments that were chomping at the bit to join NATO as quickly as possible and welcome the stationing of NATO troops and military bases along their borders with Russia. From the perspective of Russia's newly independent neighbours, the collapse of the USSR was a once-in-a-lifetime opportunity to escape the yoke of Russian influence and domination. In two of those countries, Hungary in 1956 and Czechoslovakia in 1967, Russian troops had had to be deployed to put down anti-Soviet popular uprisings.

Russia's neighbours quickly applied for NATO membership, which was just as quickly granted. From Washington's viewpoint—which ironically didn't see the breakup of the Soviet Union coming at that point in time—it was a coup de grâce. The collapse of the Soviet Union had stripped away Russia's buffer states and left it exposed. Not only were Russia's European neighbours no longer Moscow's client states, but, far from neutral, they had become in effect Washington's new states. Most held long-standing and bitter historical grievances against Moscow.

So instead of dissolving in the wake of the disappearance of the rival it existed to oppose, the NATO alliance grew by leaps and bounds, absorbing states that, until the fall of the Soviet Union, had been either former Warsaw Pact members (a group of countries founded in 1955 to counter NATO and which included Albania, Bulgaria, Czechoslovakia, East Germany, Hungary, Poland, Romania, and the Soviet Union) or were actually part of the former USSR. What was once an alliance between sixteen countries (the United States, Canada, the United Kingdom, Germany, France, Italy, Belgium, Denmark, Greece, Iceland, Luxembourg, the Netherlands, Norway, Portugal, Spain, and Turkey) doubled in size after 1991.

Bill Clinton got the ball rolling when under his presidency he allowed Poland, Hungary, and the Czech Republic to join NATO, despite vociferous objections from Russia. In 2004, President George W. Bush welcomed the Baltic states of Latvia, Lithuania, and Estonia, as well as Slovakia, Slovenia, Bulgaria, and Romania into the alliance. With the exception of Slovakia, these states all bordered Russia. In fact, the Baltic states were part of the former USSR. Albania and Croatia joined in 2009, while Montenegro joined in 2017. North Macedonia joined in 2020 and Finland in 2023, adding NATO forces to another 1,304 kilometres (833 miles) of Russia's European border. Sweden was next in line for membership approval, though the process was quickly complicated by longstanding diplomatic rifts with Hungary and Turkey.

From a Russian viewpoint, NATO's rapid expansion along most of the country's European border posed nothing less than an existential threat. Consider for a moment how Washington would feel if Chinese forces all of a sudden began helping Mexico to police its northern border. It's already freaking out about China establishing a military base in Cuba.

Virtually the entirety of Russia's European border, with the exception of Belarus and Ukraine, now houses NATO forces that could be mobilized for an invasion. Having suffered unimaginably huge losses from previous invasions by Napoleon and Hitler, both of whose armies moved through Ukraine en route to invading Russia, Russians feel a deep-seated sense of national paranoia nurtured by their history. And NATO's actions did nothing to allay those fears.

DRAWING A RED LINE IN UKRAINE

But while Moscow had lost control of its former client states, which enthusiastically joined Washington's sphere of influence en masse, it retained a strategic asset in many of those states. Some 30 million Russians now lived there. And far from celebrating the new-found independence of the countries where they lived, they pined for the good old days of the USSR, when they weren't treated as a disliked and mistrusted minority and were free to educate their children in their native Russian tongue. One of the largest of these Russian populations could be found in eastern Ukraine, where they had resided for centuries.

But when the Kiev government was toppled by Ukrainian nationalists under the guidance and direction of the American embassy in early 2014, Moscow was quick to mobilize its fifth column in Russian-speaking Eastern Europe. Putin seized Crimea, former home of the Russian Black Sea Fleet (and a gift to Ukraine from the USSR back in 1954 by Khrushchev, himself a Ukrainian, and part of Russia since 1783 when it was seized from the Ottoman Empire in the Russo-Turkish War. After the Russian Revolution of 1917, Crimea was designated as an autonomous republic within the newly formed USSR, and over the last three centuries, its inhabitants have been and continue to be Russian-speaking).[10]

Russian-speaking Ukrainians, angered that democratically elected, Russian-speaking president Viktor Yanukovych had been deposed in favour of the unelected Oleksandr Turchynov, seized government buildings in protest. When Turchynov retook them among allegations of atrocities committed by government troops, the protests spread. Russia warned the United Nations of "catastrophic consequences" if the Kiev military operation in eastern Ukraine continued, and allowed Russian weapons and "volunteers" to cross the border into Ukraine.[11]

No one should have been surprised that Russia was digging in its heels after allowing NATO to expand ever deeper into Eastern Europe. Ukraine had been part of Russia for five hundred years, and an ancient Russian state, Kievan Rus, was established around Kiev 1,200 years ago, long before Moscow ever existed. So Ukraine was very much part of Russian patrimony. It was one of the founding members of the Union of Socialist Soviet Republics back in 1921 and was the second most populous republic and home to much of the USSR's defence industry. That didn't necessarily mean that Russia was entitled to control Ukraine; only that it could be expected to respond if a rival were to lay claim to it.

That is why NATO members Germany and France vehemently opposed accepting Ukraine into the military alliance, believing that NATO acceptance would throw Europe back into a hostile Cold War environment in which they, not America, would suffer the consequences of provoking Russia. It turns out they had a point.

The consequences of 2014 were bloody and destructive, but mostly ignored. The Maidan Revolution in Kiev was soon mirrored in the formation of the Donetsk and Lugansk People's Republics in a region of Russian-speaking Ukraine known as the Donbas. Reinforced by Russian "volunteers," the breakaway regions held their own against the Ukrainian army, which resulted in a stalemate punctuated by atrocities well documented by the Office of the High Commissioner for Human Rights, primarily artillery fire on civilian neighbourhoods.

Though Vladimir Zelensky was elected in April 2019 on a peace platform, the momentum to war was too great. Soon, the formerly pro-peace president was massing troops on the violently contested borders of his breakaway republics. As many as fourteen thousand civilians were killed, making the Ukrainian government's attempt to retake the Russian-speaking republics Europe's bloodiest conflict since the Balkan Wars of the 1990s. In the early months of 2022, human-rights observers recorded a sharp increase in artillery fire coming from Ukrainian positions.

The inevitable civilian deaths created a political powder keg across the border in Russia. Putin responded by signing an executive order changing the constitution to allow the Russian-speaking provinces to join the Russian Federation. The Federal Assembly backed the changes unanimously. From that moment, any attack against those regions would be an attack on Russia itself under Russian law. As Ukrainian forces massed on the borders of Donetsk and Lugansk, Russia responded by building up forces along its border with Ukraine. As the tension built, there were diplomatic attempts to avert what promised to be a very destructive war. Russia demanded security guarantees for Russian-speakers and Ukrainian neutrality as the path to peace. The West didn't respond. In NATO's view, it was none of Russia's business whom they admitted to their military alliance.

On February 24, 2022, the world took another step into its new normal. President Putin declared a "special military operation," ordering Russian troops to invade Ukraine from Belarus to the north, from Russia to the east, and from Crimea to the south. Though Russian troops later withdrew from around Kiev and Kharkov, Ukraine's two largest cities, they seized the key port of Mariupol. This left Russia in control of a land bridge with the previously annexed Crimean peninsula and blockaded Ukrainian ports on the Sea of Azov.

Once Ukraine was invaded, the West's perception of the country as a largely corrupt backwater controlled by rogue oligarchs immediately changed. Ukraine was now a heroic defender of democracy and Western values, pitched in an existential battle against a brutal aggressor bent on stamping out democracy. The Western media enthusiastically championed the narrative, and all the reasons that Ukraine had been repeatedly turned down for both NATO and EU membership suddenly faded into the background. Any attempt to raise that past was immediately dismissed as part of Putin's "misinformation" campaign.

But America's supposedly greatest weapon against invading Russian troops wasn't the lavish military assistance that it and its NATO partners gave Ukraine instead. It was the launch of economic sanctions so severe and comprehensive that they were expected to quickly bring a shattered Russian economy to its knees. President Biden went so far as to boast that sanctions would not only lead to a decisive Russian defeat in Ukraine, but that they would also so weaken Russia that it would no longer pose any future threat to its Western neighbours (or challenge American domination of its borders).

To that end, the sanctions and other acts of economic warfare that the United States imposed on Russia were the most severe that one country has ever applied against another in the postwar era. But in today's intricately interconnected global economy, sanctions can easily become a double-edged sword that often wounds the countries imposing them.

If Russia has had lots of experience enduring sanctions, the United States, for its part, has had a long history of imposing them. Most of the sanctions imposed on Russia today were modelled on those first enacted by the United States against Iran over the course of the last four decades plus. In 1979, President Jimmy Carter first applied economic sanctions against Iran after government-supported protestors seized control of the American embassy in Tehran and held embassy employees hostage. President Ronald Reagan followed up with an arms embargo against the country during the Iran-Iraq War, coming to the aid of Iraqi leader Saddam Hussein, who America would later overthrow. Sanctions were further ratcheted up during Bill Clinton's presidency in response to Iran's nuclear program and its support for what Washington considered terrorist organizations, such as Hezbollah in Lebanon and Hamas in the Gaza Strip. The Clinton sanctions closed down all trade with Iran and prohibited investment in the country's all-important petroleum industry. Under George W. Bush's presidency, banking sanctions were imposed that excluded Iranian banks from accessing the US financial system.

That meant Iran was cut off not only from the American system and its market, but from pretty much the whole world—that is, any country that did not want to feel the bite of American sanctions. The principle, called "extraterritoriality," is based on the notion that if you want to do business with America, you must follows its laws, no matter what your nationality. If you don't, you will be prosecuted.

Some of Europe's largest banks can attest to that. They ran afoul of that principle by having dealings with Iran, and were subsequently fined billions of dollars. The list included BNP and Crédit Agricole from France, Commerzbank and Deutsche Bank from Germany, and UBS from Switzerland.

Under the Trump administration, the Chinese telecommunications giant Huawei was targeted under the principle of extraterritoriality for violating American sanctions against Iran. The Department of Commerce investigation into Huawei led to the now infamous arrest of Meng Wanzhou, CFO of the company and daughter of founder Ren Zhengfei, while in transit in the Vancouver airport on an extradition request by the United States. Meng was detained in Vancouver, leading to the retaliatory arrests of Canadians Michael Kovrig and Michael Spavor, who each spent more than a thousand days in Chinese detention before they were released following a deferred prosecution agreement between the US Department of Justice and Meng that allowed her to return to her native China from Vancouver.

Notwithstanding their longevity and scope, American sanctions against Iran have enjoyed only mixed success. Over the course of four decades, sanctions have failed to lead to regime change in Tehran, which was what Washington had ultimately been hoping for. The current Iranian government, like all former Iranian governments since the overthrow of the American-supported shah, remains virulently anti-American. And much to the chagrin of both the United States and Israel, the Iranian government continues to finance and support organizations like Hezbollah and Hamas. At the same time, the sanctions have crippled Iranian oil production, which is the mainstay of the country's economy. Iran now produces about 2.5 million barrels per day, a little over half of what it used to produce decades ago, prior to the imposition of American sanctions.

But as America and its NATO allies would discover, Iran is no Russia—a truism that created a misleading template for the use of sanctions. Not only does Russia have alternative trading relationships with a much wider network of countries, but it also has a much larger economy than Iran, and its immense resource endowments give it the ability to withdraw from the global economy and become self-sufficient in most things it needs. In its former guise as the Soviet Union, Russia had a long history of autarkic development and withdrawing from world markets. And Russia, unlike Iran, also had the means to retaliate and impose its own sanctions, which could be just as crippling, if not more so, than anything the West could throw its way.

WESTERN SANCTIONS AND THE PROXY WAR IN UKRAINE

Having borne Western sanctions since its infancy, the Soviet Union was understandably wary of developing economic relationships with Western capitalist economies. Under Stalin's successive Five-Year Plans from 1928 to 1932 and 1933 to 1937, the Soviet Union pursued a degree of economic isolation that was unprecedented for any industrial nation. Yet under those plans, the once largely agrarian Russian economy industrialized at breakneck speed.

So it should come as no surprise that the notion of self-reliance and economic isolation is still deeply entrenched in the Russian psyche. Even today, the number of Russians who favour autarky as a model for economic development outnumber by a margin of two to one those who believe in trade. Of course, today there is a third option that may be the most appealing: Russia's membership in BRICS provides an opportunity to engage in trade, but only with political allies—a Russian version of Janet Yellen's "friendshoring."

No less than eleven rounds of sanctions (with more likely to come)—including everything from personal sanctions against its leadership and its legislators to a comprehensive trade and investment ban—have been imposed, all designed to cripple the Russian economy and its government, if not ultimately intended to bring about regime change in Moscow itself.

Once targeted, Russia quickly replaced Iran as the most sanctioned country in the world, making its products and its markets pariahs in Western Europe and throughout other NATO countries. The European Union and the United States have sanctioned no less than 1,236 Russian individuals, including Vladimir Putin and his family, banning them from travel in Western countries and confiscating any financial assets they may hold in Europe or North America. A subsequent ruling by the Western-based International Criminal Court (ICC) in the Hague actually put out a war crimes arrest warrant for Putin. (Neither Russia nor the United States recognizes the court's jurisdiction. President George W. Bush withdrew America from the ICC just before America unleashed its "shock and awe" bombardment and subsequent invasion of Iraq in 2003, an operation that left hundreds of thousands of Iraqis dead in its wake.)

In an effort to target Russia's elite, the European Union, along with the United Kingdom and the United States, banned the export of luxury goods to Russia, including vehicles and high-end fashion. Similarly, the yachts of Russian billionaires have been confiscated when docked at Western ports, and then auctioned off. Russian oligarchs such as Roman Abramovich have been forced to sell their marquee sports franchises, like the Chelsea Football Club in the United Kingdom.

While all of these moves made headlines in the Western media, their actual impact has been symbolic at best. President Putin is far from beholden to Russian plutocrats, who for the most part live lavish lives outside of Russia in Western countries. In fact, with their luxury homes and yachts being confiscated, those plutocrats are more likely to spend their wealth in Russia than ever before. Nor was it likely that Putin or his family had imminent vacation plans to try their luck at a Las Vegas casino.

Far more significant were the impact of sanctions imposed on Russian companies and on Russian trade and finance. As advertised, the scope of Western sanctions imposed against Russia is truly unprecedented in postwar Europe. More than 155 Russian companies, and virtually every state-owned one, have been sanctioned. Sanctions also banned trade in over a thousand product categories, covering roughly two-thirds of EU imports from Russia, including a near-total ban on oil imports that went into effect in early 2023, as well as a ban on importing Russian coal. At the same time, the European Union banned the export of strategic goods to Russia, a move that covered roughly a third of former EU shipments to the Russian market.

The Biden administration revoked Russia's most-favoured-nation status, paving the way for the United States to raise tariffs on Russian goods not already banned from entry due to the sanctions. Products affected could include aluminum, steel, plywood, and fertilizer.

And reminiscent of the bunker coal ban imposed by Great Britain a century ago on any maritime company servicing Russian ports, most international shipping companies have refused to haul Russian products because Western insurance companies will not insure Russian cargos. An exemption was granted to Greek shipping companies to carry Russian oil to non-European ports, out of fear that if Russia could not send its oil to non-boycotting countries, world oil prices would skyrocket to levels that would be lethal to the economies of sanctioning countries due to the subsequent loss of global supply.

For similar reasons, key energy imports were exempted from sanctions, which only served to underline Western vulnerability to a loss of Russian supply. Natural gas was the most important exemption, since

Western Europe, and especially Germany, was critically dependent on it. (But just because Russian natural gas wasn't sanctioned didn't mean it couldn't be targeted through sabotage). Uranium, another critical fuel that Europe is heavily dependent on Russia for, was also exempted. Nuclear power plants in France, Hungary, Slovakia, and Finland purchase roughly $200 million worth of Russian uranium a year. And Russian diamonds were exempted at the European Union's insistence, needed as they were on the world's largest diamond market in Antwerp.

Sanctions were not only imposed against trade but were also applied in financial markets. Russian banks were, for the most part, denied access to the international banking system's SWIFT (Society for Worldwide Financial Interbank Financial Telecommunications), which is used around the world to provide banking information that facilitates cross-border money transfers and payments. Headquartered in Brussels and run by the European Union, SWIFT includes over eleven thousand banks in more than two hundred countries and territories. By denying Russian financial institutions access, NATO hoped that it would prevent Russians from being able to either send or receive money from abroad.

But like many of the sanctions imposed against Russia, the SWIFT ban was not unforeseen by Moscow. Both Russia and China had anticipated that NATO countries would at some point weaponize SWIFT against them. That is why in 2014, when sanctions were first imposed on Russia over its seizure of Crimea, Russia set up its own system, SPFS; a year later, China set up CHIPS (Cross-Border Interbank Payment System). Both provide alternatives to SWIFT to facilitate the international movement of funds.

Instead of preventing Russians from making cross-border financial transactions, the SWIFT sanctions have simply incented the development of rival systems that over time will eat into SWIFT's business. Russian bank Unistream, which specializes in international money transfers, has seen a huge boost in business since the ban on SWIFT and is negotiating to launch instant money transfers from Russia to

India, Turkey, and a number of African countries—all circumventing SWIFT. In January 2023, Russian and Iranian banks, both banned from using the Belgium-based SWIFT system, connected their interbank transfer and communications systems. More than 700 Russian banks and 106 non-Russian banks from thirteen different countries will be connected to the new interbank system.

Similarly, when global financial firms exited the Russian market in protest over the invasion of Ukraine, domestic institutions quickly moved to fill the gap. Russia's top lender, Sberbank, now provides financial information terminals to former Russian customers of Bloomberg and the London Stock Exchange Group's Refinitiv, both of whom suspended their services in Russia indefinitely. And Mir, the Russian payment system, has similarly taken up market space vacated by Visa and Mastercard when both suspended their Russian operations indefinitely.

While the mass exit of Western banks and financial institutions no doubt inconvenienced many Russian customers of financial services, it did something else as well. It incented the rapid development of alternative homegrown Russian financial service companies that very quickly occupied the market space vacated by the exiting firms. As is the case with aircraft manufacturing, homegrown Russian financial service companies may eventually even compete against those rivals in third markets, particularly in developing countries, which will likely be in BRICS's economic orbit rather than the G7's.

But as difficult as it was to hamstring Russia's financial services industry, the country's huge resource industries would provide an even greater challenge.

WHEN IT COMES TO SANCTIONS, SIZE MATTERS

The primary problem that America and its allies face with imposing sanctions on the Russian economy is that the country they are aimed at just happens to be the largest in the world. When it comes to the effectiveness of sanctions to box in an economy, size matters.

If a country has over 17 million square kilometres (6.5 million square miles) of territory, as Russia does, chances are good that nature has given it a fair share of endowments. And when that country suddenly can't export those natural endowments to foreign markets because hostile governments have closed their markets to its products, those same sanctions will materially affect the world prices of the commodities targeted. Nowhere is this more true than with the price for oil and natural gas—the lifeblood of the Russian economy (and war machine), and the very same fuels that the economies of the sanctioning countries run on and depend heavily on Russia for.

As the impacts of those measures cascade over time, it looks more and more like the Western allies are sanctioning their own economies. While the military outcome of the fighting in Ukraine remains uncertain, Russia is certainly winning the economic war that Western sanctions have waged against it.

If you want to sanction Russia, the most obvious sector to target is its oil industry—the principal source of the country's export earnings. Next to Saudi Arabia, Russia is the biggest oil exporter in the world, selling almost 8 million barrels per day of the fuel to the rest of the world (5 million of crude and another 3 million of diesel, gasoline, and other refined products). Its roughly 10 million barrels per day of total production (it consumes about 2 million barrels per day internally) single-handedly accounts for about a tenth of total world oil production. But attempts to sanction Russian oil have provided the most spectacular blowback of the economic war.

Even in the best of times, the loss of that much oil from the world market would have a dramatic price impact. But the conditions under which sanctions were imposed on Russian oil were a long way from the best of times. Globally, supply was already lagging well behind demand in the post-pandemic global oil market. With the market as tight as it was, the United States and its European allies never really intended to keep Russia from selling those 8 million barrels of oil every day on world markets. Given the lack of spare capacity in OPEC—or, for that matter, anywhere else—the sudden loss of that much supply would send world oil prices soaring above the $147 high-water mark set back in 2008. Brent, the global benchmark price, had already soared to as high as $128 a barrel when the Russian invasion began, due to fears of ensuing supply shortages. Engineering a new record high for world oil prices was an outcome that neither the Biden administration nor European NATO governments could afford, since those fuel prices would throw their own economies into deep recessions.

Instead, what the United States and its NATO allies actually hoped to accomplish was to force Russia into discounting its oil in replacement markets and hence reduce the country's export revenue, which was needed to fund the war effort. As noted back in Chapter 4, in the spring of 2022 President Biden led the charge by banning the importation of all Russian oil and oil products into the American market, roughly 800,000 barrels per day. The European Union followed suit, first banning seaborne imports of Russian crude oil as of December 5, 2022, and later banning the importation of petroleum products through pipelines as of February 5, 2023 (an exemption was granted to Hungary, Slovakia, and the Czech Republic, which are almost totally dependent on Russian oil from the Druzhba pipeline). According to the International Energy Agency, the measures forced the European Union to find another 1 million barrels per day to replace the banned Russian crude, and roughly another 1 million barrels per day to replace the banned refined oil products.

Canada also banned the importation of Russian oil, although the move by Justin Trudeau's government was entirely symbolic since the country hadn't imported any oil from Russia in over a year.

In theory, the sanctions were supposed to starve Russia of oil revenue to finance its war effort. In practice, they had the exact opposite effect. Not only did Russian oil production remain as high as it had been before the sanctions came into effect, but world oil prices skyrocketed with the banning of Russian oil to Western markets. Until the Chinese economy, the world's largest oil importer, was closed down due to stringent

COVID-19 restrictions, Brent was trading in the triple-digit range. Russia's Ministry of Economic Development announced that total earnings from energy exports in 2022 came in at a record-high $337 billion, up almost a whopping 40 percent over 2021 levels. Moreover, energy exports continued to grow in 2023 and remained higher than pre-sanction levels thanks to the expected continued strength of energy exports to key Asian markets like China and India. Both markets were of marginal importance to Russia prior to sanctions, but they have since become Russia's major energy customers—accounting for nearly 90 percent of exports in March 2023.

India, the world's third-largest oil-consuming nation, had imported a negligible amount of crude from Russia due to the high transport costs compared to the much closer Middle East suppliers. But India's demand for Russian crude skyrocketed when Russia started offering attractive discounts to attract new Asian buyers. By the end of 2022, oil imported from Russia had climbed from virtually nothing to well over 1 million barrels per day, catapulting Russia above both Iraq and Saudi Arabia to become India's number one supplier.

Not only did this shift blunt the impact of the loss of European demand for Russian oil, but it is widely reported that Indian refineries were re-exporting processed Russian crude back to European markets, providing an effective workaround when it comes to European sanctions.

At the same time, China's oil imports from Russia have also soared, reaching an all-time high and now effectively rivalling the importance of Saudi oil to the Chinese market. By the end of 2022, Russia was exporting almost 2 million barrels a day to China through the Eastern Siberian Pacific Ocean pipeline and with tanker shipments from Russia's European and Far Eastern ports, and Sakhalin, a more than 20 percent increase over the year before.

Even Saudi Arabia got into the game of snapping up Russia's discounted oil. The country doubled its imports of the Russian oil it uses at its power stations to meet summer air-conditioning demand, freeing up more of its own production for exports. And through its Kingdom Holding Company, Saudi Arabia has invested over $500 million in Russian energy giants Rosneft, Gazprom, and Lukoil since the outbreak of the conflict in Ukraine. The Saudi investment follows divestment from the sector by BP, Shell, and Exxon, all of which abandoned their very substantial Russian operations in protest of the Ukrainian invasion and absorbed billions of dollars in write-offs as a result.

Sanctions have, as intended, forced Russia to discount the selling price for its oil in order to secure new Asian buyers like China and India. But ironically, the ban on Russian oil in Western markets pushed up the price of the very benchmark those Russian discounts were based on. During the first year of the conflict, Brent traded above $90 per barrel. The increase put Russia in a position where it was getting more for its discounted oil in Asian markets than it was getting back in European markets before the sanctions kicked in.

So far, at least, the net effect of Western sanctions is that Russia is generating more revenue for its oil than it was before the sanctions were applied, and hence the impact of the sanctions, at least insofar as the critical energy sector is concerned, has been to enrich the very country they were intended to impoverish. Meanwhile, the loss of Russian supply in Western European and American markets has those countries scrambling to find substitutes at a much higher cost to their consumers, while consumers in China and India benefit by being able to buy Russian oil at a sizeable discount.

That is simply the short-run effect. But in the longer run, the sanctions on Russian oil may have more ominous implications for their principal imposer. While the United States can readily replace Russian oil imports by boosting its own production from shale fields, there is more at stake than 800,000 barrels per day of sanctioned Russian supply.

The unexpected consequences of Western sanctions show us that on the terrain of the new normal, the West no longer has the power to pull economic levers in the expectation that they can control markets. Many of the grenades the United States has been tossing into the

Kremlin have been arcing back in a swarm of unintended consequences. And those consequences continue to pile up.

Sanctions have changed not only where Russia sells its oil (and natural gas and coal), but also the currency in which it gets paid. And it's no longer dollars.

CHAPTER 10

THE DEMISE OF THE PETRODOLLAR

Up until the early 1970s, the dollar was pegged to gold at a fixed price of $32 an ounce, while the world's other currencies were in turn pegged to the dollar. That currency arrangement served as the cornerstone of what has come to be called the Bretton Woods Agreement, which anchored the workings of foreign exchange markets during the first two and a half decades of the postwar era. The system lasted until 1971, when President Richard Nixon decided to free the dollar from its gold backing and in turn allow gold to find its own price in the market. As it turns out, a few years later Nixon found a ready substitute for gold to back the dollar: black gold.

William Simon was an unusual choice for the task of building the financial architecture that would fuel the dollar with oil money. The brash, chain-smoking New Jersey native had run the highly esteemed Treasuries desk at Salomon Brothers before first joining the White House as Nixon's energy czar and subsequently becoming Treasury secretary. He was handed the seemingly impossible task of securing an agreement that would convince Saudi Arabia to invest its vast petro wealth in US Treasuries. And he was told by Nixon in no uncertain terms that failure was not an option. All Simon had going for him was the fact that, as the former head of a huge Wall Street Treasuries desk, he knew how to sell the Saudi royal family on the idea that the US government bond market was the safest, most secure place in the world for them to hold their massive petro wealth.

He pulled off the impossible over four fateful days in Jeddah, Saudi Arabia, in 1974. The United States would buy its oil from Saudi Arabia and pay in dollars; it would also sell the Saudis huge amounts of military hardware. In return, Saudi Arabia would invest the US dollars it received for its oil in US Treasuries.

The agreement was viewed by both sides as a deal with the devil. After all, the two countries had been on decidedly different sides during the recent Yom Kippur War with Israel. King Faisal bin Abdulaziz Al Saud demanded one strict condition: the Saudi oil-Treasuries accord had to be kept secret from the rest of the world. The Americans were more than happy to oblige. The less said about the deal the better. It was only in 2016, in response to a Freedom of Information Act request submitted by Bloomberg News, that the US Treasury Department reluctantly broke out Saudi Arabia's individual holdings of US Treasuries, which at the time totalled $117 billion, ranking it as one of America's largest foreign creditors. The petrodollar had been a secret for forty years.

In order to conceal the massive Saudi purchases of US Treasuries, Saudi Arabia was allowed to bypass the normal bidding process at US Treasuries auctions and buy them as "add-ons," by special arrangement with the US Treasury. The so-called add-ons were excluded from the regular reporting of official auction totals. And when the US Treasury did begin regular reporting of foreign-country holdings of Treasuries, Saudi Arabia's holdings were always aggregated with the holdings of fourteen other oil-exporting nations, making it impossible to break out Saudi holdings separately.

Moreover, not only did Saudi Arabia sell its own oil exclusively in dollars, but the kingdom was able to use its leadership position in OPEC to convince the rest of the cartel to do likewise, which cemented the role of the dollar as the world's petrocurrency. Since then, America has guarded the petrocurrency status of the US dollar forcefully. The only two OPEC countries that dared to accept alternative currencies for oil payments were forced into regime change by US military campaigns.

The first was Iraq, when Saddam Hussein's initiative to sell oil in euros instead of dollars was coincidentally followed by an American invasion, which the White House claimed was to rid Iraq of non-existent weapons of mass destruction. The second was Libya, which suffered the same fate when Muammar Qaddafi also refused to accept dollars for the country's oil exports. Even as recently as 2021, about 80 percent of the $14 trillion annual oil trade was still conducted in dollars.

The importance of the world petroleum trade to the dollar was certainly not lost on Donald Trump. Upon becoming president, his first official state visit wasn't to one of America's neighbours, Canada or Mexico, as is the custom for incoming US presidents, but instead to Saudi Arabia. The United States needs Saudi oil supply. And it also needs petrodollars to fund its huge fiscal deficits.

The world has changed radically since President Trump's visit to Saudi Arabia in 2017. The Saudi-American relationship started going downhill in the early days of the Biden administration. It began when President Biden called its old ally a pariah in the world community after the assassination and subsequent dismemberment of Saudi dissident journalist Jamal Khashoggi. That didn't go over well with MBS (Mohammed bin Salman), the crown prince and de facto ruler of the kingdom, who was implicated in ordering the killing. And the Saudi government was also less than pleased by the lack of support it had received from the Biden White House for their intervention in the Yemen war, where they were fighting against the Houthis, a proxy of their former archenemy Iran. Riyadh was even more outraged that the same Biden administration was at one point willing to negotiate lifting sanctions against Iran's nuclear program in exchange for more oil, a discovery that prompted Saudi Arabia to threaten to start its own nuclear weapons program.

The war in Ukraine and the sanctions battles that have followed in its wake have proved to be a turning point for dollar dominance in the global oil trade. Today, the world's top two oil-exporting countries—Saudi Arabia and Russia—are shunning the dollar, as is China, the world's largest oil-importing country. And the one common denominator among that group is that all three have significant grievances with the Biden administration in Washington.

None more so than Russia. Not long ago, 97 percent of Russia's oil and gas shipments to European utilities were paid for in either dollars or euros. The energy export earnings were the country's most reliable source of foreign currency. But that was all before Washington decided to weaponize the dollar.

In retaliation to Russia's invasion of Ukraine, the United States and its Western allies took the unprecedented step of freezing, or effectively confiscating, the foreign exchange holdings of Russia's central bank so that it could not deploy them in defence of the ruble. While Russia had already reduced its exposure to dollars in its foreign reserve holdings after the Crimean sanctions were imposed, dollars, euros, and pounds sterling still accounted for roughly half of its foreign reserves that were held on deposit in various banks in France, Germany, Britain, the United States, Canada, and Australia.

Had the United States and its NATO allies not confiscated these reserves during the first week of the war, Russia probably would have been more than content to continue to receive payments in either dollars or euros for its multi-billion-dollar energy trade with Europe. But that is no longer the case. Faced with this action by the United States and its allies, Russia's central bank was left with few options to defend against what was initially as much as a 40 percent drop in the value of the ruble against the dollar. But adversity sometimes comes with a silver lining.

RUBLIZING OIL AND GAS

The only thing the Russian central bank had to prop up the ruble was the millions of dollars of oil and natural gas that the country exported every day. And as the central bank would quickly discover, backing the ruble with those revenues could be a huge game changer for the currency.

On any given day over the first three months of 2022, Europe had spent as much as €800 million on purchases of Russian natural gas alone. In addition, Russia earned millions more from its oil exports to those same markets. Converting those payments to rubles would suddenly create very strong foreign demand for the currency. By "rublizing" its millions of dollars of daily energy sales, Moscow literally overnight fundamentally changed the nature of its currency. Within months of the foreign asset seizure, the ruble was trading at a five-year high against the euro, and it was the strongest currency in the world against the dollar over the first eight months of 2022. Of course, hitching your currency to oil prices is a two-way ride. The ruble surrendered a good portion of those gains as world oil prices dropped over the latter half of 2022, in line with a discernably slowing global economy. But the worldwide lack of new investment in developing oil reserves augurs well for the future of any oil-based currency. And Russia is not especially worried about exchange rates, since it has largely been cut off from dollar-denominated markets anyway. The important point for the Kremlin was that, by forcing other countries to make ruble payments for their oil and gas (or be cut off from all Russian supply), Russia had effectively usurped the role that the dollar had held for the last six decades—the ruble was becoming the new petrocurrency.

And just as the American economy had reaped huge benefits when the dollar held that position, so too should the Russian economy benefit.

Oil producers all over the world would sell their fuel in dollars and, until recently, only in dollars. They would then recycle those same dollars into dollar-denominated financial assets like Treasuries. That steady flow of petro funds gave American financial markets a huge advantage over their international competitors. Instead of petrodollars buying German bunds, Japan's JGBs, or Britain's gilts, they were buying US Treasuries. As oil prices rose, so too did the capital flows tied to the reinvestment of petrodollars back into the Treasuries market. Those petrodollar investment flows served as a critical offset to the impact that soaring oil prices had on the US economy, up until 2017 the largest oil-importing economy in the world.

Of the three dollar-shunning countries, Saudi Arabia's decision to de-dollarize its oil trade is the most shocking. In a landmark decision, Saudi Arabia effectively ended its six-decade love affair with the dollar and announced that it would now accept yuan payments for oil shipped to its largest customer, China. The move followed Russia's decision to stop accepting dollars for either its oil or natural gas exports. Moreover, both China and Saudi Arabia have signalled a willingness to bypass the dollar in much of the rest of their energy trade.

China, for its part, wants to expand the use of its yuan-priced oil contracts to suppliers beyond Saudi Arabia. To that end, when addressing the Gulf Cooperation Council during his December 2022 visit to Saudi Arabia, President Xi Jinping urged Gulf states to use the Shanghai Petroleum and Natural Gas Exchange to conduct oil and gas sales. And Saudi Arabia has said that it will consider alternatives to dollar payments for the millions of barrels per day that it exports to its customers besides China.

De-dollarizing the oil trade also means diversifying investment of petro revenues away from the Treasuries market. If you are not receiving dollar payments anymore, you don't have to reinvest those petrodollars back into buying more dollar-denominated US government bonds. Hence, as the dollar loses its grip on the payment side of the oil trade, it simultaneously loses its grip on where those payments are reinvested. Shortly after announcing acceptance of payments in yuan from China, the Saudi government stated that the kingdom would be cutting back on its investments in the Treasuries market.

It remains to be seen what impact, if any, the Saudi decision to accept yuan payments for its oil exports to China will have on other OPEC members, many of whom continue to sell their fuel in dollars. Just as Saudi Arabia convinced other OPEC members back in the 1970s to accept only dollar payments for their oil, it could today exert similar influence to accept payment in other currencies. Iraq has already signalled its willingness to accept payments in yuan. With the whole region pivoting away from American influence, and with China and India the two largest buyers of its fuel, the stage is set for other OPEC producers to join Saudi Arabia and Iraq in accepting payments in other currencies.

In the zero-sum world of foreign exchange markets, the dollar's loss in the global oil trade is another currency's gain. As the dollar continues to cede ground as a petrocurrency, some other currency or currencies will take its place. And the two currencies that have benefited the most from de-dollarization in the world's energy trade are the yuan and the ruble, which just happen to be the currencies of the world's larger energy exporter and the world's largest energy importer.

As the currency of the largest energy exporter in the world (counting both oil and natural gas), the ruble certainly has the credentials to vie for the role of the world's de facto petrocurrency. And that is exactly what President Putin had in mind when he ordered Gazprom, the world's largest gas company and supplier of roughly half of Europe's natural gas, to demand ruble payments for its gas shipments to Europe. Russian oil companies quickly followed suit.

Given the success that ruble payments for Russian oil and gas exports have had on boosting the currency, Putin has already indicated that the switch will be permanent, and will continue even if sanctions are dropped at some point in the future. Moreover, Putin has publicly entertained the idea that not only should oil and natural gas exports be paid for in rubles, but that down the road a whole range of other Russian commodity exports should also be rublized. Since sanctions were imposed, the dollar's share of total Russian exports has fallen from over half to roughly a third, while the euro's share has shrunk from 35 percent to 19 percent, as both the dollar and the euro have effectively been boycotted by the country's massive energy exports.

Like the rerouting of Russian oil and gas from European to Asian markets, the rublization of the country's energy trade—which began as a temporary measure in response to Western sanctions—has now become a permanent change in the operation of the Russian economy.

For Russia, both have become central trademarks of its place in the emerging new world order.

And Europe won't be the only region paying in rubles for Russian energy. Far more significant, given where Russia will be selling its natural gas and oil in the future, is an agreement with China to split Chinese payments for Russian gas equally between rubles and yuan. No payments will be made in dollars or euros going forward in what is likely to become, over time, the largest bilateral energy trade between the world's largest gas exporter and the world's leading gas importer.

Both Russia and China are quickly coming to realize that they can use their trading relationships with each other and beyond to not only bolster the value of their own currency, by expanding the volume of trade that is conducted in it, but also to ensure that smaller and smaller volumes of world trade are conducted in the currency of their enemies. As sanctions extend to currency markets, Russia is turning more and more to using the yuan. By the end of 2022, Russia had become the fourth-largest offshore trading centre for the currency as the yuan soared from 1 percent of the Russian foreign exchange market to 45 percent.

Like the energy sanctions that the United States and the European Union have imposed, which inadvertently led to record energy export earnings for Russia, the Western allies' plan to cripple the ruble by seizing the Russian central bank's foreign reserves has backfired. Not only has it failed to sabotage the ruble, but the plan has also had the unintended consequence of inducing a fundamental policy shift in Moscow (energy exports to be paid in rubles) has put the country's currency on a much stronger footing, which in the long run will likely come at the dollar's expense.

SETTING THE WRONG PRECEDENT WITH WORLD CENTRAL BANKS

Sanctions have done something else that the United States would greatly prefer that they hadn't. The seizure of another sovereign country's foreign reserves set a new precedent in the art of economic warfare. And that got noticed by central banks and their governments all around the world.

The implications for other central banks could be huge. The move not only brings into question which currencies central banks should hold as foreign reserves but poses a perhaps more fundamental question about how big those reserves need to be in the first place. Will central banks continue to expand their war chests of foreign reserves as aggressively as they have over the last two decades (when foreign reserve holdings mushroomed from a little over $3 trillion to over $20 trillion) now that those reserves have become, for the first time ever, legitimate targets of economic warfare?

The main reason behind the explosive growth in central banks' foreign reserve holdings was that it became necessary to buttress against the potential risk of trading shocks that have grown with the volume of international capital flows. In the early decades of the postwar era, the movement of currencies was primarily driven by trade flows. But in recent decades, those trade flows have been dwarfed by capital flows, much of it speculative in nature.

Recent decades have been replete with numerous national currency crises, as traders took aim at a currency they thought was vulnerable, for whatever reason. The Asian crisis in 1997, the Argentine crisis in the late 1990s, the Russian crisis in 1998, Venezuela in 2016, and Turkey in 2018 are a few of the more prominent in recent decades. Typically, traders would short the currency of a targeted country against the dollar, forcing the country's central bank to raise interest rates to defend its currency against the speculative attack. If the speculators kept the pressure on long enough, at some point those punishing interest rate hikes would bring about a recession, and the central bank would then have to back off and cut interest rates to revive the economy, allowing the currency to fall—just as the speculators intended.

Aside from crippling increases in a country's interest rates (that would more often than not lead to punishing recessions), the only protection against speculative assaults on a nation's currency was a central bank war chest of foreign exchange reserves that could be deployed against the speculators selling it. The bigger its foreign reserves war chest, the bigger the bear trap that a central bank could set against speculators who were targeting its currency.

But if a central bank can't use its foreign reserves in this way because they have been impounded by hostile foreign governments, what is the point of having such a huge war chest in the first place?

What the Biden administration failed to realize when it decided to confiscate the Central Bank of the Russian Federation's dollar holdings was that it was undermining one of the pillars supporting the dollar's position as the world's sole reserve currency. Instead of providing an insurance policy for financial stability, as they had in the past, the dollar holdings by foreign central banks had become a ticking time bomb. At any moment, it seemed, a political decision could be made in Washington that would freeze or seize another country's dollar foreign reserve holdings. And there is no way that a central bank could hedge the risk of a US-enacted asset seizure of its foreign reserves.

That possibility caught the attention of central banks all around the world, including the one that matters the most—the People's Bank of China, which is ironically one of the largest holders of dollars among central banks anywhere in the world.

THE NO-LIMITS PARTNERSHIP AGREEMENT AND BEYOND

Sino-Russian relations have come a long way. Just because you share a common past and a common enemy doesn't mean you've always been friends. While President Xi and President Putin both have political pedigrees that date back to the Communist revolutions in their respective countries, the two superpowers haven't always been on the same page.

Tensions grew back in the early 1960s, when Mao Zedong denounced Nikita Khrushchev's reforms as revisionism. Chinese-backed Communist parties around the world differentiated themselves from Russian-backed parties by adding the suffix Marxist-Leninist to their name, implying that their Russian-backed counterparts were ideologically impure. But this wasn't just an ideological conflict for the hearts and minds of comrades around the world; the two countries actually fought a brief armed conflict in 1969 along the Ussuri (Wusuli) River border near Manchuria.

Back then, American foreign policy toward its Communist adversaries was very different than the stance toward China and Russia taken by the Biden administration today. Two years after the border conflict between Russia and China, President Nixon made his historic visit to Beijing at the urging of his secretary of state, Henry Kissinger, to meet Chairman Mao. The goal was to try to widen the wedge between Beijing and Moscow and, in doing so, advance America's strategic interests. The visit ultimately set the stage for the opening of diplomatic relations between the two countries at the end of the 1970s. More than forty years later, the Biden administration has taken the polar-opposite approach. As it attempts to isolate Russia through sanctions, it has herded the Kremlin right into China's arms. And together, they form a formidable adversary.

Since the dissolution of the Soviet Union, relations between China and Russia have improved steadily, to the point where the two countries now enjoy their closest relationship ever. And Western sanctions have played an important, if not critical, role in both initiating and later cementing that relationship.

Bilateral relations between Russia and China got a huge boost after the imposition of Western sanctions following Russia's annexation of Crimea in 2014. Then, as now, China offered access to its huge markets to mitigate the impact of Western measures aimed at punishing the Russian economy.

The steadily strengthening Sino-Russian bilateral relationship reached its zenith in February 2022, with the "no-limits" partnership agreement announcement on the eve of the Beijing Winter Olympics, just weeks before the Russian invasion of Ukraine. In that agreement, China explicitly backed Russia's demand that Ukraine never be admitted to NATO, and Russia in turn said it would oppose independence for Taiwan. Meanwhile, officials back in the United States, who were holding a diplomatic boycott of the Olympics in protest of Chinese repression against its Muslim minority, the Uyghurs, glumly watched the two leaders as they very publicly toasted their new strategic partnership.

The no-limits agreement laid the foundation for what was to follow: a series of regular summits that saw the links between the two countries become ever stronger, bound as they were by their mutual determination to challenge what in their eyes was the hegemonic position of the United States in the world. Both leaders hailed a new world order and talked of global changes not seen for a century.

Aside from strengthening economic ties with Russia, China has steadfastly thwarted American attempts to isolate Russia in international forums like the United Nations or at G20 meetings. And both countries have been actively recruiting new allies in BRICS and elsewhere in an attempt to firm up a coalition of developing countries (or the Global South, as these countries are frequently labelled) to counterbalance Western global influence and power.

But the most alarming development—from a NATO perspective, at least—is the growing military cooperation between the two superpowers. While both Russia and China claim a formal alliance to counter NATO is not in the works, their actions suggest otherwise. The militaries in the two countries have never been closer. The Russian Ministry of Defence has already held joint military exercises with the People's Liberation Army in Russia's Far East and the Sea of Japan. Russia and China have also held joint military exercises with BRICS partner South Africa and with their Middle Eastern ally Iran. And an increasing number of joint military exercises are planned.

As prospects for conflict between Russia and NATO and China and the United States mount, so too do the prospects for some form of military alliance between the two Eurasian superpowers. Such an alignment has been crystallizing for a long time on the technological front. China has leapfrogged the world in consumer and infrastructure technology: 5G, commercial shipbuilding, high-speed trains, quantum computing. But on the military-industrial side, Russia is the senior partner. In the Russian-Chinese joint venture that is building the C'R929 airliner, the Russians are designing and building the wings, the centre section, and the PD 35 engines. But the real trust comes in sharing sensitive military technology. Russia is providing China with state-of-the-art Su-35 multirole fighters and S-400 air defence systems. It is delivering Rezonans-NE radar capable of detecting stealth and hypersonic targets well beyond the horizon (1,100 kilometres/683 miles). And while Russia would be willing to sell that kind of radar to many allies, Putin announced at the Valdai summit that Russia was helping China join a very exclusive military club. Right now, only the United States and Russia are protected by missile attack early-warning systems. Soon, China will be the third country on that list. Similarly, in October 2023, the Pentagon announced that its surveillance had shown that China had launched its first nuclear-powered guided missile submarine, first developed by Russia, to target aircraft carriers. With that, China had joined another exclusive military club that previously included only Russia and the United States.

However we choose to characterize the friendship between the largest standing armed forces in the world and the largest nuclear arsenal in the world, it is already clear that the United States and its NATO allies will not find it easy to intimidate either partner in this burgeoning relationship.

SO WHAT HAVE SANCTIONS ACHIEVED?

There is no question that sanctions are rapidly and profoundly reshaping the global economy. But that wasn't what they were originally intended to do, and the question their imposers must ask themselves is whether they are having the effect they were designed for.

Certainly, neither the threat nor the later imposition of trade sanctions has achieved its stated objective, which was to deter Russia from invading Ukraine. Nor did the confiscation of half of the Russian central bank's foreign reserves, the mass exodus of more than twelve hundred Western firms from the Russian market, or the European ban on Russian energy have any discernable impact on Russian military behaviour, foreign policy, or even industrial output. While NATO countries empty their military warehouses to allow Ukraine to remain on the battlefield, Russian missile, drone, and tank production just keeps increasing as the economy is put on more and more of a war footing.[1] Moreover, the Russian armed forces have more than doubled in size since the war began. Western military observers also note that Russian tactics and equipment have been evolving steadily, making them a more difficult opponent on the battlefield.

If, instead, the point of the sanctions was simply to impose retributory pain on Russia and its economy, there is no doubt that they have had that effect. But contrary to the initial predictions of the sanctioning countries, the Russian economy did not collapse as a result of Western sanctions. Neither did the currency, save from an initial hit that it has largely recovered from.

Although Russia's GDP did contract by a modest 2 percent in 2022, it was a fraction of the double-digit decline that was widely forecast in the West when sanctions were first imposed. Moreover, that small decline wasn't so out of line with how some of the economies of the sanctioning countries fared—particularly Germany and the United Kingdom, both of which experienced modest recessions, as did the entire eurozone economy. And the loss in Russia's economic output was more than fully recovered through economic growth in the subsequent year. Meanwhile, the unemployment rate has fallen to an all-time low. And Russia's balance-of-payments position has never been stronger, on the back of record-breaking energy export earnings (almost 40 percent higher than the year before), while its 2022 account surplus swelled to a record high (double the 2021 level).

But sanctions have fundamentally changed where Russia sells its resources and where it does not. And that trade shift will long outlive the military conflict in Ukraine. Instead of supplying North American and Western European markets with its resources, Russia has now irrevocably tilted its trade toward Asian markets, a process that it began in earnest after the initial round of sanctions back in 2014. And one market in particular is at the top of the list: China. In 2022, trade between China and Russia increased by 34 percent to an all-time high of $190 billion, up 30 percent from 2021. Bilateral trade has soared to an all-time high of over $200 billion in 2023.

While record volumes of Russian oil, gas, and coal have been sold to Chinese markets, Chinese electronic goods and vehicles have been the big beneficiaries of Western sanctions against the Russian market. Chinese automakers Chery Automobile, Great Wall Motor, and Geely Auto saw their shares of the Russian vehicle market almost triple in 2022. Since sanctions were first imposed against Russia, China has become the country's largest source of imports, accounting for over a third of total goods brought into the Russian economy.

So, by shutting Russian goods out of their markets, America and its allies have diverted trade toward an economic union between the world's largest commodity producer and the world's largest commodity consumer. And the latter just happens to be the greatest threat to the United States—a rapidly ascending superpower, China, whose economy will soon overtake the US economy to become the largest in the world.

If uniting America's two greatest rivals wasn't a bad enough unintended consequence of sanctions, consider their impact on Western economies. Sanctions have stoked inflation to four-decade highs among the G7 economies. In several, including the United Kingdom and Germany, inflation even briefly crossed over into double-digit territory.

As we saw in chapter 9, shutting Russian commodity exports out of the markets of the United States and its allies (mainly G7 and EU countries) has created a dual price for virtually every major commodity that Russia sells, as it often discounts the selling prices of its resource exports in order to attract new buyers. And given that Russia is the largest commodity producer in the world, that practice covers a lot of ground.

But the flip side of barring Russian commodities from being sold in Western markets is that the very same trade sanctions hugely push up the price of non-Russian substitutes in markets that suddenly face a scarcity of supply—whether of oil, natural gas, fertilizer, nickel, or wheat. So, in effect, the economic impact of the sanctions isn't borne just by Russian producers but by consumers of the sanctioning countries, who must now buy substitutes at much higher prices than they paid for Russian exports before the conflict began.

In turn, the huge run-up in inflation has forced an abrupt and potentially devastating U-turn for the Federal Reserve Board and other G7 central banks that could still lead to major recessions in Europe and North America. Not only has sanctions-fed inflation caused the most rapid run-up in short-term interest rates since the early 1980s, but it has forced central banks to cease their massive bond purchases under their quantitative easing programs, triggering the worst bond market sell-off in over a century.

Those are the short-term effects. Over time, sanctions are fracturing a once-cohesive global economy into rival and segmented geopolitical blocs. While that transformation is largely of America's own making, the United States and its allies are likely to enjoy a far less dominant role in the new world order that their actions are helping to create.

CHAPTER 11

CHINA AND THE NEW WORLD ORDER

Normally, annual meetings of the Shanghai Cooperation Organization (SCO) are pretty sleepy affairs—but not the one held back in 2022 in the old Silk Road trading post of Samarkand in Uzbekistan. It was the first time President Xi had travelled outside of China since the pandemic had broken out more than two and a half years earlier. It was equally significant in that it was the first meeting between Xi and Putin since the eve of the Beijing Olympics. It was also the first time the leaders actually sat across from each other, as opposed to meeting virtually.

Founded in 2001, the SCO is a Eurasian economic and security forum comprising China, India, Kazakhstan, Kyrgyzstan, Russia, Tajikistan, Pakistan, and Uzbekistan (Iran joined in April 2023). Turkey, a key player in the region and a NATO member, has formally applied to join, as has Belarus, a Russian ally.

The organization is part of the emerging landscape of the new global order. It is intended to serve as a formidable economic and political challenge to foreign powers, like the United States, who might want to gain a foothold in the region. In effect, the SCO is an expression of China's Monroe Doctrine, through which it claims authority over this region of the world just as the United States has claimed authority over North and South America for the last two hundred years. That is, the SCO is explicitly part of the map of the new normal.

But while the United States believes that it has the moral authority for dominance in its region, if not, for that matter, in the whole world, it continually challenges Russia and China on exercising the same right to authority in their region.

That salient point was emphasized at the meeting by President Xi, who called on member states to support each other in preventing foreign powers (i.e., the United States) from instigating "colour revolutions" in the region, a pointed reference to US involvement in Georgia's Rose Revolution in 2003 and Ukraine's Orange Revolution in 2004.

While Xi encouraged the group to collectively confront external threats, he also urged members to integrate their economies more closely through ever-greater intra-regional trade. And he encouraged SCO members to eschew the dollar and euro and trade with each other in their own currencies.

The group has pretty well been doing that for some time. Trade between SCO countries has soared from $667 billion at the time of its founding to $6 trillion in 2022. And more and more, trade between members is being conducted in local currencies, not dollars or euros as had been the case in the past. Several days after the meeting, at the St. Petersburg International Economic Forum, President Putin echoed Xi's remarks by declaring the end of the unipolar world where one global hegemon, the United States, could dominate global affairs and unilaterally dictate security terms to other nations.

BRICS represents an even more powerful group of developing countries that defines the new multipolar world in which we now live. The group includes the most dynamic economies in the world. Over the last two decades (from 2000 to 2020), BRICS members have led the world in economic growth, with China (1,266 percent), Russia (466 percent), India (444 percent), and Brazil (310 percent) taking the four top spots in GDP gains, and recently admitted Saudi Arabia (300 percent) claiming fifth spot. Meanwhile, the US economy registered a gain of 108 percent, ranking a distant twelfth.

And it doesn't look like BRICS dominance will diminish any time soon. China and India were on track to account for over half of growth in the global economy in 2023. And, of course, those gains are measured in dollars, as is the convention. If measured by purchasing power parity (what a ruble or yuan buys in their economies compared to what a dollar buys in the American economy or what a euro buys in EU economies), Russia's GDP recently surpassed that of Germany, the largest of the EU economies, while China has already surpassed the United States as the largest economy in the world.

The rapidly growing BRICS economies are the emerging competitors to US-dominated, Western-led blocs like the G7 or NATO. Whereas the dissolution of the Soviet Union served as a springboard for NATO's advancement, the war in Ukraine and the global economic fissures it has created seem to have become a springboard for the imminent rapid expansion of BRICS. At a pivotal meeting in Johannesburg, South Africa, in 2023, BRICS announced that it would be doubling in size by taking in Saudi Arabia, Iran, Egypt, Ethiopia, Argentina, and the United Arab Emirates (UAE). Nigeria, Algeria, Mexico, Indonesia, and Bahrain have formally applied for membership, and another six countries have also expressed interest.

If all are eventually accepted for membership, BRICS would possess 45 percent of global oil reserves and 60 percent of global natural gas reserves. Its combined GDP would be greater than that of the US economy and about double the size of the EU economies, while its 4.2 billion population would represent over half of humanity. As such, the economic clout of the group would dwarf that of the liberal democracies that America counts on for support. The G7 may believe it leads the world, but the growing lineup of countries wanting to join BRICS suggests that the rest of the world has very different ideas about leadership.

Established in 2009, BRICS has evolved into a formidable alliance. Recently, the group has assumed a distinctly more geopolitical character, with member countries openly challenging what they perceive to be American global hegemony and advocating for a move away from a unipolar world to a multipolar world where there is a more equitable global division of wealth and power.

While the group does not yet constitute a formal trade bloc like the European Union, trade between members has been growing rapidly. And in a world moving toward friendshoring, the formation of a BRICS trading group replete with its own supply chains and currencies seems like a natural course of events.

The group has already established the New Development Bank as an alternative to the World Bank and the International Monetary Fund, lending organizations that are widely perceived among developing nations to represent American and European interests. And the organization is working on developing its own currency based on a basket of member-country currencies; if this comes to pass, it will pose yet another challenge to the dominance of the dollar in global commerce.

The moves away from dollar usage parallel efforts by BRICS to set up alternative mechanisms to the Western-controlled SWIFT for international payments and funds transfers. It has even been suggested that BRICS should have its own rating agencies to compete with American agencies like Standard & Poor's or Moody's. In short, a soon-to-be expanded BRICS is establishing all the infrastructure required to offer a comprehensive alternative to the global trading and finance system currently run and dominated by the United States and the other G7 powers.

Such global redundancy is probably not optimal from an economist's perspective. Having two different interbank transfer systems, two different development banks, and two different reserve currencies seems like the very antithesis of what globalization preached. But such redundancy becomes an absolute necessity in a world where opposing blocs are intent on fighting an ever-escalating global economic war. In this new world, efficiency quickly takes a back seat to the overarching interests of national security.

WITH LENDING COMES INFLUENCE

Developing multilateral alliances with other emerging powers through the SCO or BRICS is one avenue for China to wield its rapidly growing influence in world affairs. Financing critical infrastructure throughout the developing world is another.

China has long sought to leverage its own journey from humble peasant beginnings to world superpower as a claim for leadership in the developing world. There is no better example of this aspiration than President Xi's master plan: the Belt and Road Initiative. The plan calls for China to build massive transport and other economic infrastructure like power plants in as many as sixty countries—infrastructure that will make those economies critically dependent on China. For the most part, the infrastructure being built will move Chinese-made goods to those markets and move raw materials from those countries back to Chinese factories at home, cementing China's position as the epicentre of most of the world's global supply chains.

Whether it's the flagship China-Pakistan Economic Corridor, a deepwater port in Sri Lanka, or a high-speed railway in Kenya, through its investment in and construction of these projects China is gaining a strategic foothold in recipient countries. And the projects may soon bolster its currency as well. The next phase of the Belt and Road Initiative will likely promote the use of the yuan as a settlement currency in the countries where China has projects. Beijing's intention to use the yuan in this way is part of a broader plan to promote the rapidly growing international usage and stature of its currency.

Driven in large measure by its willingness to finance so many Belt and Road projects, China has become the largest bilateral lender in the world and is by far the largest lender to the developing world. As such, China has assumed the role once played by the United States (through most of the twentieth century) and Great Britain (during the nineteenth century). Like all former leading world lenders, China gains from that role a position that yields great power and influence among countries who borrow from it.

Through the financing allocated to Belt and Road projects, Chinese investment has become pivotal to most developing countries. Billions of dollars have been spent on the projects, to be sure, but China also spent $240 billion between 2008 and 2021 bailing out twenty-two countries that had fallen behind on debt payments for Belt and Road projects—including Argentina, Pakistan, Kenya, and Turkey. The generous bailouts are as much about building long-term relationships with recipient countries as they are about building infrastructure. But that is certainly not how such projects are seen by Western powers and their own multilateral lending institutions.

As the world's largest creditor nation, China might be expected to be at the front of the line when borrowing countries default, as many are now doing. Not so, according to the IMF and the World Bank, the institutions of the old world order that have governed multilateral lending for most of the postwar era. They want China to forgive its loans so that defaulting countries are instead able to service their loans from the IMF and World Bank, and make bond payments to private investors.

Yet it is the Western policy of economic sanctions that has put many of the world's poorest borrowing countries on the edge of default. Most of their debt is dollar-denominated, and the sanctions-driven rise in inflation that has forced the Federal Reserve Board to massively raise rates has at the same time forced up the value of the dollar against the currencies of most borrowing countries, making loan repayment that much more difficult. Some, like Sri Lanka and Ghana, are teetering on the verge of default and are desperately trying to renegotiate payment terms.

Of course Beijing is balking. It's questioning why institutions where the United States has sole veto power (like the IMF and the World Bank), not to mention private investors, should have priority over China. In doing so, it is in effect challenging the hegemony of the Western-based multilateral lending institutions that have dominated global lending since they were set up after the Second World War.

At stake is the whole system of international lending. As noted above, China and its BRICS partners are establishing alternative mechanisms and institutions for multilateral lending that are in direct competition with the Washington-based IMF and World Bank. Western lending has often been criticized by recipient countries because of the strings attached to loans set out by so-called structural adjustments programs. These programs typically require recipient countries (which number among the poorest in the world) to impose extreme austerity conditions that tend to sacrifice social programs and local employment in order to qualify for financing. Since the IMF and World Bank were the only sources of multilateral financing available, recipient countries had no choice but to accept their terms. Now they are not. And lending from China and other BRICS countries is typically less tied to such rigid conditions.

Given the stalemate between China and the Western-based multilateral lending institutions on loan repayment terms, borrowing countries may soon have to choose between them. If China and the American-run IMF and World Bank cannot agree on a compromise agreement to govern debt restructuring for potentially defaulting borrower countries, multilateral lending, like trade and currencies, may soon be fractured into competing geopolitical blocs.

Political influence has come with investment and lending. When you make massive investments in or give massive loans to a country, you tend to get the government's attention. Increasingly, China is leveraging its dominant lending role to play a much larger diplomatic role on the world stage. That includes challenging American authority in the Middle East, and perhaps soon in Europe as well.

Nowhere was the mark of growing Chinese global prestige and influence more apparent than in China's ability to broker a deal between bitter Middle East rivals Saudi Arabia and Iran. In a poignant sign of how a shifting geopolitical axis can not only open new fault lines but also help close past ones, former archenemies Iran and Saudi Arabia agreed to re-establish diplomatic relations. The two countries, who have been rivals for decades, broke off diplomatic relations seven years ago. In brokering the deal, which came after President Xi visited Saudi Arabia and Iranian president Ebrahim Raisi visited Beijing,

China firmly established itself as a power broker who will play a major role in shaping the security arrangements of the Middle East.

Emerging Saudi-Iranian cooperation is nothing less than a quantum shift in the balance of power in the Middle East—one that sees China replacing the traditional power broker in the region, the United States. While America's relationship with Iran has been antagonistic since its ally the shah was overthrown decades ago, the shift in Saudi policy away from its traditional alliance with America is nothing short of a game changer for the region.

China, on the other hand, has been cultivating stronger ties with both Saudi Arabia and Iran by investing billions of dollars in key infrastructure in their economies. Back in 2021, China committed as much as $400 billion worth of investment in the Iranian economy over the next two and a half decades. At the same time, China has invested in a Belt and Road project to massively develop the ancient Red Sea port of Jizan, Saudi Arabia's third-largest port, and build the Jizan Industrial Park. In 2022, the China Harbour Engineering Company began construction of a seawater cooling system for the city.

In exchange for these and other investments, President Xi can expect the support of both of these soon-to-be BRICS members in any diplomatic initiative he may take to resolve the war in Ukraine, or, for that matter, any attempt for Beijing to assert its sovereignty over Taiwan.

The support of these two nations for Chinese diplomacy at the expense of American influence is indicative of shifting alliances throughout the developing world. While the United States holds sway over Europe and the rest of the developed world (Canada, Australia, and Japan), Western influence is rapidly ceding ground to Chinese influence elsewhere. And it's not hard to see why. The United States and its G7 allies, who consider themselves to be the global standard-bearers for democracy, often lecture leaders of developing countries on their need for better governance. But in most of the developing world, G7 countries are best known not so much as apostles for democracy but rather for their role in the developing countries' colonial past.

And it's not a role remembered with much fondness. Meanwhile, China is winning a reputation as a country that is actively bankrolling development by making huge investments in and loans to low- and middle-income countries around the world, all without inquiring about recipients' human rights records.

It's nothing less than a competition for the hearts and minds of the bulk of the world's population. And so far, at least, it's a competition China seems to be winning hands down

THE GROWING SANCTIONS WAR AGAINST CHINA

Like Russia, the People's Republic of China is no stranger to American sanctions. In one way or another, it has been on the receiving end of them ever since the People's Republic came into being. The United States maintained an economic embargo against the Communist regime from the moment it first assumed power in 1949 through President Nixon's historic visit to Beijing in 1972.

Following the Tiananmen Square massacre in 1989, an arms embargo was reimposed by the Bush Sr. administration. In 2018, the Trump administration imposed a ban on the use of Huawei and ZTE telecommunication equipment by the federal government, citing security concerns. In addition, Trump invoked national security concerns to use section 232 of the Trade Expansion Act to levy four tranches of tariffs against imports from China—the largest tariffs since the Smoot-Hawley Tariff Act of the 1930s. They included tariffs as high as 25 percent on over $300 billion worth of imports from China.

President Trump also used national security concerns to sanction specific Chinese companies. His executive order "Addressing the Threat from Securities Investments That Finance Communist China Military Companies" prohibited any American investor, institutional or retail, from owning shares in forty-four sanctioned Chinese companies. Five of those companies were forced to delist their shares from the New York Stock Exchange.

Not only has the Biden administration maintained all the tariff hikes and investment restrictions enacted by the previous administration, but, paralleling actions taken against Russia, it has also imposed sanctions on a rapidly growing list of Chinese companies, institutions, and senior government officials. From Beijing's perspective, then, it hasn't really mattered whether a Republican or Democratic administration was in charge in Washington. Both seem equally hostile.

China's rapidly growing tech sector has been a favourite target of Washington, particularly with respect to semiconductors and telecom technologies. The responsibility for Washington's efforts to deliberately contain China's telecom industry have largely fallen to Team Telecom, an interdepartmental US government agency run by the National Security Division of the Department of Justice. Its official purpose is to safeguard the American telecommunications system from cyberattack or espionage. But its unofficial purpose is to thwart the global reach of Chinese telecommunication firms, based on a fear that any advanced telecom technology developed would soon find applications in China's rapidly growing armed forces. Under this overarching umbrella of national security concerns, everything from undersea cables to 5G telecommunication towers to popular social media platforms like TikTok have been the target of aggressive American economic warfare.

For example, China's undersea cable builder HMT—which has built almost a fifth of all the undersea cables in the world over the past four years and was the fastest-growing player in the global undersea cable business over the last decade—has been sanctioned by the United States. As a result, the Chinese firm has lost out on the lucrative Singapore-to-Paris underwater cable project, as well as a number of others. And Washington has nixed a Hong Kong terminus for four planned undersea cables on the grounds that the placement would allow the Chinese government to tap the cable for sensitive information.

Meanwhile, President Biden has banned the use of the popular Chinese social media platform TikTok, owned by Chinese firm ByteDance, from all federal government–issued cellphones. Congress has even threatened to ban the use of the social media platform, which currently has 150 million viewers, entirely in the United States.

In addition, a growing number of Chinese tech firms have been sanctioned, added to the entity list that prevents them from any business dealings with American corporations. In September 2022, the Office of Foreign Assets Control sanctioned Sinno Electronics for its dealings with the Russian military. In January 2023, the US Treasury Department sanctioned Spacety for supplying satellite imagery to Russian mercenary force the Wagner Group. The following month, the Commerce Department placed AOOK Technology, Beijing Ti-Tech Science and Technology Development, Beijing Yunze Technology, and China HEAD Aerospace Technology on its entity list for their alleged assistance to the Russian military. And in March 2023, the Treasury Department added an additional five Chinese companies for their dealings with Iran Aircraft Manufacturing Industries, which produces the Shahed drone that Russia has used extensively in its war against Ukraine. The same month, the Department of Commerce added twenty-eight new Chinese firms to its entity list for acquiring restricted American semiconductor technology on behalf of the Chinese military.

Of course, it's not only Chinese firms that are affected by Washington's sanctions. So too—to their growing alarm—are American firms. In October 2022, the Department of Commerce introduced sweeping controls on the exports of advanced computing and semiconductor products to China; the goal was to deny China access to advanced semiconductors anywhere in the world that were produced with American technology. Bowing to Washington pressure, the Netherlands and Japan, each containing vital supplier links to advanced chip manufacture, have subsequently announced they will join the United States in restricting semiconductor exports to China on national security grounds. The act requires American companies and other foreign companies that use American technology to cut off all support to China's largest chip factories, with the express purpose of setting the country's semiconductor industry back by a decade.

But, as always, sanctions cut both ways. The US semiconductor industry has warned that the curb imposed by Washington on exports of advanced chips to the largest chip market, in the world will cost it between $2 billion and $2.5 billion in lost revenue in 2023. And that was before China itself sanctioned America's largest chipmaker, Micron, warning the company's large Chinese infrastructure clients that it failed to meet the country's cybersecurity standards and their further usage of its chips would compromise national security. More than 10 percent of Micron's revenue comes from Chinese sales. But other American chipmakers yet to be targeted, like Qualcomm, are over 60 percent reliant on Chinese sales, while Intel and Broadcom have between 25 and 33 percent revenue exposure. The move to deny Micron access to the world's largest chip market was widely seen as retaliation for US measures intended to curtail the export of advanced electronics to China, also on national security grounds.

Further restrictions were to follow. In August 2023, after months of back-and-forth consultations with the tech sector, President Biden signed an executive order that will prohibit American venture capital or private equity from investing in China, Hong Kong, and Macao in high-tech sectors such as artificial intelligence, advanced semiconductors, and quantum computing; it is a move that parallels actions that the Biden administration has taken on the trade front.

American venture capital firms and the tech industry itself had lobbied hard against the decision, as had a number of EU countries who feared the investment restrictions in China would adversely affect their economies. Biden's executive order targets venture capitalists who might want to make a private equity investment in Chinese tech start-ups that in turn could supply restricted (i.e., sanctioned) Chinese companies associated with the country's military. In the words of the White House, the executive order was designed "to prevent American investments from helping to accelerate the indigenization of these technologies."[1]

While the measures are not expected to impact investment in publicly traded Chinese companies (aside from those already sanctioned, like those delisted from the New York Stock Exchange) or index investments, Biden's executive order can only contribute to the growing uneasiness among Western investors about participating in the Chinese market. An increasing number of institutional funds in North America are already reducing their exposure to Chinese stock markets. While this cooling attitude may also reflect the Chinese economy's slow recovery from the COVID-19 lockdowns and growing calls in the West for supply chain diversification, it is strongly motivated by increasing anxiety over an outright economic war, if not a military conflict, between the two superpowers.

There is no question that these sanctions can harass China and poison the West's trading relationship with the world's biggest manufacturer. But can they accomplish what they are intended to do? Can they deny China access to cutting-edge chip technology? Huawei seemed to give a strong answer when it unveiled the Mate 60—a smartphone complete with 5G technology that Huawei was supposedly denied by the US government sanctions. The enabling Kirin chip was designed by Huawei and manufactured by the Chinese Semiconductor Manufacturing International Corporation, a partially state-owned company and a growing competitor of the Taiwan Semiconductor Manufacturing Company. To rub salt in America's wound, the announcement coincided with US commerce secretary Gina Raimondo's visit to Beijing, underscoring the ineffectiveness of American sanctions to stymie the development of advanced semiconductors. It was yet another example of how sanctions have spurred the development of alternatives to Western products, services, and technology.

Whether or not they realize it, the Biden administration is attempting to disrupt the force of economic gravity with its never-ending restrictions on technology transfers to China. It's a tall order, if not an impossible task. For all of Washington's efforts to thwart technological diffusion, the world's largest chip market is inexorably attracting the world's leading-edge semiconductor technology. Whether that is achieved through inventive workarounds against American sanctions or, as was the case with Huawei's new 5G phone, spurring the development of home-grown technological capacity, one way or another China is challenging America's dwindling dominance of advanced chip technology on a scale never seen before.

In fact, there is a strong argument to be made that American sanctions against China's chip industry have backfired as spectacularly as those brought against the Russian aerospace sector. The rapid development of China's chip industry has quickly become the focal point of President Xi's Made in China 2025 program. While the Chinese government, not unlike the government in Taiwan, has always supported the growth of a domestic semiconductor industry, US sanctions have been the catalyst for unprecedented levels of state funding and other forms of government support for China's chip industry. The more that massive state support enhances the domestic chip industry, the better are Chinese electronics firms able to leverage their market clout in demanding technology transfers.

Of course, the US Congress is just as guilty of creating trade restrictions as any American president. In January 2023, while the Biden administration was still working out the details of its long-awaited executive order, Congress got in on the act too, creating a special House committee that boldly branded itself as the House Select Committee on the Strategic Competition Between the United States and the Chinese Communist Party. Implicitly, the branding suggests that growing bilateral conflict between the two countries is not a clash of national interests but rather a clash between the interests of a democracy against those of a rival ideology. The characterization conveniently ignores the fact that over 95 million Chinese belong to the Communist Party, and that about a quarter of the country's 1.4 billion population can claim a member of the Chinese Communist Party as a relative. It's not exactly an exclusive club. Nevertheless, both committee chair Mike Gallagher, a Republican, and ranking Democrat Raja Krishnamoorthi have proudly proclaimed that their anti-China crusade enjoys widespread bipartisan support in Congress.

At the time of its creation, the House committee was the latest in a growing list of actions Congress had taken to effectively sanction the Chinese economy. In December 2021, Congress passed the Uyghur Forced Labor Prevention Act, which bans all products made in whole or in part from the Xinjiang Uyghur Autonomous Region of China— home to the reputedly repressed ethnic Uyghurs, whose cause has recently been championed by Washington.

Not only have sanctions failed to restrict exports from Xinjiang, but as in the case of EU sanctions on Russia, which have inadvertently triggered a revival in coal demand to replace Russian gas, American sanctions imposed against China threaten many of the Biden administration's most cherished environmental objectives. China isn't just America's largest trading partner. It's also America's—and the rest of the world's— largest supplier of the solar panels and batteries that are critical to the efforts of Western governments to decarbonize their economies. The climate diplomacy between the world's two largest carbon polluters— established during the Obama administration and including an agreement between Obama and Xi that lay the groundwork for the landmark 2015 Paris climate accord—has come to an abrupt end under Biden.

Sanctions have already severed critical Chinese supply chains that are crucial in order for the Biden administration to meet its bold environmental objective of halving American emissions by 2030. China dominates the production of polysilicon, solar wafers, and solar cells— all key components in the construction of solar panels, whose energy is being counted on to replace the energy otherwise obtained from combusting coal or natural gas.

Like most countries, the United States relies heavily on Chinese imports for the bulk of the solar panels that are installed in the country. And most of China's solar panel exports are made in Xinjiang. President Biden has championed the use of solar power in the American economy through a number of federal programs, most notably the Department of Energy's National Community Solar Partnership, which aims to create community solar systems across the country to generate enough solar power to service 5 million households by 2025. But in June 2021, the Biden administration announced a ban on imported solar panels from the Hoshine Silicon Industry Co. and a number of other companies operating in Xinjiang on the basis of allegations that they use forced Uyghur labour.

More than a thousand shipments of Chinese solar panels—worth hundreds of millions of dollars and one gigawatt of electrical capacity (enough to power 700,000 homes)—have been stopped at the US border and denied entry into the country. The shipments were from three Chinese companies (Longi Green Energy Technology Co., Trina Solar Co. Ltd., and JinkoSolar Holding Co. Ltd.) that typically have supplied about a third of all the solar panels sold in the United States. All three have halted further shipments to the American market for fear that they too would be confiscated by customs officials at the border.

Similar concerns about a growing dependence on Chinese suppliers are likely to conflict with another of the Biden administration's key environmental goals: to hit a 50 percent ZEV (zero-emission vehicle) target for all vehicles sold in the United States by 2030. China dominates the production of the high-powered electric batteries that will be needed to power those vehicles.

While environmental objectives can readily be sacrificed in the interests of economic warfare, they can also be employed as economic weapons. For example, the Biden administration's proposed Global Arrangement on Sustainable Steel and Aluminum, which it has been lobbying the European Union to join—would punish Chinese manufacturers of steel and aluminum products for their emission record with restricted access to Western markets.

And the United States is also trying to strip China of its developing nation status in international organizations like the WTO, where it benefits from preferential tariff treatment—a common complaint levelled by the Trump administration.

As American sanctions continue to pile up, China is no longer seen as the much-needed partner Bill Clinton welcomed to the ranks of the

WTO—a partner that would soon became a critical link in a global trading system that made everyone richer. While the basic economics of that relationship are still very much intact (if briefly interrupted by the COVID-19 lockdowns in China), cost factors don't seem to matter much anymore. It's not Tim Cook over at Apple who is calling the shots these days in Washington. It's the military that has the president's ear, much to the joy of a booming defence industry. Economics, like everything else, has suddenly taken a back seat to national security.

Of course, national security can mean different things to different countries. If you are the most powerful country in the world, from both an economic and military standpoint, national security is all about maintaining the status quo. But doing so is a lot harder for Washington these days than it used to be. As we've seen, Russia is no longer passively accepting NATO's post-1991 eastern expansion. It's pushing back hard in Ukraine, and it may seek to regain control of lost territory in other sections of Eastern Europe as well. China, despite the severe setbacks to its economy from the COVID-19 lockdowns, has evolved to a point where it is seriously challenging America's economic and financial hegemony. Once again, solar panels hint at the bigger story. Despite sweeping Western sanctions against products from Xinjiang, overseas shipments from the region jumped by a spectacular 40 percent to a record $409.2 billion over the first ten months of 2023. It is widely anticipated that China's GDP will surpass America's (even when measured in dollars) within the next decade, while its currency is increasingly sought around the world by its trading partners and, along with the ruble, has already begun to replace the dollar in much of the oil trade.

For the United States and its NATO allies, it's all part of an increasingly uncomfortable new normal.

XI IS ALREADY PREPARING FOR WAR

In March 2023, shortly after beginning an unprecedented third five-year term as China's leader, President Xi didn't mince words at the

National Congress of the Chinese Communist Party meeting in Beijing. He characterized American policy toward China as one of "containment, encirclement and suppression."[2] Given the escalating trade and investment sanctions that the Biden administration and Congress have been imposing against his country, it wasn't an unreasonable description of Washington's objectives.

Xi warned that the increasing use of sanctions against Chinese companies by the United States and the growing American military support for Taiwan was putting the two countries on a course for conflict and confrontation. He instructed China's parliament, as well as its political advisory body and the senior leadership of the People's Liberation Army, to prepare for war.

Whether President Xi was talking about an economic war or an actual military conflict wasn't clear at the time. But at a minimum, Xi warned that China would soon have to prepare to face the same sanctions that the United States and its NATO allies had levied against Russia. To that end, Xi stressed the importance of what the leaders of all sanctioned countries throughout history have sought: economic self-reliance. Hence President Xi's "Made in China 2025" industrial policy, which outlines a course for the country to reduce its dependence on foreign technology through the development of its own in-house capacity.

Admittedly, self-reliance is a much easier task when you happen to be home to most of the world's industrial supply chains. Nevertheless, the United States still dominates two critical facets of the world economy: technology and finance. In any full-out commercial war between the world's two largest economies, these would be the areas in which American sanctions could have their greatest punitive impact on the Chinese economy.

In an effort to minimize China's vulnerability, President Xi announced governance changes that put both the technology and the finance sectors directly under the control of the ruling Chinese Communist Party. While underscoring the critical importance of semiconductor technology, Xi went out of his way to emphasize that China must "unswervingly advance the cause of national rejuvenation and reunification" with Taiwan.[3] As it turns out, the two goals are inextricably linked.

If China's leadership entertains any plans for an invasion of Taiwan, they can be certain that the Biden administration at a minimum will respond against China with the same type of sweeping economic sanctions that the United States and its allies have imposed on Russia for its invasion of Ukraine. In this regard, how well Russia responds to and survives NATO sanctions serves as an important dress rehearsal for China. The better able Russia is to withstand American sanctions with China's support, the better the chances that the Chinese economy, with Russia's support, will be able to do the same.

Like Russia, China is not an easy target to sanction. It is a huge country that houses the second-largest economy in the world. And the magnitude of the trade flows between China and the United States is so immense that an economic decoupling would be extremely disruptive to both economies. Whereas the Russian economy was only America's thirtieth-largest trading partner, the Chinese economy is first, as measured by two-way trade flows.

And, of course, there is the looming prospect that should China invade Taiwan, the United States could directly enter the war in a military sense. The Center for a New American Security think tank ran war simulations for the House Select Committee on the Strategic Competition between the United States and the Chinese Communist Party; they project that the United States would not be able to resupply Taiwan once China begins an invasion. The simulations also predict that over a three-week full-out military engagement, the United States would lose between ten and twenty combat ships, including two aircraft carriers, and two hundred to four hundred military aircraft, and would incur losses of around three thousand troops, which is half of what America lost in two decades of fighting in Iraq and Afghanistan.

Whether or not the conflict over Taiwan escalates into a full-blown military confrontation, President Xi is at a minimum preparing his country for a protracted economic war, which will be part and parcel of the economic decoupling for which America and its allies are calling. And like Russia, China has the means to retaliate. While China doesn't have Russia's energy exports to withhold in retribution for Western sanctions, it has something just as powerful.

WILL CHINA AND THE REST OF THE BRICS DETHRONE KING DOLLAR?

One of the more curious anomalies of the former world trading system was China's willingness to fund America's massive trade and budgetary deficits. Countries don't normally go out of their way to fund their adversaries. Of course, in the old world order, China and the United States were not officially adversaries—simply interdependent competitors that mutually benefited from trade with each other.

Yet funding the American government is precisely what the People's Bank of China has been doing for decades by acquiring billions of dollars worth of US Treasuries. Only recently has China slipped behind Japan as the country that has lent the US government the most money through massive purchases of American government bonds.

Of course, those purchases weren't an act of benevolence on the part of China's central bank toward American taxpayers, even though taxpayers certainly benefited from their impact on lowering the cost of funding Washington's huge fiscal deficits. Instead, China's central bank was motivated by a need to hold down the value of the yuan against the dollar. And it had good reason for wanting to do so: China's global rival just happens to be its biggest customer. Globalization makes for strange bedfellows.

Currency markets and foreign bond purchases are closely linked. In order to buy Treasuries, the People's Bank of China must first buy dollars with yuan. The more dollars the central bank buys with yuan, the lower the value of the yuan against the dollar. And the lower the yuan-dollar exchange rate, the cheaper the price of Chinese-made goods in the American market. Ironically, the US Treasury Department actually labelled China a "currency manipulator"[4] in September 2019, even though the principal means through which the People's Bank of China manipulated its currency was by funding more US federal government borrowing through a massive purchase of Treasuries.

Whether the People's Bank of China will continue to remain so motivated to hold down the value of the yuan against the dollar is increasingly in doubt as bilateral tensions mount. If indeed America and China are about to economically decouple, as the Biden administration seems to want, the People's Bank of China may soon feel free to decouple from its massive holdings of US government debt.

As American trade sanctions pile up, restricting the importation of Chinese goods into the American market in a growing number of sectors, bilateral trade with the United States will become less and less crucial to the performance of the Chinese economy. US imports of Chinese goods plunged 25 percent over the first six months of 2023 as trade sanctions targeted at them mounted in the United States. However, the less important bilateral trade with the United States becomes to the Chinese economy, the less important holding down the value of the yuan against the dollar will become to the People's Bank of China. And that in turn means that China's central bank could start to unwind its massive position in US Treasuries.

That prospect might be more concerning to the Treasury and the Federal Reserve Board than anything Russia has done yet. It's one thing for Russia's central bank not to hold dollars in its foreign reserves (or to have them confiscated, as was the case), but it would be another order of magnitude altogether for the People's Bank of China to do likewise. The foreign reserves of China's central bank are over $3 trillion, equal to about a quarter of all central bank reserves in the world. In fact, the People's Bank of China's foreign reserves are twice as large as the holdings of the next central bank in line, the Bank of Japan. Just under $1 trillion of the foreign reserves held by the People's Bank of China are held as dollars, mostly in the form of Treasuries.

Over the last decade, China's holding of US government debt (and associated federal-agency debt like Freddie Mac and Fannie Mae bonds) has declined by about 30 percent from its peak in 2013. The process has accelerated recently, following the decision by Western authorities to confiscate the Russian central bank's dollar holdings. The People's Bank of China's holdings of Treasuries fell 22 percent in 2022, sinking to the lowest level since 2009. That process is sure to continue.

Whether motivated by a waning need to hold down the yuan-dollar exchange rate as bilateral trade shrinks or as part of a deliberate attempt to weaken the global stature of the dollar, China will be divesting from Treasuries. As it does, China will effectively be sanctioning the dollar—an act of economic warfare.

The timing of such selling could prove to be highly disruptive to the US bond market. If it occurs simultaneously with Federal Reserve Board quantitative tightening, it would pose a double-barrelled shock to market liquidity that could send US government long-term interest rates soaring. The spike in Treasuries yields would reverberate throughout the American economy and capital markets, affecting not only mortgage rates and the housing market but the stock market as well, as stocks would be forced to compete with rising Treasuries yields for investor funds. If the People's Bank of China is so inclined, America's huge borrowing needs could suddenly become a geopolitical liability like never before.

And China certainly won't be the only country lightening up on its holding of Treasuries. The weaponization of the dollar and Western-based financial institutions like SWIFT have spurred other countries to take measures to immunize themselves, should they one day become the target of American financial sanctions.

While the dollar is still by far the most heavily held asset in the foreign reserves of central banks, its dominant position has actually been declining for some time, even before the Biden administration took the extraordinary step of confiscating Russia's foreign exchange reserves. Over the past two decades, the dollar has fallen from a position of 71.5 percent of central bank foreign reserves to 58.8 percent, according to the International Monetary Fund. According to IMF data, the dollar's share of central bank forces reserves fell to 58.4 percent by the end of 2022, its lowest share since 1994.

Selling dollars from the foreign reserve war chest of its central bank isn't the only way the Chinese government can challenge the hegemony of the dollar in global currency markets. Conducting foreign trade in non-dollar currencies is another route to the same objective. And the more countries stop conducting their foreign trade in dollars, the less inclined central banks around the world will be to hold so many dollars in their foreign reserves.

De-dollarizing trade is easy enough to do. Trade markets and currency markets go together like hand and glove. In any international commercial transaction, buyer and seller must mutually agree on a currency in which to conduct the transaction. But that currency doesn't have to be the dollar anymore, as has been the case through most of the postwar era. The trade could be conducted in one of their own currencies or in another currency altogether—like the yuan, for example.

It's a message President Xi takes with him everywhere he goes, from the SCO summit in Samarkand to his visits to the Middle East and Russia. In doing so, the Chinese leader is openly questioning whether the dollar should remain the one and only reserve currency for the world economy to use. In today's environment of ever-increasing geopolitical tensions, it's a valid question to ask. Is it not possible, after all, that constantly escalating economic sanctions will fracture world currency markets just as they have already fractured world trade markets?

It seems as if more and more countries are listening to President Xi's message—which is perhaps not surprising, given that China is the top trading partner to 120 countries around the world. The message has also been greatly amplified by America's own efforts to weaponize its currency and its financial markets. Shortly after the SCO summit meeting, member countries agreed to de-dollarize their trade in favour of local currencies. BRICS members are as well. India reported that a number of its trading partners, including Russia, Sri Lanka, and Bangladesh, have agreed to conduct trade in rupees. The UAE and India were already finalizing a deal in which all bilateral trade between them would be conducted in either dirhams or rupees.

And the movement away from the dollar is gaining momentum. In February 2023, Iraq announced that, like Saudi Arabia, it would accept yuan payment for its oil exports to China. China and its BRICS partner Brazil, representing the largest economy in Latin America, have agreed to ditch the dollar and conduct all bilateral trade and financial transactions in either yuan or reais. China is already Brazil's largest trading partner, with bilateral trade in 2022 reaching $150 billion. Meanwhile, Argentina and Brazil have established a new regional currency—the sur—intended for use throughout Latin America to replace the dollar.

China has reached similar deals with Russia and Pakistan to conduct bilateral trade in their own currencies. And Russia has agreed to use the yuan, which is increasingly challenging the dollar all over the world, for settlement of trade between Russia and countries in Asia, Africa, and Latin America. Similarly, the Association of Southeast Asian Nations is developing a regional cross-border system for making trade payments in local currencies and bypassing the dollar altogether. Indonesia and Malaysia, two of the largest members, have already announced they will conduct cross-border trade using the Malaysian ringgit and the Indonesian rupiah. Eliminating the dollar is estimated to save 30 percent in cross-border transaction costs. Thailand, the Philippines, Singapore, and Brunei have indicated that they will also join in the initiative.

So far, King Dollar is still wearing its crown, but it's beginning to wobble. By March 2023, the yuan had jumped to fifth place in global currency transactions, spurred by a sharp increase in Russian demand (given that Russia is now settling much of its trade in that currency). Eighty percent of the rapidly expanding trade between Russia and China is now conducted in either rubles or yuan, while for the first time ever the yuan overtook the dollar to become the most-traded currency on the Moscow Exchange. China's share of global trade finance has more than doubled since the imposition of Western sanctions on Russia. It has a lot of ground to cover before it catches the dollar, but it is closing in fast on the euro.

As the dollar's previously unrivalled status as the world's one and only reserve currency comes under attack, so too do the benefits that come with that status. The dollar's unchallenged rule has allowed the United States to do what few other countries are capable of doing: continuing to run up massive fiscal deficits without paying a huge financial penalty. As long as King Dollar reigned, Washington could spend freely, confident that the debt it was creating would be eagerly bought by the rest of the world, who would gobble up Treasury bonds and Treasury bills. But this appetite to hold so much American government debt was created by the need to hold dollars, either as settlement for external trade or for their central banks' foreign reserves. If the rest of the world's appetite for dollar holdings diminishes due to the increased role of ascending currencies like the yuan, the willingness of other countries to fund huge American fiscal deficits also diminishes. In 2023 alone, BRICS countries, led by Chinese selling, dumped a record $123 billion of US Treasuries. If that offshore selling trend continues, Washington must either rein in its spending (and hence the size of its deficits), boost taxes, or be prepared to pay much higher interest costs to finance its deficits.

Never has this been more important to the United States than it is now. Not only did the pandemic lockdowns send Washington's budget deficit, and hence its borrowing requirements, into the stratosphere, but the Biden administration has kept federal spending in overdrive. As of December 2023, the Congressional Budget Office estimated that the federal deficit would soar to close to $2 trillion.

Washington got used to the free-spending ways that a massive monetary expansion by the Fed effectively financed at trivial borrowing costs. But an economic war between the United States and

China—where the People's Bank of China could not only refuse to finance future budget deficits but could also undo its financing of past deficits, potentially unleashing a torrent of supply onto the Treasuries market—would quickly bring that process to an end. And China's central bank won't be the only one exiting the Treasuries market. As more and more of the global oil trade is de-dollarized, fewer and fewer petro revenues will be reinvested in the Treasuries market.

Washington's borrowing costs have already soared since the pandemic as the Federal Reserve Board has stopped its once massive quantitative easing program and been forced to ratchet up interest rates by hundreds of basis points, in line with inflation. The interest rate charges on servicing the national debt have skyrocketed, so much so that high debt-servicing costs were one of the principal factors behind Fitch Ratings' 2023 decision to downgrade America's debt, stripping it of its long-held and much-coveted AAA rating.

But it's not just credit ratings that are at risk. So is the expansionary fiscal policy that has become par for the course in Washington, regardless of administration. The more expensive it becomes to fund massive fiscal deficits, the more pressure voters will put on governments to shrink them.

The pandemic inspired record-low interest rates, and quantitative easing made it easy for governments to spend far beyond their means; the weaponization of financial and currency markets will have the opposite effect. Just as American sanctions have forced the Russian and Chinese economies to become more self-reliant, hostile central banks have growing leverage over American fiscal policy. Just as Russia now has to make its own planes and China has to make its own chips, the US will soon have to pay its own debts.

Fiscal policy isn't something that immediately comes to mind when we consider the impact of the new world order. But as trans-global investment, both private and public, becomes enlisted in economic warfare, America's huge fiscal deficits are increasingly going to have to be financed at home, from the savings of American households, as opposed to by foreign central banks. And that means in the future it's going to cost the US Treasury a lot more to borrow.

As American taxpayers are about to find out, that new fiscal reality is part of the new normal that China is carefully crafting for them.

CHAPTER 12

TROUBLED WATERS

Chinese and American interests conflict all around the world. But no conflict zone is more potentially explosive than the Taiwan Strait.

A thin red line—originally drawn by an American general in 1954 during the height of the Cold War—serves as the point of demarcation between Chinese jurisdiction and Taiwanese jurisdiction in the heavily travelled Taiwan Strait, which runs between the island and the Chinese mainland. Roughly half of the global container fleet and about 70 percent of global trade in semiconductors is shipped through what is one of the busiest maritime corridors in the world.

Officially, China considers the entire strait to be within its territorial waters, since the island of Taiwan itself is seen as an integral part of China. But at least until now, Beijing has accepted the median point, as that thin red line is commonly called, as the de facto boundary for effective airspace and maritime jurisdiction.

The waters running between the island and the Chinese mainland province of Fukien have been troubled ever since Generalissimo Chiang Kai-shek fled Communist forces and established his own military regime in Taiwan (formerly called Formosa) following the Second World War. In the intervening years, there have been no less than three separate military confrontations in the strait between Communist and Nationalist forces.

The First Taiwan Strait Crisis took place in 1954 and 1955, with a brief military confrontation between the People's Liberation Army and the

Taiwanese forces over several island groups belonging to Taiwan but lying near the Chinese mainland. The Yijiangshan Islands and later the Tachen Islands were seized by mainland forces.

Three years later, in 1958, the combatants were at it again. China began shelling the Taiwanese islands of Kinmen and the Matsu archipelago, where Taiwan was attempting to build naval bases. The conflict quickly escalated, drawing America into the fray to protect commercial shipping through the strait by providing naval escorts that the mainland forces dared not attack. At the time, the Joint Chiefs of Staff had determined that the United States would defend the island from a Chinese invasion and, if need be, deploy nuclear weapons against Chinese forces as they had done a little over a decade earlier in Japan. As it turned out, other than supplying Taiwan with weapons and providing escorts, America never entered the war directly. After the fighting ended in a stalemate, the conflict concluded with the bizarre if not farcical arrangement whereby Communist forces would fire only on certain days and Taiwanese forces would fire on alternate days. But instead of firing bombs at each other, the combatants fired propaganda leaflets.

The third crisis, in 1996, was precipitated by the mainland firing a series of missile tests over the strait in an effort to discourage Taiwan's president at the time, Lee Teng-hui, from declaring the island's independence. A second set of tests was conducted just prior to the 1996 presidential elections on the island, in an effort to influence the result.

The Taiwanese government defiantly claims that the Communist government in Beijing, which came into existence in 1949, has never ruled the island nation. While this is technically true, the Taiwanese government typically fails to mention that the island has been part of China for more than four centuries. Taiwan first came under Chinese control during the Qing dynasty in the seventeenth century. However, large-scale migration of the Han people had begun two centuries earlier, and over the centuries has largely displaced the native inhabitants, who were of Austronesian ancestry. Today, indigenous people represent less than 2.5 percent of the Taiwanese population, which is now overwhelmingly Han.

In 1895, the island was ceded to Japan after China lost the First Sino-Japanese War. China took back the island in 1945, following Japan's surrender at the end of the Second World War. The Communists under Mao Zedong won the ensuing civil war, forcing the Nationalists—under Chiang Kai-shek and his party, known as the Kuomintang—to flee along with around 2 million followers to Taiwan, where they ruled for the next several decades. Ironically, the Kuomintang today is pro Beijing, in sharp contrast to the island's ruling Democratic Progressive Party

While Taiwan is always championed in the Western media as a beacon of democracy in Asia, it certainly didn't start out that way. When Generalissimo Chiang Kai-shek installed himself as the island's supreme ruler in 1949, he immediately declared a state of martial law—banning all opposition to his rule. It was not repealed for thirty-eight years, following his death in 1987. During this period, commonly referred to as the White Terror, 140,000 Taiwanese were either imprisoned or executed for alleged disloyalty to the regime and sympathy toward the mainland government.

Today Taiwan houses a vibrant and modern economy (the eighth-largest in Asia), but it is nevertheless isolated diplomatically, with only thirteen countries and the Vatican recognizing it as an independent state. This diplomatic isolation is the result of unrelenting Chinese pressure on nations around the world, including the United States, to not recognize Taiwan as a sovereign state. Nevertheless, the United States maintains both informal relations and defence ties with the island.

The 1979 Taiwan Relations Act, which governs US policy with regard to Taiwan, does not explicitly ensure that the United States would come to the military aid of Taiwan if invaded, as would be the case if it were a NATO member. However, it does require the United States to ensure that Taiwan has the resources to defend itself should it be attacked by mainland forces.

That strategic ambivalence over the precise nature of potential American military involvement served two purposes. The most obvious was to discourage China from launching an outright invasion of the breakaway republic. But the lack of certainty that America would come to its defence also restrained Taiwan from unilaterally declaring its independence from China—a move that would almost certainly trigger a declaration of war by China and a subsequent invasion of the island.

That diplomatic status quo was challenged when President Biden, in an apparent break with long-standing US policy, stated on a trip to East Asia in May 2022 that the United States would come militarily to the aid of Taiwan if it were to be invaded—the first such commitment ever made publicly by an American president. In fact, Biden went so far as to state that America's military commitment to Taiwan is significantly greater than what it is for Ukraine in resisting the Russian invasion. Needless to say, his speech didn't earn rave reviews in Beijing.

If Biden's comments weren't provocative enough, it was only a month later that Nancy Pelosi, then Democratic Speaker of the House, decided to include a stopover in Taiwan on her trip to the Far East, despite warnings from Beijing that they would consider this a further provocation. Pelosi's visit marked the first time a House leader had been to the island since Newt Gingrich stopped in back in 1997.

True to its warning, China responded to the Pelosi visit by launching unprecedented live-fire military drills that effectively blockaded the island and closed down vital shipping lanes in the Taiwan Strait and surrounding waters for three days. Its missile tests came within 19 kilometres (12 miles) of the Taiwanese mainland, by far the deepest incursion of the Chinese military into Taiwan's territorial waters to date, and for the first time, some missiles flew straight across the entire island.

In early 2023, not to be outdone by his predecessor, newly elected Republican House Speaker Kevin McCarthy offered to visit Taiwan as well, but was counselled by the Taiwanese president Tsai Ing-Wen to instead meet her in California on her return from a scheduled trip to Central America. Their meeting in early April 2023 nevertheless marked the first time that a House Speaker had met a Taiwanese president on American soil since the United States and China established diplomatic relations in 1979.

As such, the California meeting was also considered to be an affront to Beijing, which was once again quick to act. Shortly after the gathering, China responded by staging a full dress rehearsal of an invasion of the island, encircling Taiwan with its navy and aircraft during three days of military exercises that simulated an all-out attack on the island. Seventy-one aircraft and nine ships were involved, including aircraft carrier *Shandong*. The messaging was unavoidably clear. As America ramps up both diplomatic and military support for the breakaway island nation, it hastens the timing of a Chinese invasion to fulfill Xi's promise of reunification with the mainland.

As tensions rise in the Indo-Pacific, the United States has recruited Australia and Great Britain into a new NATO-type regional alliance called AUKUS (Australia, the United Kingdom, and the United States) that is focused on military cooperation. Under the pact, both the United States and the United Kingdom will assist Australia in acquiring nuclear-powered submarines, as well as sharing other key defence technologies.

Where all of this is leading is as yet unclear, but it has certainly left Sino-American relations at their lowest point in forty years, mimicking the current state of Russian-American relations. And the growing animosity between the two nations is threatening to spill over into open economic warfare, with the Biden administration announcing new sanctions against the world's second-largest economy and America's largest trading partner virtually every month.

Meanwhile, President Xi, who in March 2023 received an unprecedented third five-year term as China's president, doesn't seem to be intimidated. He has repeatedly declared that he wants the reunification of Taiwan with mainland China to be his principle legacy. And while China has claimed that it wants reunification to occur peacefully, it has threatened that it will use force to achieve the objective if necessary. Polling indicates that only 12 percent of the Taiwanese population (drawn largely from the elderly) support becoming just another province of China, so it looks as if Beijing might have to rely on the second option if Xi is to achieve his objective.

According to top US military personnel, a Chinese invasion of the island could happen as early as 2028. The United States is preparing for that eventuality by beefing up its military presence in nearby Philippines. President Ferdinand Marcos Jr. has granted America access to four more military bases, in addition to the five it already had access to under the 2014 Enhanced Defense Cooperation Agreement between the two countries. Some of the bases are located within 160 kilometres (100 miles) of the shores of Taiwan. As Washington ramps up its military support for Taiwan and its military presence in the region, it looks like the waters of the Taiwan Strait could become troubled once again.

TAIWAN'S SILICON SHIELD IS MADE FROM CHINA'S RARE EARTH ELEMENTS

While reunification of Taiwan with China has been a fundamental political objective of the Chinese Communist Party ever since it came to power, the economic and technological significance of that occurring has never been greater than it is today. When it comes to advanced electronics, the 23-million-person nation punches far beyond its weight.

Back in the 1980s, the architect of the country's economy, the all-powerful minister K.T. Li invited former Texas Instruments executive Morris Chang to build a world-leading semiconductor industry on the island. Taiwan's government funded almost half of the startup capital for the newly formed Taiwan Semiconductor Manufacturing Company (TSMC) and saw the enterprise not only as a major driver of future economic growth but as a measure that strengthened the diplomatic lifeline that ties Taiwan to the United States. Under Chang's leadership, TSMC adopted a unique business model that lay the foundation for its success. The company wouldn't design any of the chips it manufactured. Instead, it would manufacture virtually everyone else's chip designs. In doing so, it quickly achieved huge economies of scale that catapulted it to the front ranks of the world chip industry. Today,

TSMC is reputed to account for the production of more than 90 percent of all advanced semiconductors required in most military applications around the world. As such, its production is highly coveted by China, which, despite recent hostilities, is far and away Taiwan's largest trading partner. Nearly half of Taiwan's exports to China are semiconductors.

But these same chips are equally coveted by the United States, Taiwan's presumed military protector. And the US may soon try to prevent the export of state-of-the-art chips from TSMC to China, as it has done with some of its own chipmakers. The world's largest semiconductor manufacturer, along with Korean chip giant Samsung, currently both enjoy temporary exemptions from American export controls, but that could change based on Washington's fears that the company's chips will be used in the guidance systems of a new class of hypersonic missiles that China is developing.

The United States, where the semiconductor industry was first developed, was itself once a major producer of integrated circuits. But as is the case with most manufactured goods, American production of chips has fallen, from 37 percent of global supply in 1990 to about 12 percent in 2023. During that time, American electronics firms increasingly focused on chip design, outsourcing actual chip production to Taiwan and South Korea, a process that left both its industries and its military highly dependent on overseas suppliers.

The current Taiwanese government, in keeping with past governments, claims that its country is protected from a possible Chinese invasion by a silicon shield. In effect, the shield is the island's overwhelming control over the world's much-sought-after semiconductor production. Hsinchu Science Park, home to more than four hundred technology companies, including the all-important TSMC, is the Silicon Valley of the semiconductor world. The destruction of its factories (referred to as foundries in Taiwan) in any Chinese invasion of the island would create immediate chip shortages for both China and the United States, as well as for the rest of the world.

But what is seldom if ever mentioned by the Taiwanese authorities is that the island's silicon shield is built from rare earth elements (REE) that come from China. REE are a set of sixteen elements critical to the manufacture of semiconductors and other high-tech products. In actuality, REE aren't really that rare. But because deposits occur in such minute concentrations, they are extremely difficult to extract and refine (they require massive amounts of surrounding rock to be extracted and processed). Cheap labour and lax environmental regulations, together with prescient foresight, have given China a seemingly insurmountable lead in this area.

While China is highly dependent on Taiwan for semiconductors, Taiwan is equally dependent on China for the REE needed to produce electronic devices. In addition to their use in semiconductors, REE such as neodymium, yttrium, and terbium are crucial materials commonly present in an array of over two hundred electronic products ranging from cellular phones and computer hard drives to flat-screen monitors, wind turbines, and electric vehicles. They are also needed in a wide range of defence applications, including guidance systems for cruise missiles and lasers, and radar and sonar systems used in fighter jets and submarines.

Taiwan imports about three thousand tonnes of REE a year, mostly from China. And it isn't alone in depending on this Chinese supply. The United States is in the same boat, with Chinese exports composing almost 80 percent of America's REE imports. From mining to refining, China enjoys a near monopoly over these minerals. So although the global semiconductor supply chain is commonly perceived to start in Taiwan, it really starts with REE mines and smelters in China.

China may be lagging on reducing its own greenhouse gas emissions, but its meticulous planning on how to meet the energy needs of a decarbonizing world economy has been visionary. When it comes to the production of electric vehicle batteries or the strategic metals and REE needed to make them, China is light years ahead of the West. The vast majority of such batteries are produced in China, and you can't build one elsewhere without using Chinese components. It's the mirror image of America's dominance in high-end chip design.

China has not only developed its own critical materials sector (lithium, nickel, cobalt, and REE), but it has also locked up ownership of mines in other key supplier countries around the world. The country controls 80 percent of the mining of REE and 87 percent of the refining capacity for those metals, as well as 65 percent of the processing capacity for lithium, key to the production of state of the art batteries crucial to electrifying the world's vehicles. Ditto for cobalt, another key ingredient in the production of the lithium-ion batteries powering electric vehicles. China's CMOC is a major mine owner in the Democratic Republic of the Congo, which supplies the world with about 70 percent of its cobalt. Similarly, China's Tsingshan Holding Company has scooped up much of Indonesia's world-leading nickel deposits and has built smelters in the country to process the metal. Supply chain control has allowed China's CATL and domestic rival BYD to between them control over half of the global market for electric vehicle batteries. And BYD is expected to overtake Tesla to become the world's largest manufacturer of fully electric vehicles, with production expected to surpass 3 million units in 2023.

All of a sudden, the widespread goal in Western economies (the European Union, the United States, and Canada) of 100 percent zero-emission vehicle sales by 2035 is loaded with geopolitical risk. The energy transition away from fossil fuels championed by the West implies growing dependence on Chinese-made batteries and componentry. Chinese restrictions on REE exports could easily scuttle those ambitions.

Already significant, China's dominance in both the production and smelting of strategic materials like lithium and REE will become even more important as the world moves toward the ultimate goal of the net-zero-emission economies that most countries have pledged to achieve. Europe's commitment to achieve that objective by mid-century alone requires a sixfold increase in global copper, lithium, graphite, and REE production, according to estimates by the International

Energy Agency. If the rest of the world intends to achieve the same net-zero-emissions goal, the required production increases would be many times that.

In that world, the global sanctions war between the United States and Russia and China would quickly shift arenas from fossil fuels to strategic metals and REE. While that transition would lessen Western dependence on hostile oil producers, it would simultaneously leave the United States and its allies in an even more vulnerable position with regard to the supply of critical materials needed for the much-sought-after energy transformation.

There have already been trade skirmishes involving strategic materials, and more are likely to come. In the past, China had threatened a restriction in REE exports to the United States in retaliation for American measures to restrict trade and investment with China in high-end chips. In July 2023, that threat became a reality. In response to Washington's ban on exporting chip technology to China, Beijing imposed export restrictions on gallium and germanium, two rare metals used to manufacture semiconductors and solar panels. Both are on the European Union's list of materials deemed critical to its economies. China is by far the world's leading producer of gallium, and is a leading exporter of germanium as well. And in October 2023, China announced that it would require export permits for some graphite products, citing national security concerns. China refines over 90 percent of the graphite material used in virtually all electric vehicle batteries. As the Biden administration continues to tighten restrictions on technology transfers to and investment in China's electronics industry, Beijing is widely expected to ratchet up its restrictions on REE exports to the United States and its EU allies.

MOVING TO ARIZONA

That prospect hasn't been lost on the Biden administration—or on the Pentagon. American chip dependence on Taiwan certainly has huge economic consequences impacting trillions of dollars of commercial activity, but it is equally vital to the US military. The United States has less than ninety days' worth of REE inventory for its defence applications should China cut off their supply. And even rudimentary military equipment, like the anti-tank Javelin that the United States has supplied to Ukraine, uses more than 250 different electronic chips. Insufficient chip inventories have prevented America from meeting Ukraine's request for hundreds of such weapons to be delivered daily.

The need for greater self-sufficiency in semiconductor production was first highlighted by the breakdown in supply chains during the pandemic and has only gained traction as the geopolitical tensions between China and the United States increase. Biden's CHIPS and Science Act (2022) attempts to mitigate that supply dependence by promoting domestic production.

Like President Xi, President Biden has declared that achieving self-sufficiency in chip production is a national strategic objective. Both China and the United States recognize that the current status quo in the world semiconductor industry would not survive a Chinese invasion of Taiwan.

If China does invade the island, TSMC will have more to worry about than just the damage unleashed by the People's Liberation Army. A growing body of evidence points to the US Department of Defense having in place contingency plans to destroy the company's world-leading semiconductor foundries in Hsinchu Science Park in order to prevent China from capturing them. As former White House national security advisor Robert O'Brien defiantly stated in early 2023, "the United States and its allies are never going to let those factories fall into Chinese hands."[1] O'Brien likened Washington's contingency plans to Winston Churchill's decision to bomb a French naval fleet that was about to fall into Nazi Germany's hands during the Second World War.

Whatever the outcome in Taiwan, there is a strong consensus in the United States, as there is in China, on the need to build up domestic chipmaking capacity. But if the United States is to fulfill President

Biden's goal of self-sufficiency in semiconductor production, it will need access to the REE building blocks used to make such devices. As such, American self-sufficiency in producing electronic chips really implies self-sufficiency in mining and refining REE. To that end, both the United States and Canada have moved to restrict or block further Chinese ownership of critical mineral supply chains, and in some cases have demanded Chinese divestment from existing mines, although Canada's only lithium mine remains in Chinese ownership. It seems as if friendshoring doesn't just affect trade; it can be a barrier to direct investment as well.

In what has been likened to the space race between Russia and the United States during the height of the Cold War, China and the United States are now both in a frantic rush to build domestic chip capacity. According to the US Semiconductor Industry Association, thirty-five companies plan to invest $200 billion across the country in new semiconductor manufacturing plants. Much of the investment to expand American chip production is being leveraged by generous incentives from the CHIPS and Science Act, which will provide as much as $76 billion in subsidies for domestic-based chip production. (But American or otherwise, companies that have invested in chip manufacturing in either Russia or China need not apply for any funding under the CHIPS Act. They wouldn't be eligible. Even federal government procurement and spending programs have a role to play in economic warfare.)

California-based Intel has announced that it will invest $20 billion to build a manufacturing mega-site to produce semiconductors just outside of Columbus, Ohio. It's the largest private-sector investment in the history of Ohio—a state that, like many in the so-called rust belt, has lost more than a third of its manufacturing jobs over the last three decades.

But it's not just American electronics firms that are stepping up to the plate. In a telling statement of how geopolitical frictions are reshaping global supply chains in the semiconductor industry, TSMC more than tripled its originally intended $12 billion investment in a new chip plant in Arizona. The now $40 billion investment will be one of the largest foreign investments in American history. The company is also expected to build a second foundry in Japan, with construction of the estimated $7 billion plant to begin in 2024, and an $11 billion factory in Dresden, Germany, is in the works as well. While geographic diversification of TSMC's factory facilities is probably a prudent step in the face of growing China-Taiwan hostilities. It's hardly a vote of confidence in Taiwan's national security by that country's most important firm

Nor was Warren Buffett's decision to sell Berkshire Hathaway's $4 billion worth of shares in TSMC a vote of confidence in the island's future. Buffett cited geopolitical considerations as a reason for the fund's exit from its large ownership position in the company.

In a growing reflection of how escalating Sino-Taiwanese tensions could impact trade, multinational corporations are increasingly inserting clauses relating to potential supply disruptions or possible invasions in their contracts with Taiwanese suppliers. Their concerns about the security of the Taiwanese economy are shared by major insurers. In August 2023, Lloyd's of London raised insurance rates and cut coverage on risks involving Taiwan, citing the heightened risk of a military conflict with China. The move will make it more difficult and expensive to do business in the island's economy.

As noted by TSMC's founder, Morris Chang, America no longer seems to consider Taiwan a safe country for friendshoring its supply of vitally needed semiconductors. However, Chang predicted that the cost to TSMC for chip production in its new US plant will likely be double what it currently is in Taiwan.

But the company's decision to locate a mega-factory in Arizona isn't about costs. Instead, the new commercial imperative in a geopolitically fractured global economy is security. China may well invade Taiwan and seize control of the foundries in Hsinchu Science Park in the not-so-distant future, but China isn't going to invade Arizona.

As that shift in commercial imperatives continues to drive the relocation of the semiconductor industry to secure but high-cost jurisdictions, it will be reflected in the price of everything electronic, from the guidance system for cruise missiles to the latest smartphone to hit the market. And it won't just be the price of electronics that will be affected if the trade war between China and the United States reaches full fruition. Extending sanctions to China, the world's second-largest economy and home to most global manufacturing supply chains, is another order of magnitude altogether from engaging Russia in economic warfare. China's factories are so deeply intertwined with the supply chains of American firms that any sudden rupture of that relationship would affect the price of virtually everything.

As American consumers are already discovering, rejigging global supply chains that took decades to build isn't quite as easy as sanctioning the places where they once stood. They had better get used to the new prices those sanctions will bring. Although a military conflict between the two superpowers is far from certain, the economic war between China and the United States isn't simply a passing shock in turbulent times. Instead, it's part of the new normal that today's rapidly changing global order has brought.

CHAPTER 13

TURNING THE TABLES

For two years the United States and its NATO partners have been fighting a proxy war against Russia using Ukrainian troops as fodder. While the campaign has cost taxpayers billions of dollars and has depleted Western arsenals, it hasn't cost precious lives. That makes all the difference in the world when it comes to selling the Ukrainian cause to the American or Western European public. Bankrolling a proxy war comes at a much lower political cost than anything that will lead to soldiers coming home in body bags.

But the United States and their NATO allies don't hold a monopoly on using proxies to fight their battles and there are countless expendables around the world that can be enlisted for such fights for the right cause. Of all the BRICS nations, the one best positioned to wage such a war against America and its allies is Iran.

Just as February 24, 2022, changed the world in Europe, October 7, 2023, brought a new normal to the Middle East. The horrific slaughter of over twelve hundred Israeli citizens, including babies (the largest slaughter of Jews since the Holocaust), and the kidnapping of some two hundred and forty hostages by a massive and meticulously planned incursion of Hamas fighters triggered an equally horrific response from the Netanyahu government. That is the logic of terrorism—to provoke the enemy into self-harming action. Hamas couldn't have picked a more predictable target. The ruling Netanyahu government, itself the target of widespread if not unprecedented civil strife and protest in Israeli society over its attempt to weaken the power of the judiciary, was the most right-wing and anti-Arab government in the country's history.

Netanyahu didn't disappoint. He immediately gave the Israel Defense Forces (IDF) the green light to carpet bomb Gaza with seeming indifference to massive civilian casualties that have run into the tens of thousands. Outrage exploded around the world. Protests against Israel rocked capitals on every continent. At the same time, Western governments rallied to support Tel Aviv, their most important ally in the Middle East. Israel is not a member of NATO but it is viewed as part of the West as much as any member of that alliance is. Since its existence no other country in the world has received more military aid from the United States than Israel, in what has always been an American policy of ensuring that the country enjoys an overwhelming military superiority over its Arab neighbours. As the world polarized over the terrorist attacks and the decades of conflict that led to them, the best-laid plans of Israel, Saudi Arabia, and the United States suddenly went up in smoke.

Negotiations regarding the normalization of relations between Saudi Arabia and Israel had begun back under the Trump administration with the so-called Abraham Accords, which saw a number of Muslim countries—the United Arab Emirates, Bahrain, Morocco, and Sudan—establish normal diplomatic relations with Israel. Palestinians naturally saw the effort as nothing short of a betrayal and a rejection of their cause to establish an independent state.

As it turns out, the secret negotiations between Israel and Saudi Arabia were seeking to achieve a lot more than simply establishing diplomatic relations between the Jewish state and the self-proclaimed leader of the Sunni Muslim world, even though that in and of itself would have been a landmark achievement some three-quarters of a century after Israel first took its place on the map of the Middle East. In an effort to sweeten the deal, the United States had offered both

Israel and Saudi Arabia security guarantees, much like those it provides its NATO partners. So not only would the deal establish full diplomatic relations between Saudi Arabia and Israel, but they would be
soon effectively become military allies in a triparty alliance with the
United States against regional enemy Iran.

While Washington's behind-the-scenes orchestration of a Saudi
Arabia Israel accord was intended to isolate Iran, that initiative ran
directly counter to the objectives of Chinese diplomacy. China brokered the re-establishment of relations between Saudi Arabia and its
old Shia enemy Iran, consolidating the big Muslim powers and oil producers, and soothing some of the tensions within the Middle East.
Naturally, the extension of the Abraham Accord to include Saudi
Arabia was a diplomatic nightmare for Iran. Though no evidence links
the October 7 attacks to Iran, simple logic does: if Iran thought that
stirring up the decades-old Palestinian crisis would be enough to
poison Israel's deal with Saudi Arabia and other Muslim countries,
then it would make sense to do so. It would be cruelly, brutally logical.

From Iran's perspective, the prospect that its two greatest enemies were about to form a de facto military alliance was threatening,
to say the very least. While Iran wasn't technically at war with either
Saudi Arabia or Israel, the government in Tehran had been waging
proxy wars against both countries through its regional allies in Lebanon
(Hezbollah) and Yemen (Houthi). Though Hamas and Hezbollah have
long been rivals and even deadly enemies (they fought on opposite
sides during the Syrian Civil War a decade ago), the plight of the
Palestinians could plausibly have given them common cause.
Certainly, the Israeli response to the terror attacks led to immediate
statements of solidarity. (Though Iran claimed to have had no prior
knowledge of the attacks.)

Just as fifty years ago King Faisal bin Abdulaziz Al Saud couldn't
be seen publicly making deals with the likes of William Simon, the
Saudi crown prince couldn't very well been seen negotiating a deal to
establish ground-breaking diplomatic relations with Israel while the

Arab streets from Cairo to Amman to Beirut were teeming with anti-Israel and anti-American demonstrations. But after October 7, the Palestinian cause was suddenly front and centre in the minds of the whole Arab world after having been all but abandoned by Saudi Arabia and most of its Arab partners.

Saudi Arabia had already been walking a tightrope in participating in the negotiations with Israel and the United States. Despite its former heavy reliance on US military equipment, the country under MBS's direction had pivoted sharply away from the Biden administration and markedly toward China, even to the point of accepting yuan payments for its oil exports and, in so doing, bringing to an abrupt end the six-decade regime of the petrodollar. Of equal significance, Saudi Arabia had recently agreed to join BRICS along with its archenemy Iran, a move carefully and skilfully brokered by China.

But at the same time, a military alliance with Israel and the United States would give the kingdom a foot in both camps. Economically and diplomatically, Saudi Arabia could still be a proud standard bearer for the Global South. At the same time, it would enjoy powerful military protection. But as tempting as such a prospect might be to MBS, the prospect of Iran's two greatest enemies uniting was very threatening viewed from the perspective of the government in Tehran.

If the price for scuttling any deal between Israel and Saudi Arabia was the possible annihilation of Palestinian militants and civilians by the IDF, that would be a small cost for Iran to pay compared to the potential danger to its own security posed by an Israel-Saudi alliance. From Iran's perspective, Hamas (a Sunni fundamentalist movement) was expendable.

But for Hamas, Iranian support was a critical lifeline. Hamas certainly has no friends in government in neighbouring Egypt. Its parent organization, Egypt's Muslim Brotherhood, is banned in Egypt and is officially designated a terrorist organization by the government, the same designation given to it by both Israel and the United States. However, the Muslim Brotherhood's political party, the Freedom and

Justice Party, actually briefly took power in Egypt after winning the 2012 presidential election following the Arab Spring and toppling Hosni Mubarak, who had ruled the country for thirty years. But the new government was overthrown by the Egyptian military, who appointed former field marshal Abdel Fattah el-Sisi to the post, where he remains to this day.

With most of the Muslim Brotherhood's leadership incarcerated, the Sisi regime in Cairo is naturally wary of the organization's Palestinian version. Saddled already with the daunting task of feeding its population of nearly 110 million, and fearful of a reprise of the Arab Spring, the Egyptian government has little appetite for accepting another 2 million hungry Palestinian refugees, with Hamas operatives no doubt embedded among them.

Nor can Hamas count on Mahmoud Abbas's Palestinian National Authority in the West Bank for much help, aside from perhaps moral support in the form of protests against Israel. Other than facing a common Israeli foe, there is little love lost between the two Palestinian organizations. In fact, Hamas and the Palestinian Liberation Organization (PLO) were once openly at war in Gaza. After Hamas won the Palestinian legislative election over a largely corrupt PLO back in 2006, it effectively staged a coup that saw many members of the PLO opposition thrown off the rooftops of Gaza City buildings. There hasn't, of course, been another election in Gaza since, and there will likely never be one again as long as Hamas stays in power. Since then, the two Palestinian governments in Gaza and the West Bank have acted like two solitudes, precisely as Israel preferred them, since their estrangement meant there was no unified Palestinian voice to call for an independent state.

The big loser in the Israel-Hamas war, other than the twelve hundred Israelis slaughtered in the Hamas attack, the tens of thousands of dead and missing Palestinian civilians, and the millions of refugees, is the Zelensky regime in Ukraine. The conflict in Gaza has totally eclipsed the war in Ukraine in the Western media. And as the old adage attests, "out of sight, out of mind." Despite the White House's attempt to link additional military aid to Israel with an even greater aid package for Ukraine, the proxy war in Europe quickly became a political liability in Congress, where Republicans were balking at continuing to provide carte blanche support to Kiev to fight a proxy war against Russia. The effects were soon being felt on the battlefield. Ukraine's much-vaunted counter-offensive to regain lost territory during the spring and summer of 2023 fell largely on its face. Without an ever-increasing supply of American and NATO military equipment, fighting a war of attrition with a much larger Russian opponent could only be a losing strategy for the country. Since the October 7 Hamas attack on Israel that has dominated the global spotlight, maintaining prior levels of military aid to Ukraine seems increasingly unlikely in the future.

Of course, the United States stands to lose as well, and not only in its proxy war with Russia in Ukraine. It may soon, to its dismay, find itself fighting on three separate fronts. In addition to fighting Russia in Ukraine and dealing with growing military friction from an increasingly belligerent China in the South China Sea and the Taiwan Strait, it must now deal with a potential third front in the Middle East, where the tables have suddenly been turned. Instead of America waging a proxy war, now it is its military bases in Syria and Iraq, as well as its strategic ally Israel, that find themselves on the receiving end of missiles fired by Iran's proxy armies in the region, much to the delight of Iran's BRICS partners. China and Russia have patiently watched the conflict in Gaza from the sidelines. Both countries have officially called for a ceasefire and condemned attacks on civilians, but neither has explicitly denounced Hamas's attack on Israeli civilians. While it is doubtful that either had a role in or even advance knowledge of the event, both clearly understand its wider geopolitical significance and implications. The war has roiled up passions across the Middle East, most of it vented against Israel and against America itself. It has left both countries isolated in the region. Arab leaders refused to meet President Biden on his sudden trip to Israel during the crisis for fear of provoking a violent backlash among their populace. Even so, there were violent demonstrations in the West Bank and Jordan.

Whatever status quo emerges in the aftermath of the conflict, it will likely see America playing a smaller role in the region and China taking on a larger role. Like Russia, China has staked out a strong position that a condition for peace in Palestine is that Israel respect UN resolutions calling for it to return to its 1967 borders, a position that won't resonate well with anyone on the political spectrum of Israel's highly fractured politics.

If Hamas is removed from power by the IDF, Gaza is likely to be governed by a UN peacekeeping force, possibly under the auspices of the West Bank's Palestinian National Authority. As may well be the case in eastern Ukraine, another battlefront where UN peacekeeping troops may be stationed in the not-so-distant future, representatives from the People's Liberation Army could be part of such an undertaking. If so, slowly but surely China would be spreading its wings around the world to places such as Eastern Europe and the Middle East where its military presence has been all but non-existent in the past.

As in Eastern Europe and the South China Sea, the notion of normal is changing markedly throughout the Middle East. For Israel, normal used to mean building a few new Jewish settlements in the West Bank and tolerating the odd sporadic missile launch in protest from Hamas in return. Meanwhile, Israel continued to expand the number of Arab countries that it had established full diplomatic relations with, without having to make any meaningful concessions on the Palestinian front, like suspending the construction of new Jewish settlements in the occupied West Bank, let alone providing any credible plan to grant the Palestinians their long-sought independent statehood. Now normal has changed. The IDF may take out any future security threat to its citizens from Hamas in Gaza, but in the process of destroying Gaza and killing thousands of innocent civilians, it has put the Palestinian cause of independent statehood back under the global spotlight. And that, in turn, can only lead to mounting international pressure on Israel to negotiate statehood with its Palestinian neighbours.

For most Arab countries, including Saudi Arabia, normal meant distancing themselves as far as possible from the radical Hamas government in Gaza while still paying lip service to their cause of an independent Palestinian homeland. With millions of Palestinian refugees now reduced to living in rubble, that is going to be much harder to do. And they all fear a broader regional conflict if Iran is drawn into the fighting. If that happens, regimes may topple, oil may stop flowing through the Strait of Hormuz, and the superpowers may find that they too are drawn in. American carrier strike groups steamed to the region shortly after October 7, where they were joined by Canadian and French vessels. Meanwhile, Russian MiGs armed with hypersonic missiles took up around-the-clock patrols, capable of striking NATO assets within minutes, and a small Chinese fleet entered the Persian Gulf, too small to be a military factor, but a tripwire to a much greater crisis should the ships somehow come to harm.

A dangerous wild card was added to the deck when the Yemeni Houthis interdicted cargo to and from Israel and western seaports. Only Chinese and Russian aligned freight was allowed to pass safely. Because of the Houthi missiles and the caution of maritime shippers, the rest of the world's freight would have to travel around Africa, adding 5,000 miles to a voyage from Asia to Europe that would normally have traveled through the Red Sea and the Suez Canal. That could only stoke inflation, lead to industrial shutdowns, and exponentially raise the risk of escalation. Airstrikes to re-open the shipping lanes quickly brought the ships of the US and Royal Navies under fire. The devastation of Gaza and its inhabitants has reverberated throughout the world. Antisemitic attacks skyrocketed across Europe as aggrieved Muslim communities vented their anger at their Jewish neighbours. But in turn, their actions endangered themselves by boosting support for right wing anti-Muslim groups like Geert Wilder's Party of Freedom, whose shocking victory in the Netherlands in the November 2023 election puts him in a position to lead the next government in what has traditionally been one of Europe's most liberal and tolerant countries. Wilder not only wants to end immigration from the Middle East but he wants to restrict the cultural and religious freedoms of Muslim immigrants already in the country. From Viktor Orban's Fidesz in Hungary to the Alternative for Germany Party, there are many in Europe who share Wilder's perspective. And perhaps it's no coincidence that all three parties favour discontinuing military aid to Ukraine.

Where the emerging new fault lines in the Middle East will lie is unclear but a protracted war between Hamas and Israel would put the region back into strife. And make no mistake about it: while the conflict between Israel and Hamas has regional roots dating back decades, it has now become part of a much broader conflict between a rising new global order and the one it hopes to replace.

CONCLUSION

TERRA INCOGNITA

Where does an ever-escalating global trade war lead? Can the West still win such wars? Or is there a new world order emerging in which the United States and its allies can no longer use their once unchallenged economic and military power to unilaterally dictate security terms to the rest of the world?

A growing number of economic heavyweights in the developing world are lining up to join America's principal opponents, Russia and China, in an already expanded BRICS that now includes once bitter enemies Iran and Saudi Arabia, as well as Egypt, Ethiopia, and the United Arab Emirates. Dozens more are waiting to join. Together, these nations are challenging the dominance of Western economies on a scale not seen in a century.

Implicitly, if not explicitly, BRICS nations are calling for a new world order, where they—and not the United States and its NATO allies—set and enforce global rules. And they seem more than prepared to throw their considerable economic weight (and possibly, in the near future, their rapidly growing military weight) behind achieving that objective.

As BRICS membership grows, the reach of Western sanctions shrinks. Instead of isolating Russia in a unified world community condemning its invasion of Ukraine, sanctions have instead fractured the global economy into competing and opposing geopolitical blocks. For many in the Global South, the conflict in Ukraine is a European war that has little to do with them. For others, Western sanctions provide their economies with unique new opportunities to expand trade and, at the same time, lessen their financial dependence on Western powers. And most of the developing world now looks to China, not the United States, for global leadership.

But there is much more than shifting perceptions of global leadership at stake. Worse than the loss of international prestige and influence, America's and its NATO partners' pervasive use of sanctions has set in motion economic processes that do not auger well for the future performance of their own economies.

THE LEGACY OF SANCTIONS

As the war in Ukraine drags on with no apparent end in sight, it has become abundantly clear that Western sanctions, advertised as the most crippling ever imposed, have not only failed to bring the Russian economy to its knees but in many cases have backfired on their imposers. China and India have more than replaced Western markets through record purchases of sanctioned Russian exports, in the process ignoring the warnings and threats from America and other sanctioning countries.

Whereas the loss of European energy markets would have once proved fatal to the resource-based Russian economy, record purchases by Chinese and Indian buyers—reflecting, in turn, their own economic power and massive appetite for energy—have driven Russian energy exports to all-time highs.

While sanctions have failed to shred the Russian economy as intended, they have managed to shred the very global trading order that we have been told was the basis of our collective prosperity over the last couple of decades. The exclusion of Russian, and possibly soon Chinese products too, from Western markets, as well as the ban on investment in those countries, undermines the very foundation of the old neoliberal global order that was predicated on the free flow of goods, capital, and technology around the world. And that fundamentally changes how our economies operate.

Instead of fostering the highly specialized division of labour that globalization compels, sanctions encourage economies to look inward to meet the needs of their own domestic market. Adapting to a world of sanctions requires that a local economy become a jack of all trades, as opposed to a specialist in whatever its natural comparative advantage might be. And that transformation is happening not only in the economies of sanctioned countries but in the economies of sanctioning countries as well.

For nations that lack the resources to be self-sufficient (and most do), friendshoring provides the new chart book for navigating the many obstacles that now stand in the way of global trade. Friendshoring essentially means trading with your political allies at the exclusion of trading with hostile nations.

Decoupling or derisking as it is now more commonly referred to is the flip side of friendshoring—and its goal is nothing short of turning the very dynamics of international trade (comparative advantage) on their head. Decoupling and friendshoring are driven by geopolitical imperatives, not economic ones. For the most part, America's allies are highly developed economies paying wage rates not different from its own. Moving supply lines to those countries may make them a lot more secure and reliable, but whatever they are going to deliver will cost a lot more than what consumers have been used to paying.

Nowhere is friendshoring more important than when it comes to achieving energy security—the new preoccupation of governments far and wide. On both sides of the sanctions war, the new imperative of energy security is spurring massive investment in new infrastructure that will lock in for decades to come the massive shifts in energy flows that have occurred during the Russia-Ukraine war. In some cases, those shifts make a lot of economic sense. Bringing together the world's largest natural gas exporter (Russia) and the world's largest gas importer (China) is a case in point. In other cases, though, the shifts make no economic sense. Consider, for example, replacing cheap natural gas delivered through Russian pipelines to energy-hungry Western European markets with expensive American LNG.

Without Russian natural gas, power prices in Europe have spiked to unheard-of levels, and the soaring cost of energy has already dragged the whole EU economy into recession. Most affected is Germany, which not only faces economic stagnation in the near term but is also looking at a long-term prospect of deindustrialization marked by a secular decline in the country's all-important but power-hungry manufacturing sector.

THE BROADENING SCOPE OF ECONOMIC WARFARE

Historically, trade restrictions have been the normal realm of economic warfare, but today's sanctions have spread like some terrible contagion to financial and currency markets as well. Just as sanctions have reshaped trade flows, they are now reshaping investment and financial flows.

The free flow of capital, goods, and technology is the foundational pillar of the old neoliberal global economic order. But it is screened through the prism of all-encompassing national security interests. Investments in semiconductor technology, as well as in strategic metals and REE, are now strictly governed by government watchdogs. That means no new Chinese investment in North American strategic minerals or REE, and no North American investment in or sales of technology to China's semiconductor industry—all in the name of ensuring national security.

Currency markets have also been enlisted in the war between the United States and its Western allies and the rapidly ascending BRICS challengers. What is at stake in this battleground is nothing less than the continued reign of King Dollar as the world's unchallenged reserve currency—another hallmark of the postwar financial order that is now being challenged like never before.

Gone already are the days of the petrodollar, when virtually all of the world's oil trade was conducted in greenbacks, with many of them recycled back into the US Treasuries market to finance America's huge budgetary deficits. And it's not just the oil trade that has turned its back on the dollar. Just as Russian exports are being shut out of Western markets, China, India, Brazil, Argentina, and a growing list of countries are shutting the dollar out of their foreign trade. And let's not forget that, thanks to the aggressive, ground-breaking, American-led measures that confiscated roughly half of the Central Bank of the Russian Federation's foreign reserves, the dollar is losing ground in central bank reserve holdings all around the world as well, and nowhere more so than with the People's Bank of China, which holds nearly $1 trillion worth of Treasuries. China's central bank, which holds more reserves than any other central bank in the world, can just as easily weaponize its reserve holdings as the United States and its EU allies can.

And what of the effectiveness of sanctions themselves? Instead of piling on more and more rounds, maybe it's time to step back and take a good long look at what they have actually accomplished.

While the United States promised its NATO allies that the Russian economy would quickly collapse, no such collapse has occurred. Instead, the Russian economy has proved remarkably resilient. In part, this resilience attests to the degree to which the Kremlin had already sanction-proofed its economy after the penalties the United States and its allies imposed following the annexation of Crimea. It also reflects the degree to which Russia has pivoted toward Asia, and in particular toward its BRICS partners China and India, whose massive markets have welcomed with open arms Russian exports denied access to Western markets.

The ultimate economic impact of sanctions may yet boomerang on those countries that impose them. Instead of forcing Russian consumers (and perhaps, soon, Chinese consumers as well) to go without Western goods, sanctions have created a vacuum that is quickly being filled by the growth of indigenous companies that not only replace Western firms, as they have in the aerospace industry, but over time may come to compete with them in other markets as well, particularly those in BRICS countries. If Russia and China were laggards in technology and finance, sanctions that target those key areas are the strongest incentive possible to rectify those deficiencies. Having spurred the development of alternative services and industries in BRICS countries, have the United States and its NATO partners incented the development of new competitors?

WHAT HAPPENS TO YESTERDAY'S GLOBAL INSTITUTIONS?

A changing global order requires changing global institutions. What will become of the once esteemed economic institutions of the old global order, like the World Bank, the International Monetary Fund, and the World Trade Organization? Will they become dysfunctional or, even worse, simply irrelevant as BRICS sets up competing institutions like the New Development Bank?

What about the political institutions of that same dying order, like the United Nations or other multilateral forums such as the G20? How much longer will countries like India or Brazil be kept from gaining a seat at the United Nations Security Council, while both the United Kingdom and France enjoy the perks of exclusive membership? Does membership in the body—with which comes veto power—reflect the world today, as it did when it was established in the aftermath of the Second World War?

Is the G20 any more relevant as an international decision-making body than the United Nations, which is now largely seen as dysfunctional? Recent G20 meetings have been so divided that the release of a joint declaration has been impossible, despite it having always been their custom. Will future meetings simply mark occasions where the two opposing geopolitical blocs, with very different ideas about how to resolve the world's problems, continually admonish and denounce each other for the benefit of the domestic audiences watching at home?

Even the West's ultimate economic alliance, the G7, is increasingly showing fault lines and divisions. While the United Kingdom and Canada, for reasons of either history or geography, readily accommodate Washington's interests and agenda, how much longer will France and Germany stand meekly at America's command?

President Emmanuel Macron has already declared that France shouldn't be drawn into any conflict between China and the United States in the South China Sea. In June 2023, shortly after Macron made that statement, a European Council on Foreign Relations poll of eleven EU countries found that the majority of respondents in each agreed with him, believing that Europe should stay neutral in any conflict between the United States and China over Taiwan. And the Scholz government in Germany, trying to fight off the rising tide of the right-wing Alternative for Germany party, has had to dial back earlier calls for a decoupling of its economy from that of its largest trading partner, China, as the economic ramifications of such action began to sink in for an already struggling German economy now cut off from cheap Russian natural gas.

And if the G7's economic alliance could fracture, so too could NATO'S defence alliance. In its enthusiasm to surround Russia by recruiting all of its neighbours, has the alliance taken into its ranks fifth columns like Hungary and Turkey whose dissenting votes and actions will continue to frustrate, if not undermine, NATO actions?

And what of Ukraine, where the new normal began to take shape? By late 2023, it began to look as though the Ukrainians' successes early in the conflict were illusions brought on by the fog of war. A Republican-controlled House has already balked at approving more military aid to Kiev and looming on the horizon is the possibility of a second Trump presidency. A defeat for Kiev would mean a defeat for NATO and its biggest champion. If so, what began as an existential threat for Russia may become one for NATO instead.

WHAT HAPPENS AFTER THE NOVEMBER 2024 ELECTION?

Donald Trump has long argued that Ukraine is not of strategic importance to the United States. It's a viewpoint that has, over time, become widely held by Republican lawmakers whose control of Congress has stymied the Biden administration's attempts to provide additional tranches of military aid to Kiev. Should Trump prevail in the November 2024 elections, the flow of military aid would be summarily halted. Even in the event of a Biden victory, without the Democrats controlling both Congress and the Senate, aid would slow to a trickle of its former flow. According to Ukraine's former top general Valery Zalnzhny, with the battleground resembling the trench warfare of the First World War, it's only a matter of time before the Zelensky regime (or some authority from the Ukrainian military) is forced to the negotiating table, likely leaving Crimea and the already-occupied portions of the Donbas in Russian hands.

While a peace treaty will undoubtedly preserve the survival of an independent Ukraine, NATO may be less fortunate. The Western alliance, already highly fractured by the strain and stress of an almost two-year long war, may no longer be sustainable in its present form.

For Germany and France, a Trump victory would be a double-edged sword. Both countries have expressed growing concern about the duration and widening scope of the war and would welcome its end. Moreover, NATO's military stockpiles have been dangerously depleted while decades of globalization have hollowed out the manufacturing industries needed to replace them.

At the same time, Trump's return to the White House would pose other challenges. At minimum, a Trump White House would demand that its NATO partners shoulder a greater share of the alliance's military spending. But an even greater concern would be just how the United States' continued commitment to a joint defence treaty in Europe will fit into an America First Policy of a second Trump administration, if at all.

And let's not forget that the United States won't be the only super-power holding an election in 2024. So will Russia, where Vladimir Putin will likely ride a military victory in the Donbas to another term as president. That means a further deepening of the No Limits Partnership Agreement with China, which is likely to take the form of a de facto military alliance. Can we expect to see the presence of the People's Liberation Army on European soil, possibly as part of some UN peacekeeping force, stationed in a demilitarized new border between Russia and a downsized Ukraine?

Whatever the terms of a peace settlement, one thing is already clear: NATO's relentless three-decade long expansion into Eastern Europe has come to a screeching halt, and some of it may yet be reversed.

Emboldened by its success in the Donbas in conjunction with a potentially isolationist post-election White House, will Russia seek to undo some of NATO's past gains? There are almost a million restive ethnic Russians living in the Baltic states. Will the Russian minorities living in Estonia, Latvia, and Lithuania be called upon to play the same role that they did in Donbas and Crimea?

The United States' withdrawal of its military would leave Europe appended to the western edge of Eurasia but dependent on American natural gas and markets. Over time, will Western Europe be reduced to a small promontory on a massive Eurasian land mass dominated by BRICS powers China, Russia, and India? Perhaps, but whatever the terms of a peace treaty in Ukraine, the map of what is normal in Europe will have been indelibly changed.

IT ISN'T REALLY ABOUT DEFENDING DEMOCRACY

The United States spends nearly $1 trillion on its defence budget every year—a total that is larger than the next ten leading defence-spending countries in the world put together (China, Russia, India, Saudi Arabia, the United Kingdom, Germany, France, South Korea, Japan, and

Ukraine). In part, the massive size of the American defence budget reflects the size of the tax base and the economy that supports it. But even more important is the priority given defence spending by both Republican and Democratic administrations, highlighted by the fact that nearly half of all discretionary spending by the US federal government is on defence. This prioritizing is the principal reason why America's defence budget is so much larger than those of other countries. While China's GDP is almost as large as America's, for example, its defence budget is only a quarter of the size.

America justifies its massive defence budget, as well as its generous military support for the Zelensky regime in Ukraine, as a defence of democracy. But that justification is increasingly suspect, given both what has happened in Ukraine and what is occurring in the United States itself.

Ukraine, whose historical commitment to democracy has been tenuous at best, is currently governed by a regime that has banned all political opposition on the grounds that it is simply a front for invading Russian forces, as well as any public demonstrations. And it has banned all military aged men (27-60) from leaving the country. Moreover, the government in Kiev has canceled the 2024 elections. A poll conducted in late 2023 by Ukraine's Razumkov Centre found that over half of Ukrainians expect that their next leader will come not from the ranks of political parties but rather from the military.

More important still, support for democracy, or at least American institutions of democracy, is also suspect in the very country that claims to be its guardian angel. The fog of political war makes it impossible to know exactly what is afoot. Is the Democratic White House really a nest of corruption and drugs? Is the former Republican president really guilty of the charges that have kept him entangled with the courts for the better part of a decade? Or are the charges simply a politization of the justice system, designed to intentionally obstruct the process of electing the next president? Fierce opinions are in ample supply on both sides of these questions. While both sides of the political aisle sing the praises of democracy, neither actually believes that voting will yield the outcomes they stand for. The real action is in the courts, in the streets, and in the back rooms, and perhaps most of all in the pathways or propaganda eagerly provided by a highly polarized media. Is this really the ideal model of government that America so fervently believes the rest of the world should follow? And is safeguarding this ideal the real reason for justifying a defence budget equal to the entire GDP of Africa?

As Americans continue to lose faith in their democratic institutions, they may come to see the true nature of the proxy war the Biden administration is fighting in Ukraine (and perhaps soon in conflicts in the South China Sea and the Middle East as well): nothing more and nothing less than a great power's pursuit of its strategic interests and attempt to maintain its influence and standing around the world. Stripped of its ideological trappings, this noble pursuit is no different from those of America's adversaries Russia and China. So why should one be deemed morally superior to the other?

Maybe we will come to recognize that, contrary to what our media repeatedly tells us, the conflict in Ukraine isn't simply "Putin's War." The much-despised (in the West) president isn't the only Russian (among 144 million) who feels surrounded and threatened by the NATO forces that have weapons pointed along almost all of the country's European frontier.

At the same time, we might ask ourselves whether our differences with China are really only with the ruling Communist Party, as both Congress and the Biden administration would have us believe. Is it possible that they are much broader, and really arise from the national interests and aspirations of the rising Asian giant? Are the Communist Party's agenda and interests really so different from those of the majority of the Chinese people? Do we really think President Xi Jinping and the other 96 million members of the Chinese Communist Party are the only ones among a population of 1.4 billion who want their country to become a great power rivalling the United States?

It's been over three hundred years since China could claim world dominance. Back in the seventeenth century, as now, trade was the source of much of the country's power; it filled China's treasury with most of the world's silver, just as today it fills the country's central bank with record holdings of foreign exchange. Back in 2017, President Xi boldly declared that China must once again be at the centre of the world. Most of his countrymen wholeheartedly agree, just as most Americans believe their country should hold the same position.

Of course, questions like those posed above cannot be asked in today's media. In time, perhaps they will be, as the fog of war eventually clears. But however Western governments and media demonize their opponents, the underlying reality is that the world is changing, and with change comes conflict. At the end of the day, a once all-powerful America will have to share global power with its adversaries. And contrary to what the current administration in Washington claims, sanctions will only hasten that adjustment. By attempting to enforce its economic power, America risks losing much of it.

WILL CLIMATE CHANGE CONTINUE TO BE A CASUALTY OF WAR?

The world is changing in other respects as well. Mass evacuations from burning infernos have become the norm for people from Maui to Yellowknife to Greece as atmospheric carbon and with it global temperatures reach new highs. How will the growing spectre of global conflict between the West and BRICS affect the transition to a more sustainable world economy—one that no longer feeds an already warming atmosphere with a steady diet of heat-trapping greenhouse gas (GHG) emissions?

When push comes to shove, will America and its EU allies dial back their world-leading emission-reduction targets for fear of compromising their national security? Or as raging forest fires, devastating droughts, and disastrous flooding become ever more commonplace, are the United States and the European Union prepared to allow BRICS powers to dominate tomorrow's clean energy markets even more than they dominate today's fossil fuel markets?

If nuclear power replaces coal-fired power in much of the developing world, as we all hope it will for the sake of reducing future global GHG emissions, most of that world will depend on Russia to both build and operate their nuclear power plants, and to provide fuel. Through Rosatom, Russia is the world's dominant builder, operator, and fuel supplier of nuclear power plants. Even the aging reactors in more than one hundred nuclear power plants in the European Union that will likely be kept running well beyond their prescribed operating lifetimes will run largely on Russian-enriched uranium.

Meanwhile, China dominates production of the lithium-ion batteries needed to electrify the world's vehicle stock, as well as the REE and strategic metals that go into building them. The Biden administration has already chosen to sacrifice its lofty targets for solar power by closing the border to Chinese solar panels, and has threatened to do the same for Chinese-made batteries, which would likewise sabotage Washington's zero-emission vehicle targets. Will future administrations in Washington make the same choices?

INFLATION IS HERE TO STAY

While its foundation was poured by the huge monetary and fiscal expansion that occurred during the pandemic, inflation is now sustained by a far more powerful and lasting dynamic. Economic warfare promises to finish the job that the economic lockdowns from the pandemic started—the massive realignment of global supply lines. In the process, sanctions are removing what unquestionably has been the single largest brake on inflation in the postwar period: the ability for foreign trade to replace goods made by workers in high-wage economies like North America and Western Europe with goods mass-produced by low-wage workers in China and elsewhere in the developing world.

But in a time of conflict and sanctions, it is security, not costs, that matters most. All of a sudden, the domestic labour force in high-wage countries is in hot demand as supply chains manned by cheap overseas workers are no longer deemed secure. But it is far from clear whether that domestic labour force—members of which built up sizeable nest eggs from generous handouts during the pandemic—wants the work, or what wage it is willing to work for.

In any event, the new mantras of friendshoring and reshoring have put the American worker back in the driver's seat. And those workers, once the victims of globalization, are now driving wages ever higher, putting in place a wage-price spiral that threatens not only food and energy prices but prices for just about everything sold in the economy.

The realignment of global supply lines already well underway could very quickly go into overdrive should geopolitical conflict worsen between the two largest economies in the world. The impact on supply and prices of a full-fledged sanctions war between the United States and China would dwarf the impacts of Western sanctions against the resource-rich but relatively small Russian economy.

What would a full-fledged sanctions war against China look like, for example, for Apple, the world's most valuable company, with a market capitalization around $3 trillion? In a mere two days of trading, the company's share value fell over 6 percent, shaving off $200 billion from its market capitalization after it was erroneously reported that government employees in China would no longer be allowed to use iPhones. But such a restriction would be just the tip of the iceberg for Apple if a full-fledged sanctions war broke out between China and the United States.

In a time of war, China can live without Apple. But can Apple live without China and its skilled but cheap labour force? The world's largest smartphone and computer manufacturer finds itself straddling a China-US fault line that may soon become chasm-like in proportions.

Over 95 percent of Apple's iPhones, AirPods, Macs, and iPads are made in China. On its own, Foxconn (ironically a Taiwanese company), which is Apple's largest supplier in China, employs 500,000 people in its Chinese factories. And behind those factories lies an intricate web of subcontractors. In addition, more than a quarter of the fifteen hundred components that go into Apple's iPhone are manufactured in China. Of the 188 suppliers that Apple disclosed in public reporting in 2023, 151 (or 80 percent) had production facilities in China, and 41 had facilities in Taiwan.

If Apple suddenly can't access supply from its Chinese factories, what will it cost to buy whatever Apple may produce somewhere else? While the firm is now trying to diversify production to India and other locations in Asia, there is really no other place for Apple to go, at least not if it wants to manufacture its products at the same quality and price levels that it does today in China. India has the population to match China, but it lacks the skilled labour force and industrial infrastructure to replace it as the centre of global supply chains. Moreover, shifting a sizeable proportion of Apple's production to India is something that might occur over a decade, not in the time frame of a year or two. Besides, India is a founding member of BRICS and diplomatically close to Russia, so who knows what trade relations between India and the United States will look like down the road? Vietnam, another growing manufacturing hub for electronics, has a labour force that is one-twentieth the size of China's and not nearly as skilled. Mexico, the closest cheap labour force to the United States, is in the grip of cartels that pose huge security costs to anyone who wants to produce there. And like so many other countries in the Global South, Mexico has applied for BRICS membership, wanting to hedge its bet on the US-Mexico-Canada Agreement on trade that it signed with the Trump administration.

China is where Apple manufactures almost all of its products. It is also one of the company's most important markets. Apple's sales in China have tripled over the last decade, reaching $70 billion in 2022.

What holds true for Apple holds true for countless other American-based companies that rely so critically on Chinese supply chains and markets.

WHETHER CENTRAL BANKS REALIZE THAT OR NOT

Whether the potentially enormous inflationary implications of economic decoupling have been recognized by central banks is at this point an open question, since none have spoken publicly on the issue. Chinese wages may no longer be ten times lower than those in North America, but the minimum wage in China is still about four times lower than in the United States and considerably lower still when compared to wages in many EU countries.

While some central banks have warned that interest rates will not return to the record lows seen during the pandemic, none has yet abandoned the sunny forecasts of inflation returning to a target range, as if nothing has changed in the world that might impact future price behaviour.

And to make matters worse, the potential loss of low-cost Chinese supply lines comes at a time when workers in North America and Europe are rediscovering their long-lost bargaining power. No longer fearing that their jobs will be offshored, workers in North America, the United Kingdom, and other Western economies are finding that tight labour markets are rewarding them with wage gains not seen for decades. Take, for example, the 20 percent plus increases in recent contracts signed in the North American auto industry. But to their chagrin, they are also finding that most of those wage gains are being eaten up by inflation— a scenario that is encouraging labour to ask for even bigger pay hikes to compensate for the loss of their wage's purchasing power.

What, then, are the implications for monetary policy and the future direction of interest rates? Since China's admission to the WTO, Sino-American trade has increased almost sixfold, from $100 billion in 2001 to almost $600 billion in 2022. If these trade links are about to unwind due to policy-induced decoupling, that swing could have just as dramatic an impact on inflation as offshoring did, only this time in the opposite direction.

In the newly emerging world of friendshoring and reshoring, are central banks now misguided in their attempt to wrestle inflation back down to the previous 2 percent target range? Is that still attainable? If not, then why sacrifice millions of jobs trying to attain it through policy-mandated recessions that drive up the unemployment rate in order to drive down the inflation rate? The pre-pandemic, pre-sanctions global economy is an entirely different animal than the post-pandemic, sanctions-fractured global economy we live in today. When will central banks recognize this new reality and recalibrate their inflation targets?

SO WHAT DOES ALL OF THIS MEAN FOR YOU?

As the wider world changes, so too will your world.

In the past, I have argued that volatile energy prices would, as I put it back in 2009, "make the world a whole lot smaller." My argument then was that scarcity, coupled with rising demand, would put pressure on oil prices, which would violently oscillate, damaging both supply and demand and creating a cascade of downstream consequences for trade, industry, and even politics. What we are seeing take shape today in a world of ever-increasing sanctions can only make that world smaller still.

What happens in Ukraine or Taiwan or the Middle East may seem far removed from your daily life, but the impacts will be felt wherever you live. You may not be losing sleep over the emerging new world order and the profound balance-of-power changes that it brings, but you can't help but have already noticed its impact on your daily cost of living. All of a sudden, something that was supposedly long buried— inflation—has been resurrected and is making daily life challenging in a manner you've never seen before. As more and more sanctions are applied to China, the soaring cost of living is only going to get worse. And as the cost of the goods and services you buy continues to rise, so too will the cost of the money you borrow to buy them.

Even though interest rates have already risen at the fastest clip in decades, rate levels are still nowhere close to reflecting current inflation; this is particularly true of long-term interest rates set in the bond market. Adjusted for inflation, a long-term bond (10-plus years) still offers investors little or no return. More importantly, long-term bond yields are actually lower than short-term interest rates. This is a rare phenomenon in the bond market known as a yield curve inversion, and it occurs when the bond market believes that central banks will lower interest rates in the future so that tomorrow's borrowing rates will be significantly lower than today's. But the longer inflation persists, the less likely those rate cuts the bond market is counting on will occur, in which case bond yields may still have lots more room to rise—all the more so if central banks like the Federal Reserve Board continue with their quantitative tightening program or if the People's Bank of China continues to decouple from its huge holdings of US Treasuries.

If you're an investor, the prospect of even higher bond yields puts your portfolio at risk. As central banks have discovered to their dismay—thanks to the plunging value of their bloated balance sheets—rising bond yields translate into falling bond prices. And rising bond yields are not exactly bullish for the stock market either. How will your stocks fare when instead of swimming downstream alongside plunging bond yields they have to swim upstream against a raging current of steadily rising interest rates?

Nowhere might that be felt more than in the value of tech stocks, which have driven recent stock market gains through the surging share prices of artificial intelligence stocks like NVIDIA. If tech companies are suddenly cut off from their supply lines in China, forcing Apple to produce your iPhone or Mac in California, you probably don't want to own the manufacturer any more, even if it's the highest-valued company in the world (at least today). And if the Taiwan Semiconductor Manufacturing Company is now making the electronic chips that go into your smartphone or your computer in Arizona instead of Taiwan, you probably don't want to own it either—or, for that matter, any other chip company that is manufacturing semiconductors in North America and paying North American wages to do so.

The greatest fear around tech stocks used to be Federal Reserve

Board tightening, since such monetary action would slow the economy and hence stand in the way of companies meeting the soaring sales growth projections so generously built into their share prices. But now such stocks may soon face a much greater obstacle, and one whose impact would last much longer than that of a temporary cyclical tightening in monetary policy. If severed supply lines with China are replaced by friendshoring or reshoring, a sector that has built its Moore's law growth rates on falling prices could instead find itself at the vanguard of inflation.

An outright trade embargo between China and the United States would be disastrous for the global economy, but even a Chinese blockade of Taiwan and the resulting disruption of logic chip production would cost electronics producers globally an estimated $500 billion in lost revenue from products that critically depend on chip supply. Of course, Taiwan doesn't just produce logic chips. It is also a major producer of printed circuit boards, other electronic components, and casings and lenses that all are integral to the iPhone and most other end-use electronic products. Rhodium Group research estimates that the economic impact of a Chinese blockade of Taiwan on the world economy would run around $2 trillion—an impact of roughly the same magnitude as that of the COVID-19 pandemic.

Of course, tech won't be economic warfare's only casualty in the stock market. If sanctions-fed inflation is going to ensure that central banks keep their foot on the brakes and push interest rates ever higher and hold them there for much longer then yet suspected, most of the stock market might become quite unappealing.

But what about people's most valuable asset, which typically isn't their investment portfolio (unless their wealth puts them in the top 10 percent of the population) but their home? The stock market isn't the only asset class whose fortunes are leveraged (or deleveraged) to the cost of borrowing. If inflation is the new normal, so too are today's mortgage rates, or even higher ones in the future. How will the housing market fare as it recalibrates to the contours of elevated mortgage rates, with every increase in borrowing costs disqualifying more and more potential homebuyers from the market?

Those particularly at risk are homeowners who financed their homes at the record-low mortgage rates offered during the pandemic. While those who chose variable-rate mortgages have already felt the bite of soaring interest rates, many homeowners who had locked in their mortgages near or at all-time lows during the pandemic have yet to do so. The Bank of Canada estimates that homeowners who will refinance their expiring fixed-rate mortgages in the next three years will face monthly payment increases of between 20 and 40 percent. Mortgage holders in other OECD countries face similar scaled increases.

As more mortgage holders have to refinance at much higher borrowing rates, will home ownership become a luxury that many households will simply no longer be able to afford? By many measures, housing affordability is already at an all-time low. Will the flip side of housing's unaffordability be soaring rental prices as more and more households are forced to rent instead of buy? And what of the office property market that today looks half abandoned as employees who worked from their homes during the pandemic decide to continue working from home long after there is no public health reason to do so? In the face of unprecedented office property vacancy rates throughout North American cities, will those half-empty towers be converted into much needed rental space for the households whose home-buying plans have been stymied by soaring mortgage rates?

If office conversion proves to be the solution to the emerging rental crisis, it will be noteworthy how the pandemic first encouraged a massive wave of migration away from cities to more remote locations, while the echo effect from this exodus—the conversion of downtown office space into residential rental units—could pull many of those same people back into revitalized downtowns.

And in what currency should you hold the savings you've put aside to one day buy a home? You might think twice about holding the once almighty US dollar. As more countries in the Global South de-dollarize their trade, and as more and more central banks reduce the dollar weighting in their foreign reserves, the greenback will lose much of its global lustre.

Will that extend to the junior dollars as well? Could the Canadian and Australian currencies also be targeted in global economic warfare? Both countries have gone out of their way to provoke America's rivals. Calls from the former Australian prime minister to investigate the Chinese origins of the COVID 19 virus resulted in a temporary suspension of Chinese purchases of Australian coal and timber beginning in late 2020. More recently, Beijing can't be too enthralled by Australia's decision to join AUKUS—the NATO-type alliance it has formed with the United States and the United Kingdom to counter Chinese influence and power in the Indo-Pacific region.

It's certainly no coincidence that China is taking steps to reduce its dependence on Australian iron ore, which accounts for 60 percent of its imports of the metal. China has recently announced a partnership with global mining giant Rio Tinto to build a trans-Guinean railway. The project will take iron ore from a new $15 billion mine being built in the world's largest untapped supply of high-grade iron ore to a deepwater port, from which the ore will be shipped to China. The new supply from Africa is expected to replace much of what China currently imports from Australia.

Canada, too, has gone out of its way to provoke China's wrath. It began with the arrest of Meng Wanzhou on an American extradition charge, which in turn triggered, among other responses, the suspension of Canadian canola exports to China in 2019, which lasted for three years, and a Chinese ban on Canadian beef imposed in 2022 that is still in effect. There could be more trade reprisals in response to widespread reports in the Canadian media of Beijing trying to intimidate members of Parliament with Chinese family ties. In response, China has kept in place a ban imposed during the pandemic for group-sized tourist travel to Canada, even after lifting such restrictions against Australia and the United States. Prior to the pandemic, Chinese tourists spent more money in Canada than those from all other countries combined. While Canadian politicians and media can grandstand their allegations of Chinese political interference with impunity, the same unfortunately can't be said for the more than 2 million Canadians who work in the country's tourist industry.

Even if neither country's currency is directly targeted, the fortunes of the junior dollars are very much linked to that of their much larger cousin. Global investors tend to treat Australian and Canadian dollar securities as part of the same dollar block portfolio in which they hold Treasuries and other US-dollar-denominated assets. So, if they lighten up on US dollars as part of a strategic geopolitical realignment of their portfolio, they will probably reduce their Australian and Canadian dollar holdings as well. If you're living in Sydney or Toronto, you might want your currency to be called something other than a "dollar." Maybe an "aussie" or a "loonie."

And what about food? It too has become a battleground in the sanctions war. The United Nations warns that the world is currently facing its greatest level of food insecurity in the entire postwar period. Russia has terminated the Black Sea Grain Initiative, choking off wheat, corn, and oil seed supply from the Ukrainian breadbasket. India, the world's largest exporter of rice, has unilaterally moved to restrict rice exports in favour of supplying its domestic market. Other food exporters may follow suit.

In a world where sanctions promote autarky, will food shortages compound themselves by encouraging food-producing countries like India to horde their agricultural output for their own populations and cut back on exports? We've already seen that play out during the initial global shortages and subsequent price spikes in the early days of the Russian-Ukrainian war. Food export bans followed on the heels of similar export restrictions that became commonplace during the pandemic with respect to vaccines, respirators, and masks.

How will soaring food prices affect shoppers? Skyrocketing grocery prices have already seen North American and British shoppers flock from full-price grocery chains to discount supermarkets and start buying canned goods instead of fresh produce. Are we on the cusp of economically induced dietary changes as households adjust their spending budgets to the new reality of soaring grocery bills?

In the midst of so much change and upheaval, we can no longer count on what we used to take for granted—most of all, a world trading system that we were told made all of us better off. While with every passing day we get a better glimpse of what our future will look like, the precise contours of the rapidly emerging new world order are yet to be fully revealed. But amidst all the uncertainty that surrounds us, one thing has become increasingly clear: as we sail farther along this course of seemingly inevitable global conflict and accompanying profound economic change, there is no turning back to the world we once knew. It simply no longer exists.

ACKNOWLEDGEMENTS

I would like to thank Nick Garrison, Linda Pruessen, and Zainab Mirza for their careful editing of the manuscript as it evolved over the last two years.

What started out as an investigation into the economic aftermath of and consequences of the COVID-19 lockdowns grew into a much larger project, whose scope broadened significantly from what was originally intended as events unfolded in Ukraine and Taiwan. Hence *Is There Any Light At The End of the Tunnel?* morphed into *A Map of The New Normal: How Inflation, Sanctions, and War Will Change Your World Forever.*

There were more than a few twists and turns in the process, and I would like to once again thank Nick and the rest of the editorial team at Penguin Random House Canada for their encouragement and support.

I would like to thank Maurice Smith, Harvey Bradley, Murray Miskin, Phil Sokolowski, and Gregor Robinson for their helpful comments on subjects covered in the manuscript.

And I would like to acknowledge the great work and efforts of my intrepid publicist Sharon Klein, who has also supported me on my previous books.

Jeff Rubin
Toronto, Canada
May 2024

NOTES

CHAPTER 2: INFLATION

1. Alex Seabrook, "People in Bristol using log burners could face £300 fines," BBC, September 4, 2023, https://www.bbc.com/news /uk-england-bristol-66709740.

2. Graeme Wearden, "Brits 'need to accept' they're worse off and stop pushing wages and prices higher, says BoE chief economist—as it happened," *The Guardian*, April 25, 2023, https://www.theguardian .com/business/live/2023/apr/25/price-rises-nestle-profits-uk -grocery-inflation-cbi-business-live.

CHAPTER 3: BROKEN LINKS

1. Josh DuBose and Rachel Menitoff, "22 Arrested in Massive Train Cargo Burglary Ring in Los Angeles; $18M in stolen goods recovered," KTLA News, November 17, 2022, https://ktla.com/news/local-news /22-arrested-in-connection-with-l-a-railroad-burglaries-18-million -in-stolen-merchandise-recovered/.

2. Bethany Allen-Ebrahimian, "Europe Turns on China," Axios, September 20, 2022, https://www.axios.com/2022/09/20/europe -turns-on-china.

CHAPTER 5: DELEVERAGING

1. Gareth Hutchens, "RBA Deputy Governor Michele Bullock Says Outlook for Global Economy Is 'Quite Worrying,'" ABC News, September 21, 2022, https://www.abc.net.au/news /2022-09-21/rba-says-outlook-for-global-economy-is-worrying /101461316.

CHAPTER 6: WINTER IS COMING

1. Jon Shelton, "US Warns Nord Stream 2 Firms to 'Immediately Abandon Work,'" DW, March 18, 2021, https://www.dw.com/en /nord-stream-2-us-warns-companies-to-immediately-abandon -work/a-56920315.

2. Caitlin McFall, "State Dept Vows Nord Stream 2 Will Be a 'Hunk of Metal at Bottom of the Ocean' if Russia Invades Ukraine," Fox News, January 27, 2022, https://www.foxnews.com/politics/state -dept-vows-nord-stream-2-hunk-metal-bottom-ocean-russia -invades-ukraine.

3. Dave DeCamp, "Blinken Says Nord Stream Sabotage Is a 'Tremendous Opportunity,'" Scheerpost, October 3, 2022, https://scheerpost.com/2022/10/03/blinken-says-nord-stream -sabotage-is-a-tremendous-opportunity/.

4. Isabel van Brugen, "Russia Issues Warning to US After Nord Stream Sabotage Allegations," *Newsweek*, February 9, 2023, https://www.newsweek.com/russia-warning-us-white-house -nord-stream-sabotage-1780101.

CHAPTER 8: THE HUNGER GAMES

1. Ragip Soylu, "Why Ukrainian Grain Is Not Going to Countries with a Food Crisis," Middle East Eye, August 13, 2022, https://www.middleeasteye.net/news/russia-ukraine-turkey -grain-deal-explained.

2. Lisa Cleaver, "Report: Ukrainian Grain Fed Pigs in Spain," Feed & Grain, February 16, 2023, https://www.feedandgrain.com /grain-supply-chain/news/15384273/report-ukrainian-grain-fed -pigs-in-spain.

CHAPTER 9. AVIATION

1. "Russia Fly-Around a Source of Tension for Airline Industry," France 24, June 5, 2023, https://www.france24.com/en/live -news/20230605-russia-fly-around-a-source-of-tension-for -airline-industry.

2. "US-Bound Chinese Flights Avoiding Russia's Airspace—Reuters," RT, June 2, 2023, https://www.rt.com/business/577346-us-chinese -airlines-avoid-russia/.

3. Andrei Martyanov, "It Is the Devil You Know—II," Reminiscence of the Future (blog), October 11, 2018, https://smoothiex12.blogspot .com/2018/10/it-is-devil-you-know-ii.html.

4. Joanna Bailey, "The MC-21 Wing—Why It's a World's First," Simple Flying, November 26, 2021, https://simpleflying.com /mc-21-wing-world-first/.

5. Valius Venckunas, "Russia to produce 1000+ new airliners by 2030— Minister of Industry and Trade," Aerotime Hub, June 16, 2022, https://www.aerotime.aero/articles/31333-russia-to-produce-more -than-1000-new-aircraft-by-2030.

6. Valius Venckunas, "Boeing, Airbus planes will "never be delivered" to Russia again: Rostec," Aerotime Hub, September 29, 2022, https://www.aerotime.aero/articles/32285-boeing-airbus-will- never-return-to-russian-market-rostec#:~:text=%E2%80%9CWe %20believe%20that%20this%20process%20is%20irreversible% 20and,delivering%20any%20new%20aircraft%20or%20parts %20to%20Russia.

7. Nicholas Mulder, "The History of Economic Sanctions as a Tool of War," Yale University Press, February 24, 2022, https://yalebooks

.yale.edu/2022/02/24/the-history-of-economic-sanctions-as-a
-tool-of-war/.

8. Michael Thumann, "Hate message from Moscow," *Zeit Online*,
December 22, 2022, https://www.zeit.de/2022/53/angela-merkel
-russland-krieg-wladimir-putin.

9. Mulder, "History of Economic Sanctions."

10. Crimea had been part of Russia for almost two hundred years
before Khrushchev, himself a Ukrainian, transferred it to Ukraine
from Russia back in 1954, when both belonged to the USSR. At
the time, it was seen as a gesture of eternal friendship between
the Ukrainian and Russian republics. Obviously, times have
changed. Before Khrushchev's decision to give the region to
Ukraine, Crimea had been part of the Russian Empire since 1783,
following the Russo-Turkish War, when it was taken from the
Ottoman Empire. After the Russian Revolution of 1917, Crimea
was designated an autonomous republic within the newly formed
USSR. Over its history, the majority of inhabitants in Crimea
have been and continue to be Russian-speaking.

11. Luke Harding and Julian Borger, "Ukraine crisis: Vladimir Putin
warns of 'consequences' after Slavyansk skirmish," *The Guardian*,
April 25, 2014, https://www.theguardian.com/world/2014/apr/24
/vladimir-putin-consequences-slavyansk-ukraine.

CHAPTER 10: THE DEMISE OF THE PETRODOLLAR

1. The evidence for Russian industrial output comes in many forms:
the steady output of tanks, missiles, and shells in spite of predictions the Russians are about to run out is one piece of evidence, as
are the claims of the Russian authorities. *The New York Times* con-
firms many pessimistic western appraisals of Russian industry:
Julian E. Barnes, Eric Schmitt, and Thomas Gibbons-Neff,
"Russia Overcomes Sanctions to Expand Missile Production,
Officials Say," *The New York Times*, September 13, 2023,

https://www.nytimes.com/2023/09/13/us/politics/russia
-sanctions-missile-production.html.

CHAPTER 11: CHINA AND THE NEW WORLD ORDER

1. Jenny Leonard, "Biden Signs Narrow China Investing Rules as US Seeks Better Ties," BNN Bloomberg, August 9, 2023, https://www .bnnbloomberg.ca/biden-signs-narrow-china-investing-rules-as -us-seeks-better-ties-1.1957014.
2. James Crabtree, "Biden and Xi Are Doomed to Escalation," *Foreign Policy*, March 15, 2023, https://foreignpolicy.com/2023/03 /15/china-us-biden-xi-competition-escalation-aukus-geopolitics/.
3. Rhoda Kwan and agencies, "Xi Jinping Vows to Oppose Taiwanese "Pro-Independence" Influences as Third Term Begins," *The Guardian*, March 13, 2023, https://www.theguardian.com/world/2023/mar /13/xi-jinping-taiwan-independence-china-parliament-national -peoples-congress.
4. "Treasury Designates China as a Currency Manipulator," US Department of the Treasury, August 5, 2019, https://home.treasury .gov/news/press-releases/sm751.

CHAPTER 12: TROUBLED WATERS

1. Britney Nguyen, "US Would Destroy Taiwan's Semiconductor Factories Rather Than Letting Them Fall into China's Hands, a Former National Security Advisor Says," Business Insider India, March 15, 2023, https://www.businessinsider.in/tech/news /us-would-destroy-taiwans-semiconductor-factories-rather -than-letting-them-fall-into-chinas-hands-a-former-national -security-adviser-says/articleshow/98614453.cms.